THE ROOKIE

THE
ROOKIE

AN ODYSSEY THROUGH CHESS
(AND LIFE)

STEPHEN MOSS

B L O O M S B U R Y

LONDON · OXFORD · NEW YORK · NEW DELHI · SYDNEY

John Wisden & Co Ltd
An imprint of Bloomsbury Publishing Plc

50 Bedford Square
London
WC1B 3DP
UK

1385 Broadway
New York
NY 10018
USA

www.bloomsbury.com

WISDEN and the wood-engraving device are trademarks of John Wisden &
Company Ltd, a subsidiary of Bloomsbury Publishing Plc

First published 2016

www.wisden.com
www.wisdenrecords.com
Follow Wisden on Twitter @WisdenAlmanack
and on Facebook at Wisden Sports

British Library Cataloguing-in-Publication Data
A catalogue record for this book is available from the British Library.

Library of Congress Cataloguing-in-Publication data has been applied for.

ISBN: HB: 978-1-4081-8970-2
ePub: 978-1-4081-8971-9

2 4 6 8 10 9 7 5 3 1

Typeset in Adobe Garamond Pro by Deanta Global Publishing Services, Chennai, India
Printed and bound in Great Britain by CPI Group (UK) Ltd, Croydon CR0 4YY

To find out more about our authors and books visit www.wisden.com.
Here you will find extracts, author interviews, details of forthcoming
events and the option to sign up for our newsletters.

For my parents,
Raymond and Kathleen Moss,
who gave me the freedom and
self-confidence to play.

CONTENTS

HANDSHAKE

'Chess is my world. Not a house, not a fortress where I hide myself from life's hardship, but indeed the world. The world in which I live a full life, in which I prove myself'

— *Mikhail Tal, world champion, 1960–61*

Chess games traditionally begin with a handshake. You loathe your opponent; you want to maim, kill, destroy him – almost invariably it will be a him – but you must observe the proprieties. Hence the handshake. Usually, your opponent's hand will be limp and lifeless; there may be dirt under the fingernails; chess is not for the well-scrubbed. But ignore any physical repulsion and shake hands. 'Hello. Nice to meet you. Have a good game.' In other words, 'Die, you detestable worm.'

This book is about my struggle to be a good chess player. The inspiration had something to do with love, a renewed affection for this odd but glorious pursuit after a long break in which I had foolishly put life ahead of the 64 squares, but the trigger was fear. Of calumny, ruin and possible imprisonment. After playing the game to a moderate standard at school and university in the 1970s I had more or less given up until I discovered you could play real-time chess over the internet against anonymous opponents of wildly different standards: six-year-olds from Minnesota who barely knew the moves; grandmasters from Minsk who annihilated me. One Saturday evening I was playing a few unimaginative games on the unimaginatively named Internet

1

Chess Club site when my opponent propositioned me in the thin space below the on-screen board where you were allowed to mock your opponent's moves.

'Hi, I'm Pamela.'

'Hello,' I said, pondering my reply to her opening move.

'What's your name?'

'Stephen.'

'I'm 19,' said Pamela. 'How old r u?'

'25.' This was actually about half my age, but you know how it is.

'r u single?'

'Yes.' OK, another lie …

'Do u want to have sex?'

'Sure.'

'Do u like it rough?'

'Very.'

By this stage we had played about six moves each (perfectly conventional, not at all rough). I was about to castle, putting my king in safety and preparing for a long tactical battle. (While offering hot sex, Pamela was actually playing a pretty conventional Four Knights opening.) Suddenly the machine froze with my king in mid-procession and we were logged off. Someone at AOL, or ICC, or maybe the Metropolitan Police's internet porn unit, had decided the conversation was too racy. Ever since I have been waiting for the knock on the door. Hence the need for the book – a seminal survey of the true sport of kings, but also an exhibit to use in evidence if the case ever comes to court. Because, m'lud, I WAS JOKING. I knew that Pamela, 19, was actually Norbert or Nathan, or Bill or Brian, 56, a man living in Wallington or Workington who had such a wasted life that he spent his Saturday evenings playing dull openings and pretending to be a youthful nymphomaniac. I was playing a game – in every sense. Please believe me, and please don't confiscate my hard drive. We chess-playing middle-aged men have our foibles; that's why we are so devoted to it. Chess, that is. We feel content on these 64 squares; it's the rest of the world we have a problem with. So before you lock me up please let me explain.

I started playing chess when I was 11. A friend showed me the moves. I think his father had shown him. Fathers usually feature somewhere in the chess learning process. Prodigies can beat them by the age of six. Killing the father is an oedipal imperative for great chess players. I was certainly no prodigy. For one thing I started too late – some 11-year-olds are virtually grandmaster standard. I was OK but, as with most other things in my life, didn't work hard enough at the game. I wanted instant brilliancies; refused to do the slog of reading books (especially on opening theory); saw chess as an art not a science; had a friend who saw it as a science not an art, who did read books on opening theory, and who always beat me. I played for my school and had a reasonable record because I used to insist on playing on the lowest boards in the six-strong team. Already my lack of ambition was apparent. What I mainly remember is that we always got biscuits and orange juice before each match. Schools admired boys who played chess. Sadly the same couldn't be said for the girls, who tended to favour rugby players. I played in an under-18 chess congress in Newport, my home town in South Wales, came third and got a certificate. My science-not-art friend came first, damn him. At university I once beat grandmaster John Nunn in a simultaneous display. He was playing about 30 other people, but a win is a win. I was 19 – Pamela's age – at the time and felt pretty good about things. Nunn made a blunder – the light in the dingy room where the university chess club met was very poor – and resigned in disgust. No doubt had he played on, he would have recovered and won. As far as I know my science-not-art friend never beat John Nunn.

Generally, though, the move from school to university was not good for my chess. I recall entering the university championship, losing my first four games in grisly fashion and retiring from the battlefield. These were serious players, and my lucky win against Nunn counted for nothing. Whereas at school I had been in the top six in chess terms, at university I was a nothing. That hurt, though not enough to start studying the game systematically. It seems I learned early to take the line of least resistance. If I didn't play I couldn't lose, which might be good for one's self-confidence but guarantees you will never become a better player. Don't be scared of losing is every grandmaster's mantra – that's how you learn. At 20 I was too callow to realise that.

For a couple of decades after university I didn't play, except on a cheap, pocket-sized computer that played very basic chess. Like most early chess computers it was obsessed with material. If you fed it pawns, it would always grab them, not realising checkmate was imminent. This was good for my ego but very bad for my chess. I occasionally played an over-the-board game if I stumbled across another aficionado, usually in pubs, but at the age of 45 I was still playing to the same feeble standard as at university. I could avoid blunders, which is enough to beat rank amateurs (especially in darkened pubs after a couple of pints), but I couldn't play with any imagination. I didn't remotely understand chess.

Then around 2004 I started playing higher-level computer chess; played on the internet; started playing over-the-board games fuelled by ambition rather than alcohol. My chess got slightly better, a little more creative, but I was still moderate: an average-to-weak competition player. I joined a chess club, which meant I was playing against experienced players who had what are called chess grades – numbers, not unlike golf handicaps, that designate how good they are. Grades, which are calculated by the English Chess Federation (ECF), count for a great deal in domestic chess. The top-rated player in the UK has a grade of around 280; a player with a grade of 200-plus would be deemed very strong; a player graded more than 175 would, in my estimation anyway, qualify as an expert; my grade as I embarked on this book was 133. As I began my odyssey I tentatively hoped I might be able to improve on that. Sometimes I felt 175 and above – true chess expertise – was reachable; sometimes 150 seemed more realistic; in my darker moments I feared my grade might actually fall and I would be exposed (or perhaps confirmed) as a charlatan.

To complicate matters there is also an international system of ratings, developed by Hungarian physicist Arpad Elo (they are sometimes referred to as Elo ratings) and overseen by FIDE, the world governing body of chess (FIDE stands for Fédération Internationale des Échecs, but increasingly it distances itself from its French origins and styles itself the World Chess Federation). A 'weak' grandmaster (in chess everything is relative) will have a FIDE rating around 2550; the top grandmasters are rated 2750-plus. Former world champion Garry Kasparov, the undisputed king of chess in the 1980s and 1990s, had a peak rating of 2851; Magnus Carlsen, the young Norwegian who has inherited Kasparov's mantle as world number one, surpassed even that, though because of ratings inflation direct comparisons across generations are treacherous. The numbers for both the national grades and the international ratings are normative. They have no meaning in themselves; all they do is establish your strength relative to other players. If I beat a player with an English Chess Federation grade of 150, I am awarded 200 points (150 + 50); if I lose to him, I get 100 (150 - 50). These are averaged over about 30 games, by which point it is reckoned you will have an accurate indication of your relative strength, your place in the pecking order. Some players are very protective of their grades and ratings. It is the chess equivalent of penis size. But perhaps this is territory into which we should not stray.

To convert a UK grade into a rough international rating equivalent, you multiply by seven and a half and add 700. Thus for me 133 x 7.5 = 998 + 700 = 1698. A quintessentially average rating. I was probably the most average chess player in the world. But there came a point where being average was no longer enough. I had become good enough to know how bad I was. I was attached to two clubs, Surbiton and Kingston, and was mixing with players who were very good, players who were 200-plus in UK chess money, players who had international master titles, one notch below the coveted grandmaster title. I wanted to be like them. I wanted to feel as at home on the 64 squares as they did. Hence this book: an attempt to understand chess and the people who play it; to learn to play better; to relate something of the game's history; and to try to explain why it has been played throughout the world for at least 1,500 years. It sets out to be an examination of the soul of chess, but it is possible that from time to time my own troubled soul will make an appearance too.

I was a middle-aged man who had done OK in life: good degree, relatively successful career in journalism (mainly with *The Guardian*), a wife who somehow had managed to stick with me for more than 30 years, a son I was proud of. But there was something missing. I hadn't created anything substantial; hadn't climbed Everest or crossed the Sahara; hadn't mastered a discipline. Journalism is the occupation par excellence for dilettantes and perpetual outsiders, for commitmentophobes wary of putting down roots. We glide across the surface of life, stopping here and there to make an observation or pass some half-baked judgement, but in the end what does it add up to? The cliché is that statues are never erected to critics, but I suspect even fewer are raised for journalists. I craved substance and saw in chess a possible way of laying down a marker. I would pursue true excellence, become an expert, demonstrate that I wasn't just a dilettante. I would for once in my life settle at something and show I could conquer a metaphorical continent. That, at least, was my hope.

When players keep score in a game, they do so in what is called algebraic notation. Each of the 64 squares has its own designation (shown in the diagram below).

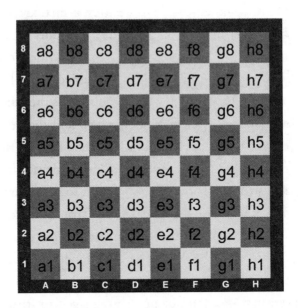

I have tried to imagine my odyssey as if I were a piece – or more properly, like Alice on the other side of the looking-glass, a pawn – making an uncertain progress across a chessboard. There are eight files on a board, a to h, and I have followed that nomenclature for the eight chapters in this book. Each of those eight files comprises eight squares, so each of the chapters will contain eight elements. Chess players are nothing if not logical. Black and white squares alternate on a board, and that alternation will dictate the flow of the book. The black squares will represent my experiences, the games I play, marked by misunderstanding and error. The blackness is appropriate. The white squares will be the counterpoint, offering illumination as I explore the history, literature and philosophy of chess, and meet great players who have cracked the code. This is the promised land I can see in the distance but have difficulty locating. Think of me as a chess Everyman, searching for salvation. But be warned. If you look at a chessboard, which is always set up with a white square on the right-hand side ('white on the right' – the first thing you tell a beginner), you will see that in notation terms you begin on black (a1) and end on black (h8). This does not bode well for my journey.

This book will have failed if it is read only by chess players. I want to proselytise on behalf of a game that has slipped off the radar of the mainstream media since the defining world title match between the suave Soviet champion Boris Spassky and the crazed American challenger Bobby Fischer in Iceland in 1972, and the interminable struggles between the Soviet players Garry Kasparov and Anatoly Karpov in the mid-1980s. That determination to reach out beyond the 15,000 or so competition players in the UK means the book must be comprehensible to the general reader. I have kept detailed analysis of moves out of the main body of the text, instead putting scores of my key games in an appendix for those who want to chart my progress (or lack of it) more deeply. Another appendix provides an explanation of algebraic notation for non-players who want to understand the lingo and follow the games.

This is emphatically not a learn-to-play-chess book. My goal is to capture the essence of the game – psychological, philosophical and cultural – and look at why we play it, why it has endured, and why the hell I am so bad at it. We are in this together, and by the end we will understand chess and, more importantly, understand life – the search for knowledge, control, perfection. After decades of chess mediocrity, I set out to achieve excellence, for the first time in my life to master a world, to become good – not just good at chess but good at the act of living, for as the 17th-century priest and chess lover Pietro Carrera pointed out in his seminal work *Il Gioco degli Scacchi* (*The Game of Chess*, published in 1617), only the man who is truly at one with himself can play good chess. 'Someone who has to play an important game should avoid filling his stomach with heavy foods since these are prejudicial to serious mental activity and affect the vision,' wrote Carrera. 'A chess player must practise sobriety.' No more beer; no more pie and chips; only unwavering concentration on the 64 squares.

OK, now we are ready to play. Have a good game – and this time I mean it.

FILE A
From Bournemouth to Bunnysville

'Every chess master was once a beginner'
– Irving Chernev, prolific chess author

A1: BALD TRUTHS

Bournemouth seemed an appropriate place to begin my quest. The bathos was appealing. 'No one plays chess in Bournemouth,' a friend who was born in the town told me. Hastings, just along the coast, is the famous chess resort. But the inaugural Bournemouth Grand Congress in the spring of 2012 intended to change all that. This was an event with pretensions. The prize for the 'Open' event, for the strongest players, was £1,000 – enough, in this underpaid world, to attract four grandmasters (GMs), the elite of the world game. Even the 'Challengers' event which I entered, for players with an English Chess Federation grade of 155 or below, was worth £300 to the winner. Not that, with my grade of 133, I expected to come anywhere near winning. Respectability would be enough. There were five rounds spread over a showery weekend, starting on Friday evening and ending late on Sunday afternoon. Players had two hours each for all their moves, so potentially a game could take four hours. Twenty hours of chess out of 48. A daunting prospect.

I felt strangely confident as I set out, taking the train from Clapham to Bournemouth on a bright Friday afternoon. In retrospect, I should have realised that my preparations were not ideal. I had planned to take a carefully selected range of fruit and salads to see me through the weekend, but ran short of time and ended up having to grab a packet of chocolate digestives from Sainsbury's and four hot cross buns. Pietro Carrera would not have been happy with these choices. The upside was that large stomachs are almost de rigueur among middle-aged male chess players, who form a substantial majority at chess weekenders, so I would blend in well. I had failed to book in time to get the £30-a-night special offer at the Carrington House Hotel, the venue for the congress, so ended up at the Days Hotel on the other side of town. It was a pricey £167 for two nights. Add £51 for the train ticket and £35 for the entry fee, and even winning the Challengers section would give me only a minimal profit. I checked in and prepared myself for my date with destiny, still feeling sure I would give a good account of myself. After all, 150-graded players are nothing special.

The first game, against a balding man in his late fifties who had come all the way from Llangollen to play, went reasonably well. I lost, but put up a very respectable fight, though this being my debut in a proper weekend tournament I got confused when we had to exchange and sign each other's scoresheets at the end. 'Is this your first weekender?' he asked, with what sounded like a note of pity. Ignoring the faux pas, I had taken the game well into the fourth hour and felt I'd given him some problems. A loss against one of the highest-ranked players in my section did not seem like the end of the world. There would be weaker players ahead, and to lose in the first round in these so-called 'Swiss' events – where you are paired in each round with players on the same score as yours – can in some cases be an advantage. Fly high early and there may be a danger of coming up against a series of strong players. So I was not downhearted by this first defeat.

The Bournemouth Grand Congress had attracted a good turnout, including a group of blind players who used Braille boards and had to be told the moves. Almost the only sound in the large room – the hotel's 'presidential suite' – was the clack-clack of the blind players' boards, and their opponents' sotto voce recitation of the moves. Altogether there were more than

150 players in the three sections – Open, Challengers and Minor (for players graded less than 125). I counted just four women. The majority were middle-aged men, some rather infirm but all sternly competitive. One of my opponents did not point out that I had forgotten to press my clock after making a move, and made a point of dwelling on his reply to use as much of my precious time as possible, moving only when I eventually realised my oversight. The will to win in chess is ferocious, even among the most mild-mannered of players. It is kill or be killed. Part of the game's perverse appeal is that you sit there in silence and observe superficial pleasantries – perhaps offering to bring your opponent a glass of water if you are getting one yourself – while all the time wanting to destroy him. Did I have that desire?

My second game was against a player who had an estimated grade of 124 but was clearly much stronger. When I looked him up later on the internet, I discovered that ten years previously he had had a grade of 153. He is what we bad losers call a 'bandit', playing off a grade that bore little relation to his real ability. Admittedly he might have been rusty – he said he had had a long lay-off and was just coming back to competitive chess – but good players usually keep the essence of their strategic ability, even if their tactical skills lessen as middle-aged brain cells die. This was the best game I played in Bournemouth (the moves are given on p379, as the first of ten key games which punctuate this journey across the chessboard). I even managed a knight sacrifice, giving up material to get a sharp attack. While speculative – a good player would have calculated more carefully – it was at least interesting and gave me good chances. When the first time control arrived – we each had to play 40 moves in 100 minutes and the rest in another 20, to make four hours in all – we could both take a breather. We happened to head to the loo together – the mental overload of chess is very tough on the ageing bladder – and I was feeling rather chipper. At the very worst I was sure I could get a draw. Perhaps, with king and five pawns to his king, bishop and two pawns, I could even contrive a win. If only. Rusty or not, he outplayed me in the endgame, I blundered, his bishop gradually exerted control, my king was rendered impotent, I lost.

This was the turning point. Had I managed even half a point in that game – the usual scoring system is a point for a win and half a point for a draw – I'm convinced things would have gone better for me thereafter. But the loss undermined me psychologically. I had played eight hours of exhausting chess against two seasoned campaigners and had nothing to show for it. Worse, I had had a few beers the evening before after what I considered my noble effort against the bald man from Llangollen, and the effects of the Nurofen I had taken that morning to counteract my hangover were starting to wear off. I had ignored Carrera's dictum that to play well you had to practise abstinence and was paying a heavy price.

I bought a sandwich and went to sit forlornly on the seafront in the one-hour break between games two and three. As I sat there with my plastic bag, windswept, dejected and emitting a nervous hum while trying to read a newspaper that kept blowing away, a stag party went past – Bournemouth is the Blackpool of the south coast, full of young hedonists dressed as cardinals or courtesans. They looked at me quizzically and one of the young men started to imitate my hum. Suddenly I felt like many other chess players must feel – marginalised, detached, a figure of fun. The difference was that some of these unconventional, unworldly figures – men who find a world they understand on the 64 squares – have the solace of being good at chess. I was a loser, as I proved in the afternoon when I was crushed in 21 moves, playing feebly and imploding in little more than an hour's play against another of those bronzed, balding, retired accountant types who spend their weekends on the chess circuit.

I was now plumb last and would have to take a bye in the next round on Sunday morning. I didn't fancy playing a friendly or walking along the blustery seafront for four hours, so decided to withdraw. It would look terrible on paper, and indeed online, where in the final results I was shown as 36th and last in my section. People would think I'd quit in a fit of *amour propre*, but that's life. I tried to convince myself that this terrible beginning was at least good for the book's narrative arc. I also tried to imagine myself returning to this benighted place in a couple of years and sweeping all before me, beating a succession of gnarled, elderly men clutching plastic bags. I would be avenged. For the moment I took solace in more beer and went home, wishing it was as easy to escape from a bad position on the board. It was one of the most dismal weekends of my life, but things could only get better. Couldn't they?

A2: IN SEARCH OF A GURU

 'Education in chess goes on in a most haphazard fashion,' wrote Emanuel Lasker in his *Manual of Chess*, published in 1925. 'Most chess players slowly climb to a certain rather low level and stay there.' This is a fair summary of my life in chess. Forty years of mediocrity. Yet Lasker, who was world champion for 27 years from 1894 until 1921 (the longest reign in chess), insisted it was possible to train anyone to become a very good player. He even specified how long it would take – 200 hours, divided between rules of play and exercises (five hours), elementary endings (five hours), openings (ten hours), tactical combinations (20 hours), position play (40 hours), and play and analysis (120 hours). Bill Hartston, British champion in 1973 and 1975, made a similar point when I went to meet him at the *Daily Express*, where he wrote the Beachcomber column. 'I think anyone of reasonable intelligence ought to be able to become close to international master standard,' he said encouragingly. The sky was the limit. In theory, anyway.

I thought I could manage Lasker's 200 hours, but was less sure about Malcolm Gladwell's recipe for expertise. In his book *Outliers: The Story of Success*, he puts his cards on the table pretty early on: 'To become a chess grandmaster seems to take about ten years … and what's ten years? Well, it's roughly how long it takes to put in 10,000 hours of hard practice. Ten thousand hours is the magic number of greatness.' That's 20 hours a week for a decade. I'd given myself just three years to make the grade.

Andrew Soltis's *What It Takes to Become a Chess Master* was similarly discouraging: 'Only a tiny fraction of people who play chess become masters. In fact, only 2 per cent of the people who take chess seriously make master. Why?' His answer is that most players will hit a wall. It will come at different points for different people – a rating of 1500 for some, 1700 for others, 2100 for stronger players – but it will come. And when it comes you have to learn to be a different type of player. Previously you could rely on opponents of a similar strength to you making a blunder – all you had to do was play steadily. But as you got stronger and started to encounter better players, they would not self-destruct. Then you had to learn to play a more subtle kind of chess. You had to forget the kind of player you had been and almost start afresh. But I was getting ahead of myself. Perhaps the wall would come, but first I had to lay a few bricks.

I needed to recruit some experts to help me. John Saunders, a former Welsh international and a chess writer who had edited both of the UK's best-known chess magazines (though, as he liked to point out, not at the same time), lived near me in south-west London and offered to give me some lessons. We went through the games I played in Bournemouth, and he concluded that what was lacking was precision. I had some reasonable ideas, but didn't execute them properly. In the second game – the one with the knight sacrifice which defined the tournament for me – he pointed out a line which would almost certainly have won the game. It needed a bit of serious analysis to find, and instead I had played a more obvious but weaker move – the sort of move chess players, real chess players, dismiss as 'plausible'. It looks good but isn't; is optically attractive but ultimately leads nowhere.

Good players talk about the 'truth' of a position; today's all-seeing computer programs can penetrate that truth. But mediocre players like me are bewitched by superficially attractive moves which promise more than they deliver. Saunders called the missed move – a thrust with the bishop instead of the knight check I had played – a 'tragic missed opportunity', which might be overstating it, but that was how it felt at the time. 'In chess, as in life, opportunity strikes but once,' said Soviet grandmaster David Bronstein, who came agonisingly close to winning the world title in 1951. You reach a decisive moment in the game and have to nail it. Miss it and it's gone for ever. The tiniest change in the position can mean your chance has evaporated. It's why in classical chess – where players have a couple of hours to play 40 moves – they might ponder a single move for an hour. They know this is the crisis and that they have to get it right. Don't play plausibly, play well. 'When a weak player thinks a lot over a move,' Hartston told me, 'he always makes a mistake. When a strong player thinks a lot over a move, he plays the right move. You think a lot when you don't know what to do, and the weak player talks himself out of the good moves.'

After Bournemouth I played in the Felce Cup, in effect division three of the Surrey individual championship. Division one, for the top players, attracts those with grades of 180-plus; division two is for the 140 to 180 group – near-experts and those who reckon they can mix it in that company; division three is for the 110-140 brigade; then there is a division four (described as the 'Minor' in many events) for novices. The precise numerical divisions will vary from tournament to tournament, but those four categories give a representative breakdown of the structure of chess in the UK. In retrospect I realised that the under-155 category in Bournemouth had been pitched a little high for me – those old blokes knew their way around a chessboard. The Felce was more my level – you had to be graded 140 or below to qualify – but the downside was that you came up against talented youngsters.

Playing children is a no-win situation. Unless they are prodigies, you are expected to beat them, and it's ignominious if you don't. I lost my first game in the Felce to an 11-year-old girl who spent most of her time looking bored. I played abysmally – the only mitigating factor was that I had been working unusually hard and arrived late for the game, losing what proved to be an important quarter of an hour on the clock (your clock is started at the designated time whether or not you have arrived at the board). This defeat distressed me even more than Bournemouth. That night I replayed the game in my head as I lay awake – it had turned on one crazy move where I had completely misunderstood the position and failed to calculate the variations properly. It was infantile stuff, with me rather than my 11-year-old opponent cast as the infant. Coming so soon after Bournemouth, it reduced me to something close to despair. But Saunders offered some sage advice when I met him to analyse the game a couple of days later. 'Psychologically it can be quite hard to face children,' he said. 'The best advice is simply to be objective and non-discriminatory, and treat them as you would any opponent. By the same token, don't get too depressed if they duff you up. Good chess players come in all shapes and sizes.' He also pointed out that the girl I played was the fourth best female of her age group in the country; if she stuck with chess she would one day be very good indeed.

Saunders had an unusually testy exchange with me a few weeks later. I had recovered in the Felce Cup with two victories and told him I was trying out some new openings, including one called the Slav, which I hoped would solve the problems I repeatedly had as black when white opened by moving his pawn to d4. He dismissed my suggestion that a new repertoire of openings would in one bound set me free. 'Let's nail the opening fallacy once and for all,' he declared. 'Club players buy opening books by the bucketful simply because they misdiagnose their problems. The chess book industry is of course more than happy to feed their pointless addiction. Just as a bad workman blames his tools, the bad chess player blames his opening repertoire. It is possible to reach a remarkably high standard in chess with only the sketchiest knowledge of openings, acquired simply via practice. To improve, you need to read some chess books. But don't waste money on opening books; try to make it fun by working through puzzle books to sharpen your tactics. And find something elementary and enjoyable on the endgame. Sit down and work through the book, take it on journeys, read and re-read.'

Hartston had told me one of the reasons he gave up playing competitive chess at the age of 40 was that, with his days in the England team over as a new generation emerged in the 1980s, he had returned to playing club chess and was coming up against people he had played as he was rising through the ranks 20 years earlier. 'They were still making the same mistakes they'd made all those years ago,' he said. 'I thought this is a terrible rut to get stuck in, and it raised the question, why was I playing at all?' Emanuel Lasker, the world champion who said it should be possible to become an expert after just 200 hours of study and play, also despaired of the fact that so few students of the game made progress. 'There are a quarter of a million chess amateurs who devote to chess at least 200 hours every year and of these only a thousand, after a lifetime of study, attain the end [of true expertise].' In his *Manual of Chess* he lays out his solution: 'Education in chess has to be an education in independent thinking and judgement. Chess must not be memorised, simply because it is not important enough. If you load your memory, you should know why. Memory is too valuable to be stocked with trifles. Of my 57 years I have applied at least 30 to forgetting most of what I had learned or read, and since I succeeded in this I have acquired a certain ease and cheer which I should never again like to be without.'

For Lasker the key was to forget facts and dicta about chess, and concentrate on understanding the principles of the game: 'You should keep in mind no names, nor numbers, nor isolated incidents, not even results, but only *methods*. The method is plastic. It is applicable in every situation ... He who wants to educate himself in chess must evade what is dead in chess – artificial theories, supported by few instances and unheld by an excess of human wit; the habit of playing with inferior opponents; the custom of avoiding difficult tasks; the weakness of uncritically taking over variations or rules discovered by others; the vanity which is self-sufficient; the incapacity for admitting mistakes; in brief, everything that leads to a standstill or to anarchy.' Lasker's lessons attracted me because they could also be applied to life: don't take the easy option; avoid rote learning; work it out for yourself. If I could become a better player, I really would be on the way to becoming a better, more rounded person.

A3: THE TIGER AND THE MONK

If Bournemouth and my loss to the 11-year-old in the Felce were bad, there was soon worse to come. I hadn't given chess a thought for a fortnight and, tentatively returning to the fray, played some late-night games on gameknot.com – one of the weaker sites, where you can normally rack up a few easy wins. I was abysmal. You can tell immediately when you are playing poorly: your mind is dull; instead of seeing moves in clumps – an indication that you are functioning well – you play single, disconnected moves that lack structure and pattern. The essence of good chess is to build a sound foundation – this is the strategic bit – from which good moves and combinations (the tactics) flow. In many ways it resembles football: both games are about the exploitation of space, the nagging away at weak points in your opponent's defence, constantly probing until a gap appears. Goals rarely come out of the blue; they arise from concerted pressure over time, creating openings in attacks where you might have three or four different ways of getting the ball in the net. But instead of playing like Barcelona I was playing like Barnsley.

My bad night on gameknot came on top of several other worrying signs. I had lost my first league game of the season to a player graded only 107. In reality he was perhaps a bit better than that – he was young and his grade was still catching up with his ability – but I played abysmally and had a lost position by about move 12. He played an opening called the English (pawn to c4 followed by pawn to g3 to plant a powerful bishop on g2), and it flummoxed me. 'You don't know much about the English, do you?'

my opponent said to me after the game. Frankly I thought that was unnecessary. The awfulness of the defeat wasn't the only thing about the evening I hated. The room was packed – several league matches were in progress at the same time. It was stuffy and the BO from a couple of dozen middle-aged male chess players was even worse than usual. I sat squashed in my seat for two and a half hours and squirmed in the face of inevitable defeat. Why was I doing this? Rather than making the progress I'd hoped for, I seemed to be getting worse.

I had signed up to play in a weekender at the London Classic at Olympia in west London, the nearest thing the UK has to a festival of chess, where nine super-GMs were playing alongside a host of amateurs. I hoped to imbibe some of their greatness by osmosis. At the very least I hoped the place wouldn't smell. Happily it didn't, and I got even closer to greatness than I'd anticipated, taking a pee when I got there at the urinal next to the Armenian grandmaster Levon Aronian, who was then rated the second best player in the world. I couldn't, in the circumstances, quite bring myself to ask for his autograph. The chess was less inspiring. My first opponent, on a cold Friday evening, was a young Spanish girl. Her father, a strong player, patrolled nearby, though not so near as to attempt to influence the game. When I first saw her – as usual I was a bit late arriving – I anticipated an easy win. Her rating was not especially high and she looked angelic; not like a chess player at all. How appearances deceive. She proved to be a tough nut, playing steady, pragmatic chess. I established a slight advantage, then blew it as time started to run short, losing the thread of the game. It was a banal defeat.

I put on my coat, scarf and beanie hat – I at least looked like a chess player, unkempt, tubby, derelict – and melted into the night. Another weekender had started badly. It wasn't, though, another Bournemouth, thank God. I won my Saturday morning game against an elderly man who played very passively. Even then I couldn't quite finish him off, and he could have drawn if he had played soundly, but he went wrong in time trouble (when you have to play your moves with virtually no time left), gave away a pawn and allowed himself to be mated. I was ecstatic. I had recorded my first victory in a serious tournament. I put it down to better organisation. I'd got there early that morning, made sure I had a proper pen to record the moves, eaten a decent breakfast, tried to be coherent. It worked. Carrera was right: eat well, live well, play well.

Jonathan Rowson, a former triple British champion who was playing in the very strong Open tournament at the Classic, wrote about his preparation in his weekly chess column in the Glasgow *Herald* newspaper. He quoted former world champion Alexander Alekhine, who said that 'during a competition a chess player has to be both a beast of prey and a monk'. Rowson, who was in his mid-thirties and now a part-time chess player with a wife, a small child and a paying job (all of which should be anathema to the committed player), said he could no longer approach the game in the way he had when he was a fully fledged pro: 'Part of me would like to ascend to the roof terrace, and pay obeisance to the rising sun with 12 surya namaskaras, before preparing oatmeal porridge, solving a few tactical exercises and then getting stuck into three hours of intense opening preparation on ChessBase, but the reality has been rather different. I wake from a disturbed night in gentle desperation for a coffee that I barely have time to drink, negotiate various timings with my wife Siva, and then wrestle with my three-year-old son Kailash who never wants to wear his gloves on his way to nursery, despite the freezing cold. I get a walk of sorts on the way back home, and feel ready to get focused, but who's going to clean the kitchen? Call the childminder? Buy the Christmas tree?' Neither monk nor beast of prey, then, but doting dad.

Being a grandmaster with a FIDE rating close to 2600, Rowson still did OK, but he wasn't at quite the level he had been ten years earlier. In the primeval struggle that is a game of chess, focus, desire, stamina and the sheer will to win count for a great deal. The mental energy demanded by a four- or five- or, at the very highest level, six- or even seven-hour game is huge. Multiply that by five for a weekender played over two or three days, or ten – with a game a day, as in the Open at the Classic – and it becomes a draining experience. You need the porridge and the mental warm-ups; maybe even the yoga exercises. 'Preparation is partly about conditioning your nervous system for the delicate balance of imperious desire and contemplative restraint,' explained Rowson. The killer instinct of the tiger and the self-denial of the monk – this was the combination I had to seek. I feared that with me it was the other way round. But, still, I had won a game and felt pleased with myself as I consumed a half-cold piece of flan and slightly soggy scone in the Tesco just down the road from Olympia.

In the afternoon I reverted to type and played like a soggy scone. Again I was guilty of underestimating my opponent, a rotund old gent in a suit who kept falling asleep when it was my go. This, plus the fact he played a very odd move early in the game, made me think I would win easily, but thereafter he played OK while I lost my thread in the middle game and ceded him an advantage which he never quite relinquished. Again I felt I hadn't quite done myself justice, though I wasn't completely despondent. I was becoming more used to tournament conditions, had managed to register my first win, and wasn't beaten up in any of the three games. John Saunders, whom I now saw as my chess

27

doctor, summed up the third game as 'a bad opening but thereafter quite a good grovel'. I fought; I didn't just collapse as I had at Bournemouth. Once again, as at Bournemouth, I didn't appear for the third day, but at least this time it was because I had another engagement rather than because I was bottom of the entire competition and being forced to sit out a round. I wasn't quite a beast of prey yet, but nor was I any longer a sloth. I had graduated to the level of anteater. It was a start.

A4: A BRIEF HISTORY OF CHESS

 Chess has been played for more than 1,500 years, with most authorities plumping for India in or before the sixth century AD as its birthplace. H. J. R. (Harold) Murray, who wrote a vast history of the game published in 1913 and a condensed version which appeared posthumously, argued that chess originated in India, and his thesis has held sway ever since. He argued that it was 'the conscious and deliberate invention of an inhabitant of north-west India who flourished not earlier than the Huri domination of north India which lasted from AD 455 to 543'. Murray, a keen player as well as historian of the game, was in no doubt that the inventor had produced something of lasting value. 'This Indian, who well deserves his traditional title of philosopher from the benefit which he conferred on mankind by his invention of chess, set out with the intention of making a game which should symbolise a battle between two Indian armies as they existed in his day, and he named his game chaturanga, "the army game", using one of the current Sanskrit terms which meant "army".'

Harry Golombek, a prodigious writer on chess, questioned Murray's hypothesis in his history, published in 1976. He pointed out that other board games had been played for millennia before chess, and hypothesised that chaturanga might have been derived from a Chinese game. Nice though Murray's notion of a single begetter was, Golombek reckoned it was more likely to have evolved over centuries as merchants plied their trade in Asia. He did, though, accept that the game was codified in India, as a game played on 64 squares between two rival armies comprising a king, a minister, elephants (which moved diagonally as bishops do now), a horse (equivalent to the knight with the same peculiar – and, in Lewis Carroll's view, unstable – movement), and a chariot (equivalent to the rook). It wasn't quite the game as we now know it, but the family resemblance is instantly recognisable.

From India chess migrated to Persia and on to the Middle East. The numerous references to the game in *The Arabian Nights* attest to its popularity, which survived attempts by Islamic sects to outlaw it, though their opposition did result in the game being played with abstract pieces because of the Koranic ban on figurative images. From the Middle East it moved with the Muslim armies into Spain and thence to the rest of Europe, where from the 11th century on it became, literally, a game of kings and queens. Richard Eales, in *Chess: The History of a Game*, published in 1985, dates the first European reference to the game to a monastery at Einsiedeln in Switzerland just before the year 1000, but he reckons it was played in Europe for a generation before that. Murray argues for an even earlier date, suggesting that it may have been learned by Europeans who had visited Moorish cities such as Seville as early as 900. The English word 'chess' comes via the Latin '*scacci*' from the Arabic word 'shah'. Chess has always been, and remains, a gloriously global game.

Murray suggests King Cnut played chess, and was a very bad loser. Knights played the game on the crusades; Robert, the brother of Henry I of England, played while in prison in Cardiff Castle; and King John was also a mean chess player. The Vikings became keen on the game, and were responsible for the much-admired 12th-century Lewis chessmen, found on the Isle of Lewis in the Outer Hebrides in 1831 and now competed over by museums in England and Scotland (the British Museum holds 82 of the 93 artefacts, with the rest at the Museum of Scotland in Edinburgh). By the 12th or 13th century the game had also reached Russia, though patriotic historians in that country have at times tries to push the date back by a millennium or so.

The courts of medieval Europe changed the game in what Jenny Adams, an authority on chess in the late Middle Ages, calls 'a conscious attempt to map its own social structure on to the game'. In her book *Power Play* she traces the evolution: 'In a departure from its eastern predecessors, medieval chess in Europe featured a queen rather than a counsellor, a judge or bishop rather than an elephant, and a knight or horseman rather than a horse, names that made the game correspond to social classes of the cultures that played it. Particularly striking was the change of the Arabic *firz*, or *firzan*, a word that describes a male counsellor, to the European queen, or regina.' It is a peculiarity – one much commented on by psychoanalysts of a Freudian bent – of the game that has been handed down to us that the queen is the most powerful piece on the board, wreaking havoc as she flails in all directions, while the poor, emasculated king hides behind his pawns, emerging only at the end of the game when the battlefield has been cleared and he can shuffle around, a mere one square at a time, in relative peace, trying, usually when his queen is dead, to help another pawn to the eighth rank to create a new mate (and protector).

In the 15th century the game, enjoying its own version of the Renaissance, speeded up. Pawns were allowed to move two squares forward as their first move, the range of the bishop was extended and the queen became the all-powerful piece it is today, combining the diagonal movements of the bishop with the lateral movements of the rook. Golombek argues that the new form of the game preserved its popularity in a more demanding age, while Eales, who rubbishes the notion that the queen's new power reflected a change in the social status of women in the period, says play was revolutionised. 'The new chess must have struck the casual player as a rather different undertaking from the medieval game,' he writes. 'The increased striking power of the forces on both sides meant that the speed of attack and defence was quickened, while the consequences of a single weak move could be much greater.'

This more dynamic form of chess produced a generation of experts who began to lay the foundations of modern chess theory. The Portuguese player Pedro Damiano, who was born in 1480, wrote one of the first widely distributed treatises on the game, published in Italy in 1512. In the second half of the 16th century Ruy López de Segura, a Spanish priest who later became bishop of Segura, expressed himself dissatisfied with Damiano and published his own primer, *Libro de la Invención Liberal y Arte del Juego del Axedrez* (*Book of the Liberal Invention and Art of the Game of Chess*) – Renaissance writers did not favour snappy titles. The Ruy López opening (1. e4 e5 2. Nf3 Nc6 3. Bb5) is named after him, and also called the Spanish Game in his honour. He analyses the opening in detail in his book, but was not its originator – it is one of the 12 openings discussed in the so-called Göttingen manuscript, the earliest text on modern chess, which dates from the 1490s.

In the 17th century the experts from the Iberian peninsula gave way to Italians: Pietro Carrera, my mentor on clean living; Alessandro Salvio, a better player than Carrera and author of *Trattato dell'Inventione et Arte Liberale del Gioco Degli Scacchi*, published in 1604 in Naples, where Salvio founded a chess academy; and Gioachino Greco, a short-lived, much-travelled Calabrian (he was called 'Il Calabrese') who was reputed to be a brilliant attacking player and developed several famous gambit openings which are still widely used today. Mikhail Botvinnik, the great Russian-born world champion and founder of the Soviet school of chess, considered Greco the first true chess professional – he used to wager on the games he played – and admired his style of play. 'Greco introduced combinations into chess,' said Botvinnik in an interview published in 1988. 'Before his time there had been no such thing. It was a major step forward.'

In the 16th and early 17th centuries chess became a game for experts, and not everyone appreciated the fact. 'Chess-play is a good and witty exercise of the mind for some kind of men,' wrote Robert Burton in *The Anatomy of Melancholy*, first published in 1621 (almost exactly contemporary with Carrera's *Il Gioco degli Scacchi*), 'but if it proceed from overmuch study, in such a case it may do more harm than good; it is a game too troublesome for some men's brains, too full of anxiety, all out as bad as study; besides it is a testy, choleric game, and very offensive to him that loseth the mate.' This was one of the earliest suggestions that chess excellence and mental instability were closely related.

Literature, though, clung on to an older conception of chess. Shakespeare has Ferdinand and Miranda play chess at the end of *The Tempest* ('Sweet lord, you play me false,' she complains) in a scene which is both a neat commentary on the capture by Prospero of the usurper Alonso and a reflection of the acceptance of the game as a noble pursuit for courtly lovers. 'At chess the sexes met on equal terms,' Murray points out, 'and the freedom of intercourse which the game made possible was much valued. It was even permissible to visit a lady in her chamber to play chess with her.' In 1624 Shakespeare's contemporary, Thomas Middleton, wrote a play called *A Game at Chess* which used the game as an allegory for the conflict between Britain (the white side, naturally) and Spain (black), with pieces and pawns employed to lampoon political figures. It was banned after nine performances, but its popularity suggested that a wide public had no difficulty understanding what the game represented. Chess, *pace* Shakespeare, was being democratised.

As Carrera's book shows, by the 17th century the names of individual chess players were becoming known. Chess was changing from courtly pursuit to coffee-house pastime, and expertise now counted for more than chivalry. Carrera's is a treatise on how to play the game, and emerged in a period when Italian and Spanish players were for the first time mapping out the game as a competitive sporting endeavour founded on a body of theory and analysis. This, the so-called heroic age of chess, was the true beginning of the modern game. 'From now on,' argues Eales, 'chess grew and flourished because of its intellectual and sporting qualities rather than its symbolic prestige.' It had ceased to be a courtly diversion and became a subject of serious study and semi-organised competition, and in Greco it had the first example of a player who could earn his living at the game. Modern chess was born.

In the following century the centre of gravity in the chess world shifted from Spain and Italy to France and the UK. Chess is a very good barometer of power. As nations rise they tend to dominate the sport, which is why in the past couple of decades we have seen the emergence of India and China as leading chess nations. Chess relies on leisure and a growing middle class enamoured of a game which is perceived to be intellectual – as well as on infrastructure for training and on money to pay players and run tournaments. These are now in place in the big Asian economies just as they were in France and Britain back in the 18th century. Slaughter's Coffee House in St Martin's Lane, close to Covent Garden, became a magnet for London's best players. None, though, could compete with François-André Danican Philidor, a musician and chess genius who dominated the game in the second half of the 18th century. Philidor, who wrote a hugely popular chess manual and memorably pronounced that 'pawns are the soul of chess', was a subtler, more positional player than his contemporaries and revolutionised thinking about the game. According to Murray, 'he was the first player to realise the underlying principles [of chess] and to attempt to embody them in a definite system of play'. Philidor was also a notable exponent of blindfold chess, playing multiple opponents, and gave exhibitions which astounded audiences.

The greatest player of the early 19th century was another Frenchman, Louis-Charles Mahé de La Bourdonnais, unofficial world champion from 1821 until his death in 1840, when he was in his mid-forties. 'The quickness with which Bourdonnais calculates the *coups* is a beautiful part of his game,' wrote an English admirer in *Fraser's Magazine* in the year of his death. 'When I first had the honour of measuring weapons with Bourdonnais over the chessboard, his rapidity was to me positively terrific. I was lost in the whirl ... He seems to be a species of chess automaton, wound up to meet all conceivable cases with mathematical accuracy.' In 1834 Bourdonnais had an epic series of encounters with the Irish player Alexander McDonnell, prefiguring the great chess rivalries of the next two centuries – Steinitz and Lasker, Alekhine and Capablanca, Fischer and Spassky, Karpov and Kasparov, names forever intertwined. Bourdonnais also set something of a precedent for later chess masters by dying in poverty. Touchingly, chess player and author George Walker ensured that the Frenchman was buried close to his old rival McDonnell, who had died five years earlier, in Kensal Green cemetery, north-west London.

Bourdonnais was succeeded as unofficial world champion by the Englishman Howard Staunton, who gave his name to a design of chess pieces ('the Staunton pattern') that became standard throughout the world, gradually replacing the designs which had until then been characteristic of each of the leading chess-playing countries. The first major international tournament, which was organised by Staunton, was held in London in 1851 to coincide with the Great Exhibition – and competition players needed a standardised pattern. The design was commissioned by the English company Jaques and is usually attributed to Nathaniel Cook, with Staunton endorsing it in what was in effect the first big sports sponsorship deal.

Staunton gave way to the German-born Adolf Anderssen, who won the 1851 tournament and was accordingly recognised as world number one, but in 1858 Anderssen was decisively beaten by the brilliant young American Paul Morphy, who proceeded over the next three years to beat all comers before retiring. This early retirement and the fact he all but disappeared from view for two decades before his death at the age of 47 inevitably links him to his fellow American Bobby Fischer, who, after reaching the summit by winning the world title in 1972, peered over the other side, didn't like what he saw and stopped playing. In Morphy's case it can perhaps be explained by the fact that, as the scion of a wealthy professional family in New Orleans, chess was not seen as a fitting occupation, so he followed his father into the law. By all accounts he was a decidedly unsuccessful lawyer, but he refused to return to chess and died of a stroke in the bath in 1884, a bathetic (in every sense) end to one of the shortest, strangest yet greatest of chess careers. Philidor and Morphy are perhaps the two immortals of the era before the official world championship was instituted in 1886, though I retain a soft spot for Bourdonnais and his whirling fingers and obsession with the game. The report in *Fraser's* said he played from noon to midnight seven days a week, and 'if you are very slow he does not hesitate to tap the table lustily'.

The first official world champion was Wilhelm Steinitz, a mathematician born in Prague who later emigrated to the US, changing his name to William. He had been the world's strongest player since the mid-1860s, but was given the title officially only when he won a match with Johannes Zukertort that was deemed to have been 'for the Championship of the World'. The later world champion Botvinnik, in the interview in which he hails the greatness of Greco, names three other 'masters to whom chess players are especially indebted'. Greco represented the 17th century and was recognised as one of the founding fathers of the game for his combinative play; Philidor was chosen from the 18th century because, according to Botvinnik, 'he drew attention to the assessment of positions that are determined by the pawn structure'; Morphy was chosen because 'he demonstrated positional understanding in open games, where the pieces are mobile and the pawns play a subordinate role – what pawns were to Philidor, pieces were to Morphy'; and, finally, Steinitz was admitted to the pantheon because he 'contributed an understanding of closed positions [where the pieces are locked in by the pawn structure].' Greco, Philidor, Morphy, Steinitz – modern chess history in capsule form. 'Afterwards, all these ideas were developed,' said Botvinnik, 'but in the last hundred years there has been nothing fundamentally new.'

Steinitz was world champion for eight years, until he was defeated by Emanuel Lasker in 1894. Lasker, whom Mikhail Tal considered the greatest player of all time, was champion for 27 years – the longest reign of anyone and unlikely ever to be beaten now that title matches are more frequent and players' careers at the very top tend to be shorter. Steinitz and Lasker, by each dominating chess for a generation (the former was acknowledged as the world's best player for a couple of decades before he won the official title), became flag-bearers for the game and made the role of world champion all important. The fact there have been so few champions – Magnus Carlsen, who won the title in 2013, is only the 16th holder of the undisputed title – gives it extraordinary power. The British chess writer Bernard Cafferty has likened the roll-call of champions to an 'apostolic succession'.

Some of the magical 16 may be greater than others, but there are no duds. Occasionally chess writers pop up suggesting that the world championship be decided by an annual knockout event – a kind of Wimbledon of chess. When Carlsen challenged Viswanathan ('Vishy') Anand for the title in November 2013, US national master Matt Gaffney wrote a blog on the Slate website advocating ditching the world championship in favour of a tennis- and golf-style structure which combined a live ratings system to determine rankings and four 'grand slam' tournaments which would provide a framework for the chess world. The latter is certainly desirable: the current 'great' tournaments are rather random in terms of when they take place, whether sponsors can be found and who gets invited, and FIDE's grand prix system is still in its infancy. So four slams – in, say, Moscow, New York, London and Paris or Amsterdam – would be tremendous. But something crucial might also be lost if world champions came and went annually; that something is the way one player can define a generation. Yes, a Nicklaus or a Federer can still emerge in a slam system – players who are unquestionably first among equals – but would we get a Lasker, a Fischer or a Kasparov? Their longevity, or in Fischer's case the way he singlehandedly wrested the title from the Soviet Union, gave them a transcendence which even Nicklaus and Federer lack. These are not merely great players from chess history; they define that history and the way we think about it.

Each of what we might call the 16 'apostolic' champions holds a special place in the heart of chess players: Steinitz and Lasker, who between them founded the dynasty; José Capablanca, whose classical style is beloved of purists; the great tactical genius

Alexander Alekhine; the upright Dutchman Max Euwe, whose victory over Alekhine in 1935 shocked the chess world; the steely Botvinnik, who set the benchmark for 40 years of Soviet domination of world chess in the middle of the 20th century; Vasily Smyslov, Mikhail Tal, Tigran Petrosian, Boris Spassky – Soviet players who maintained their country's grip on the title until Bobby Fischer, the most charismatic player since Morphy, overturned it in the greatest match in chess history in 1972; Anatoly Karpov, who inherited Fischer's crown in 1975 without the American defending the title and as a result has sometimes not been given his due by the wider public, though the chess cognoscenti recognise his greatness; Garry Kasparov, a contender for greatest ever player; Vladimir Kramnik, the stately, sophisticated Russian who caused another upset when he defeated Kasparov in London in 2000; Viswanathan Anand, the first Indian champion, taking the game back to its birthplace and unleashing a chess boom there; and now Magnus Carlsen, the highest-rated player of all time.

The English grandmaster and chess journalist Jon Speelman, who was rated number four in the world in the late 1980s, said that picking the very greatest players among this 16 is a largely fruitless exercise. Kasparov, he suggested, was probably a stronger player than Fischer, but that is to miss the point. 'Every great player,' he said, 'creates a whirlwind in his time and the full force of the storm is not easily forgotten.' A magnificent phrase that sums up what each of these 16 players achieved. The game's future may be uncertain – will computers solve chess? Can it reclaim its place in the public affection? Will the Fischer–Spassky match prove to have been the zenith of the sport? – but its past has been a glorious one. Truly, as the Dutch grandmaster Hans Ree said, a game 'beautiful enough to waste your life for'.

A5: EPIPHANY IN CHESS-TER

 After the London Classic – by no means a triumph but not quite a disaster either – I played a couple of league matches for Surbiton, one of my two clubs. One was an emphatic win in which I really did, almost for the first time, feel I knew what I was doing, though my opponent was an elderly bloke who played very poorly and contrived to hand me a piece on about move eight, so any progress may have been illusory. In the other game, against a stronger opponent, I scraped a draw, having been up against it for the whole game – another triumph for the art of chess grovelling so admired by Dr Saunders. When you manage a draw in those circumstances it feels as good as a win.

The other step forward was that Saunders had shown me how to set up a chess database. I now had hundreds of thousands of grandmaster games on my hard drive, which I could play through and analyse with the help of a computer program stronger even than the world champion. (What I didn't have, of course, was the time, will or powers of application to do this hour after hour in true Gladwellian fashion.) More importantly I was able to start inputting and analysing my own games to see where I was going wrong, allowing the computer to show me the vast array of possibilities I had been missing. Imagine a game played by me as a walk down a single, straight, rather featureless road. Suddenly, thanks to the computer, I could begin to see the whole map – the maze of other streets, all the directions in which one could have gone. I was not going to play like an Aronian, no matter how often I peed next to him, but the computer and my database allowed me to begin to understand the complexity of a grandmaster's thought processes.

I felt I was making progress and, though it was the middle of winter and the country was blanketed by snow, I decided to enter a tournament in Chester. It appealed for several reasons: I had never been to Chester; the hotel in which it was being played was offering cheap deals and had a swimming pool; and, best of all, there was an under-135 section. With my grade of 133 I would be near the top of the handicap list. There were sure to be a large number of dangerous juniors playing, but there might also be some bald blokes I could actually beat. I prepared properly: took the day before the tournament off; gave myself plenty of time to get there; avoided alcohol; told myself to eat well. I felt I could make a mark in this event. At the very least I felt I could manage to play all five rounds. And who should I cross paths with in the hotel driveway as I arrived? Grandmaster Mark Hebden, a fiftysomething veteran who had been playing these bread-and-butter tournaments week in, week out for decades. I took our simultaneous arrival as an omen. This was going to be my moment. I had prepared like a monk – give or take the sausage roll and custard tart I felt compelled to buy on my way. Now it was time to unleash the tiger.

It didn't feel like that in the first game, in which I played black against a crusty old retainer who, despite a grade of just 110, seemed to know his way round the chessboard. I played a dull opening; he exerted a tiny bit of pressure; then, after 24 moves, he offered a draw. Seeing only a long grind ahead, and thinking that if anything he had the most microscopic of edges, I accepted. Maybe this was pusillanimous. There was £300 for the winner of this section of the tournament and I ought to have been chasing every point. I tried to reason that I was playing the long game (ironically by playing a short game in the first round). I knew it was a bit feeble, yet after my earlier losing starts in tournaments I was pleased to be on the scoreboard. The early finish meant I could also retire to the hotel bar for two post-match beers. This was hardly monastic, but I needed to loosen up a bit.

It also gave me the chance to talk to a nice man from Liverpool, who had won the game on the adjoining table to me when his opponent – like me graded 133 – had blundered horribly. The Liverpudlian was besotted with chess. He had taken it up at the age of 32, but had the enthusiasm of the latecomer, took lessons, knew his openings thoroughly, played by the book. He didn't have a job, was unmarried, and chess had become fundamental to his life – the board as world, a world which made sense. I had noticed during the game how heavy his breathing had become when he was under pressure and it looked as if he would lose – his higher-graded opponent had a stronger position but threw it away. His breathing had sounded more like sexual congress than a chess congress, and made me think that for many of these middle-aged chess players the game offered something of the excitement of sex, a distant memory for most of us. Why else would we be turning up for long weekends in anonymous hotels?

Once again the great majority of the participants were male: Asian schoolboys with eager mothers in tow; the obligatory old blokes who had played chess since its heyday in the 1950s; and a few men of indeterminate age in between. Whether 30 or 50, they largely conformed to type: bespectacled, unathletic, receding hair, computer programmers to a man. There were exceptions, of course, but the stereotype held true in a surprising number of cases. Chess Man exists. Some had brought their partners along, and Chess Woman, too, conformed to type: a very large type; some so large they could barely move from their seats in the bar.

Part of my preparation for the Chester Congress had been watching an episode of *Midsomer Murders* called 'The Sicilian Defence' in which a serial killer runs amok at a chess club. The programme got quite a lot wrong: you do not shout 'check' in the middle of the tournament room; indeed there is no obligation to tell your opponent his king is in check – any self-respecting player will be aware of that. And few games will get as far as checkmate. Most players will realise the game is up before the denouement and resign. But it also got a surprising amount right: the long-haired kid with the pushy mother; the middle-aged loner who lives for chess; the earnest health freak (they do exist amid all the beer bellies) focused on the game, seeing it as part of the Darwinian struggle to come first in life. The world outside is stuck on the oddness of chess players, and while the suggestions of lunacy – the genius-next-to-madness line – can be overdone, there is some truth in it. This is an odd, hermetically sealed world. I heard one of the chess wives explaining to a woman staying in the hotel but not connected to the tournament that she and her husband quite frequently spent their weekends in this way. The woman being initiated into the ways of chess weekenders was incredulous and quickly switched the conversation to the iciness of the road from Runcorn.

The second day was frustrating and exhausting. By the end, after eight hours of grinding chess, I was spent – and a little depressed. I had played OK in the two Saturday games, but no more than OK. I won a game I should have drawn and drew a game I should have won. I had two points out of three and would be out of the money – one player had three out of three and three others had 2.5. Tomorrow would be a very long day. My opponent in the game I won but should have drawn was deeply irritating. He kept offering me draws, and in the end I had to ask him to be quiet. Then I made him play on in a position which was technically drawn, and he blundered away a pawn and lost the game. He then had the gall to imply that I was unsporting for making him carry on in a drawn position. Early in the game he had spilt a cup of coffee over himself, so perhaps he was a little perturbed. I also noticed he made no attempt to keep an accurate score of the game – scribbling nonsense on the scoresheet to save himself time. I would have lodged an official complaint if I hadn't won the game. Perhaps I was developing that necessary core of steel.

Towards the end of my Saturday morning game, I was so irritated by my coffee-stained opponent that I kept telling myself to 'play like a machine' – a variant, perhaps, of Alekhine's 'beast of prey'. Show no emotion, no sympathy, just kick the other guy as hard and as often as possible. But in the afternoon, despite having my opponent on the run for almost four hours, I couldn't quite manage to secure the victory. I should have won, could have won, but he outplayed me in the endgame – I was in time trouble, with just a few seconds to play each move – and he escaped with a draw. I was dejected: that half-point made a big difference. I couldn't face spending a second evening surrounded by men with chess programs, so took a taxi into Chester. But the half-timbered houses and deserted streets depressed me even more. I'd hoped to have a pizza, but Chester's gastronomic delights were limited and I ended up having a cheeseburger and chips for £2.08 in McDonald's. Truly I had become a tournament chess player: prone to depression and obsessed with economy.

The following morning I woke feeling a little better – and determined to enjoy the games I still had left to play. Because I was the joint highest-rated player in my section of the tournament (remember, this was division three), I had been playing under a burden of expectation. I expected to be in with a shout of winning the first prize of £300. As a result I had lost sight of the potential beauty of the game, of the free play of the imagination, and been playing too mechanically. I needed to learn how to delight in the Zen-ness of the game, to lose myself in its boundless possibilities. Winning was the objective – playing a beautiful game was a distant second – yet to win you had to free yourself from that mechanical mentality. That was what Andrew Soltis, in *What It Takes to Become a Chess Master*, meant when he said you had to remake yourself as a player as you went up the rankings: mechanical chess was good enough to beat weak players, but more sophisticated strategies were needed against more seasoned campaigners. Against anyone of any ability, to win you needed to pursue many lines of thought rather than just one, to light small tactical fires all over the board (a skill I had noticed Emanuel Lasker had in abundance). But by playing with more imagination, you might also have to open yourself to the possibility of defeat. Greater complexity could mean greater danger: anyone unwilling to accept that risk was destined to chess mediocrity.

On Sunday morning, after a refreshing swim in the hotel pool, it was time to put my new theory of open, flexible, dynamic, uninhibited chess to the test. And do you know what? It worked. I felt more relaxed, in control, had some reasonable ideas and was enjoying it. Thanks to a powerful attack, I managed to win my first game after a couple of hours' play. The second game was even better – a tense struggle which, despite having the disadvantage of playing black, I eventually won. In both games, against capable opponents, I felt I could play. These two wins meant I ended up on four points out of five – enough for a share of first prize in my section. The three joint winners of the under-135 event shared £525. I had won some money at rapidplay events before, but this was my biggest purse. For the first time I felt like a chess pro and started to resent the idea of having to do things other than study and play chess. I was still at a low base, but I was convinced I was making progress. The ghost of Bournemouth had been exorcised. Chess-ter, as a friend of mine insisted on calling it, was my salvation. That slog through the snow, the headaches induced by close on 20 hours of chess, had all been worthwhile. I was happy. Bobby Fischer was right: winning chess games is better than sex. Not that we committed chess players are really in a position to make a comparison.

A6: GRAND MASTERY

I had met Stuart Conquest, British champion in 2008 and an itinerant grandmaster then living in Spain, a couple of years previously while I was spectating at the annual Hastings tournament, and liked him immediately. He was amusing, apparently free of hang-ups, more worldly than the average GM. He was a friend of John Saunders and occasionally slept on his sofa while visiting London. He was also organiser of an annual tournament in Gibraltar in which I was about to make my international debut. I was looking for a grandmaster with whom to build a working relationship, and Conquest seemed a possibility. To test the water we spent an afternoon together in Bristol, where he was visiting his father. Spending time with his dad must have made him nostalgic because when we met he brought along the pocket chess set on which he used to play as a boy, his old trophies – he was world under-16 champion in 1981 at the age of just 14 – and some of the books that had inspired him as a youngster.

Conquest was in his mid-forties at the time of our meeting in Bristol and his competitive chess career was winding down. Forty is often a watershed for chess players – brain cells start to decay, powers of calculation diminish, stamina is reduced, the slide down the rankings accelerates. Some older players carry on, content to play at a diminished level – Viktor Korchnoi, the Soviet dissident who played against Anatoly Karpov for the world title in 1978 and 1981, was still in the world top 100 at the age of 75 and only a stroke at the age of 81 quelled his extraordinary will to compete – but others pack it in. Conquest surprised himself and the chess world by winning the British championship in 2008, after he had passed that watershed birthday. But when we met he was developing an alternative career as a coach, commentator and tournament organiser. A year or so after our meeting in Bristol he moved to Gibraltar to take a full-time role running junior chess there and co-ordinating the big open tournament held every January. He is literate, quirky and quick-witted; his chess is highly creative, and he describes his playing style as 'irresponsible, inventive, chaotic'. It sounded wonderful.

Sitting in a canal-side café in the centre of the city, I asked whether his love of chess remained undimmed 40 years after he first learned the game. He paused. 'My respect for it is,' he said. 'My appreciation of it. I will still gladly pick up an old chess book, and I had the thrill of my life recently when I discovered the Zukertort grave.' On a walk in Brompton Cemetery in west London, Conquest had happened on the grave of Johannes Zukertort, the Polish-German player who lost to Steinitz in 1886 in the encounter now seen as the first official world championship match. The grave was overgrown, and Conquest had to clear away weeds to read the inscription. So moved was he by the discovery and by Zukertort's story – Zukertort died two years after the title match at the age of 45 – that he determined to clean up the grave and erect a new memorial, which was unveiled on one of the few sunny days of the summer of 2012, one top-class player paying homage to another across the centuries. So the love remained, but not what Conquest calls the 'lust' for chess. He no longer felt the need to play all the time. 'I'm not training and working at chess as much as I used to,' he admitted.

Among the precious items he brought from his father's house to show me was the first book that inspired him – Irving

Chernev's *The Golden Dozen: The Twelve Greatest Chess Players of All Time*. 'I loved the cover,' he said. 'Maybe I became a chess professional because of this book.' The cover shows chess pieces on pedestals; on each pedestal is the name of a legendary player – Alekhine, Bronstein, Smyslov, Fischer, Spassky, Botvinnik, Nimzowitsch, Capablanca, Tal, Rubinstein, Petrosian, Lasker. 'There was a pedestal free,' explained Conquest, 'and I remember thinking, "Maybe I can get on that one."' The book had a lovely inscription from his father, who gave his nine-year-old son the book in 1976: 'To Stuart, because he has worked so hard, all my love, Daddy.'

He grew up in Hastings (where else could a Conquest hail from?), home of an internationally renowned tournament and a well-established chess club. His first teacher, apart from his father, was Arthur Winser, a player with a grade of 200-plus who won the Hastings club championship on many occasions. Winser, who died in 1991 at the age of 84, must have been a delightful teacher. Conquest showed me another of his boyhood books, this time with an inscription from Winser: 'To Stuart on his 10th birthday, with Faith that he will achieve greatness, Hope that this will bring him joy, and Love that now surrounds him will continue all his days.' The words Faith, Hope and Love were picked out in orange felt pen. Despite the inscription's peculiar syntax, it was clear Winser worked as hard on the gift as he did on his chess. 'Arthur always said to me, "Stuart, the endgame is vital – you have to learn about endgames. And not just learn them, but appreciate and love them."' Conquest showed me a famous endgame study which inspired him. It was devised by Richard Réti, born in Prague at the end of the 19th century and another of his heroes, in part because of his early death at 40. Conquest was evidently a romantic.

This is the position dreamed up by Réti, a noted composer of endgame studies.

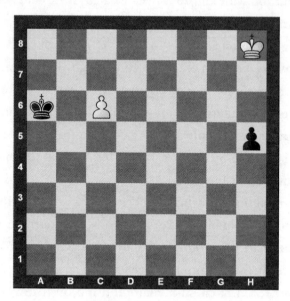

White to play and draw

It is white to move, playing "up" the board, but the situation looks hopeless. The black pawn must surely reach the first rank and become a queen. Yet, incredibly, the white king can catch the pawn by moving along the diagonal and keeping alive the threat of promoting its own pawn and being first to queen. White must play Kg7; black responds with h4 – again it looks utterly lost for white, but appearances deceive. White plays Kf6 and now black must lose a tempo (in effect a move but with the suggestion of time – in chess time is everything) by playing Kb6 to stop the white king coming to the aid of the pawn and allowing it to queen first. White now plays Ke5 and suddenly black can no longer win. If the black king captures the white pawn, the white king has time to scuttle across to intercept the black pawn. If black chooses to push the pawn instead, the white king can retreat to d6 and help his own pawn to reach the eighth rank and become a queen, leading to a theoretically drawn position with king and queen against king and queen. This study encapsulates all the wonder of chess, a wonder that conquered the young Conquest and won him for life: on the surface, the game is up for white, yet with precise calculation it can be drawn. It is an example, frequent in chess, of appearance and reality being at odds. One reason computers are so proficient at chess is that they do not play optically; they simply calculate. All they are interested in is the truth of a position.

Conquest told me these endgame studies were 'priceless' and hymned their intrinsic beauty. 'They are like a microcosm of chess,' he said. 'This is the nuts and bolts of chess and, stripped down like that, it becomes a Zenny motorbike kind of thing.' I had already been thinking of my odyssey as an attempt to embrace the Zen of chess, so it was pleasingly synchronous that Conquest should allude to Robert M. Pirsig's bestseller, *Zen and the Art of Motorcycle Maintenance*, which like everyone else I had read as a student in the 1970s in the search for enlightenment. When we left the café, we immediately came across Pirsig's book on a bookstall beside the canal. This must, I felt, be ordained, so I bought it for £3.50.

As the work he had done in building a proper memorial to Zukertort demonstrated, Conquest was in love with the history of the game. He said he was glad he had learned to play in the pre-computer era because he had been forced to absorb the game from the great masters: 'You do feel when you see these 14- and 15-year-olds with a rating of 2580, and playing endless games, that they are probably ignorant of lots of chess history. I was taught by people who'd played these great players in their day, and I was lucky as a child to play in simultaneous displays against some of the greats – Spassky, Karpov, Korchnoi, Kasparov, even Botvinnik. How about that? Then when I was older, I beat Tal and drew with Smyslov playing them one to one. Amazing. I was very lucky.'

He decided to become a professional chess player after his A levels and gave up a place at Cambridge, where he had intended to study modern languages. He said he now regretted not going, but the decision is one professional chess players frequently make. Conquest became a grandmaster in his mid-twenties. I asked him what it meant to get that mystical title. 'It's something many people would sell their grandmother for,' he said. 'It was the result of hard work, commitment and following one's dream.' Some players, especially those in middle age, believe the title has been devalued because of the proliferation of grandmasters over the past couple of decades – that ratings inflation problem again – but Conquest has no such doubts. He reckons the title still encapsulates mastery, mystique, a dash of magic. Grandmaster v grandmother? No contest.

A7: SHORT AND ALMOST SWEET

 The Tradewise Gibraltar Chess Festival is one of the most prestigious tournaments in the world – 260 entrants, 50 grandmasters, a battery of international masters and other titled players. The centrepiece is a terrifyingly strong open tournament played in the Caleta Hotel, which is perched on the Rock, overlooking the Mediterranean. I had booked to play in one of the satellite competitions spinning round this gallery of international talent – a five-day tournament for players rated under 1900; quite a bit stronger than Chester and potentially painful. I would need to be at maximum Zen readiness, but I was far from that blissful state. I was tired, in the middle of a complicated domestic falling-out, lacking all focus. It would, I told myself, be impossible to play in this condition. I would make a fool of myself – in front of 50 grandmasters. In front of my chess doc, too – John Saunders was doing the online reports and games analysis for the event.

British grandmaster and former world championship contender Nigel Short was also in Gibraltar. A few years previously I'd worked with him on a chess column for *The Guardian* in which he passed on grandmasterly tips to me. We never really made much progress, finding it more congenial to drink large amounts of red wine at his home in Greece (he is married to a Greek woman and has two children) as we ramblingly discussed chess, but I'd enjoyed the encounters and they made me want to test whether it really would be possible to achieve a marked improvement as a chess player at my advanced age. (*The Guardian* column was called 'The Rookie', so the way those meetings in Athens sowed the seeds of this odyssey are fairly obvious.) Short lost horribly against a much weaker Spanish player on the day I arrived in Gibraltar, and I wondered how approachable he would be, but he greeted me warmly in the bar afterwards, and I joined him and a group of his fellow players for a meal later. It was a joshing affair, with Short holding court among mostly younger GMs and IMs. There was much more discussion of sex than chess. Had it been a group of, say, top Bulgarian rather than English players, then no doubt discussions of the latest developments in opening theory would have been more prominent, but Short is not made that way. Chess is his life – he has played since he was six, was a great prodigy, beat the former world champion Anatoly Karpov in a famous match, challenged Garry Kasparov for the world title in 1993, has strong claims to be considered the greatest ever British player – but, unlike some players, he is aware of life beyond the board.

Short, as ever, was the life and soul of the evening, amusing, scurrilous, mostly keeping on the right side of good taste. There was some discussion of his afternoon demolition. Though he was putting a brave face on it, the defeat had clearly hurt him. He said he hadn't been playing well for some time and needed to put in some serious work to re-oil the mental cogs – he was close to 50, geriatric for a chess player, though up to this point he had managed to a remarkable degree to maintain his strength and was still close to a rating of 2700, giving him the distinction of being the oldest active player in the world top 100. One of the GMs present, Joe Gallagher, another former British champion, stirred the pot a little: 'But maybe it's all over, Nigel. Perhaps at 50 no amount of work is going to reverse the effects of anno domini. Short was not quite sure how to take this and there was a brief silence. Amid the joshing it was a serious question – when is enough enough?

'I suppose I am reaching the point where I can soon wave my bat to the pavilion,' said the cricket-loving Short. But it is a fair bet he never will. Besotted with chess, he will probably play until he drops. Whereas Conquest was happy to segue into a career as teacher, organiser, guru, Short needed to test himself at the board. The urge to compete was seemingly unquenchable.

The next day he was asked in an online broadcast how he coped with such a dramatic setback. 'Usually after losing I am pretty bad company,' he said. 'But this game was so bad it didn't feel like it was me playing. I felt very detached before the game and therefore it hurt less. When it is an unmitigated disaster it is almost funny.' He demonstrated his capacity to recover from a disastrous defeat, winning a string of games. He finished as one of four top-scoring players and came second in the play-off, edged out by the Russian grandmaster Nikita Vitiugov. It was a remarkable performance by Short and showed his competitive edge was as sharp as ever.

Would meeting Short again inspire me? It seemed unlikely. I found the hotel in which the tournament was played oppressive. All that combined chess power intimidated me. The players would form little cliques – English, Spanish, Russian – and it was hard to break in. Gibraltar itself is an insular place – a little bit of old England under a Spanish sun (and, in January, quite a lot of Spanish rain). The chess hotel felt like a hermetically sealed world existing within another hermetically sealed world – a series of Russian dolls. The local paper gave huge coverage to the event, and dignitaries would arrive every day to give it their blessing, but very few members of the public came to have a look.

I was staying across the Spanish border in La Línea – in part because it was cheaper, but also because I'd had a premonition that I would find a week in Chessville claustrophobic. It worried me that this might mean I wasn't obsessive enough about the game to make the great leap forward I hoped. I wanted my chess to have wit and life, and I didn't believe I could achieve that if I tunnelled into this labyrinthine world; I wanted to arrive by air. That was my excuse for breaking away one afternoon and going down the coast to Tarifa, the most southerly point in Europe. I walked across the causeway to the fort beyond the beach and stood alone in the sand-filled wind and the spray – the most southerly human on the European mainland. I misunderstood the timetable at Tarifa bus station and ended up having to wait two hours for the bus back to La Línea. There was nothing for it but to study some chess. I had brought three books on chess with me for my week in Gibraltar, plus two non-chess books. So far only the latter had been consulted, but with the moment of my entrance into the tournament imminent I had taken only a chess book to Tarifa and, as I sat there marooned in the rain and a force nine gale, I had no alternative but to look at it. It was a book on an opening called the Scandinavian Defence (a bizarre name, given that it originated in Spain in 1475), where black plays pawn to d5 in response to pawn to e4. I had had terrible trouble finding a good response to pawn to e4 – a rather fundamental problem for a chess player since this is the most common opening move, at amateur level anyway – and hoped the Scandinavian, which cuts out lots of theory and gets white playing on ground chosen by black, would be the answer. Even if it didn't, at least it passed the time waiting for the bus.

The sun shone the next day – and it especially shone on me. I managed a quick win with some tactical shots that lifted my mood hugely. Although the English Chess Federation had published their half-yearly revised grades that morning (and, worryingly, I had gone down to 128), this win against a 150-rated opponent (admittedly quite an elderly man whose best days at the board were behind him) and the still luminous memory of the

Chester triumph made that seem irrelevant. I convinced myself I was on the verge of a breakthrough.

My second game in Gibraltar was a short draw against an ex-pat who lived in Algeciras, a large Spanish town on the other side of the bay. He was a decent player and I didn't feel like a long-drawn-out battle, so we agreed a draw and settled on the hotel terrace to drink beer in the pale January sun. I was pleased with my performance so far, and the upside of not winning the game was that I wouldn't be paired with one of the half-dozen players who had won both their games.

I was very keen to win my third game against a Romanian whose strength was hard to gauge. One observer, having looked at some of his games on a database, assured me my opponent was a 'fish' (Soviet chess-speak for a weak player ready to be netted), but I wasn't so sure. I had black for the second game in a row and, because my opening theory on the black side was even sketchier than when I played with the white pieces, I wasn't confident. Perhaps I would prove to be the mackerel. But the incentive if I won was that I would be in the top four or five for the fourth round, with my game broadcast live online by webcam and shown on the display boards in the hotel lounge for all the grandmasters who would be playing later in the day to admire (or, more likely, mock). It was a big incentive, but also added pressure, and I had no idea how I would respond.

Perhaps in the end it meant too much. I played well and had a small advantage after being on the defensive for much of the game, but then I blew up, missing a move that would have given me very good winning chances (see Game 2 on p380). In the opening my opponent had played aggressively and gone for a mating attack on my kingside, but I defended well. I then surprised him – and myself too – with a knight sacrifice that left me a pawn up. I thought I could make the pawn count in the endgame, but made a series of blunders in my customary time trouble and collapsed. My lack of experience in a tight position where I had no more than ten seconds to make each move meant my brain froze. After four hours of fierce combat I had lost. It was a desperately disappointing defeat. No showboards, no webcam, no grandmasterly attention, just mid-table mediocrity and, over the next two mornings, a couple of largely meaningless games – one a victory, the other a defeat which my plain-speaking chess doc described as 'a fiasco'. My opponent in that defining third game, who had a FIDE rating of 1790, had been a bit stronger than I had expected. Certainly no fish. But nor was he a shark, and with correct play in the endgame I could have won, and should at the very least have managed a draw. He had missed my neat knight sacrifice and congratulated me on it after the game – an act of graciousness he might not have extended if he had lost. Later I bumped into Nigel Short and told him I had lost in distressing circumstances. Any advice on what I should do to cope with the pain of defeat, I asked. Try suicide, he suggested helpfully.

A8: THE VIEW FROM BUNNYSVILLE

One evening at Gibraltar, I attended a masterclass by the Soviet-born grandmaster Gata Kamsky, who moved to the US when he was 15. He had been a world top-ten player in the 1990s, then taken an eight-year break from chess, and had now returned for a second career. At the board he had an aggressive demeanour, with his close-cropped hair, square head and tendency to scowl. As with many great chess players, he exuded intensity. But in this late-evening setting in a crowded basement room at the Caleta, analysing a complex game that had given him great pleasure (a win, of course), he was almost endearing. He talked about two of his chess heroes – the Armenian-born world champion Tigran Petrosian and Akiba Rubinstein from Poland, an artist of the chessboard from the early part of the 20th century who many believe is the greatest player never to have become world champion. Kamsky said he did not like to subject games by Rubinstein and Petrosian to computer analysis in case he found holes in them. 'Computers are too strong nowadays,' he complained. 'Leave me with the dreams of my youth.' I warmed to this romantic vision of chess and his talk of the beauty of the game. Like any hard-headed pro he needed to make a living, but winning wasn't everything – there was still scope to enjoy the game and respond to it aesthetically. I might not have been able to understand all Kamsky's play, but I could identify with his motivation for playing and maybe even his need to take a long break from the game, which can grind you down if you are playing badly.

One advantage of playing in an international tournament was that I would start to build up a bank of FIDE-rated games on which an international rating would be based – useful if I wanted to play more tournaments outside the UK. With two wins, a draw and two defeats, my performance in Gibraltar was rated 1674, respectable enough in my first tournament abroad. I hadn't been humiliated – that was the main thing. It was January, but when the sun came out it was warm, and I had a celebratory swim in the bay at the foot of the ridge on which the hotel stood. I felt free, and content with what I had achieved. I almost felt like a chess player.

The games in the Masters event started at 3pm, and many were still in progress six hours later. Some of those competing had also played in the satellite tournaments in the morning, so it was a monumental mental and physical effort. I got to know the young English GM Stephen Gordon a little during the tournament, and noticed he used to take two bananas in to each game – something I made a mental note to emulate. I'd been taking in a Twix and eating it by about move eight. I also looked for an at-board style to emulate. I admired Joe Gallagher – the veteran English GM who had given Nigel Short pause for thought in the restaurant – for the way he put his nose close to the pieces on his side of the board and rocked back and forth. He was close to 50 and had played more professional poker than chess over the preceding decade, but he still played a mean game and did very well in the tournament.

It was fun to wander round the big room in which the tournament leaders played (one of the subsidiary rooms, to which the laggards in the tournament were consigned, was cruelly nicknamed 'Bunnysville'), rubbing shoulders – or more often stomachs – with these legendary figures as they paced back and forth: the great Ukrainian Vasily Ivanchuk, Alexei Shirov from Latvia, the Russian Artur Jussupow. I made a point of trying to brush against them in the hope that some of their chess magic would rub off. One evening I inveigled Emil Sutovsky into the hotel restaurant for a long chat about the state of chess. Sutovsky, a delightful man who speaks five languages, was uniquely well placed to explain how the sport currently stood because as well as being a wonderfully creative player – former youth world champion and European champion – he was also president of the Association of Chess Professionals, the GMs' negotiating body, much needed in the murky world of international chess.

Sutovsky wasn't having a great tournament, but he was still happy to talk – more than many self-absorbed players would be willing to do. As president of the chess pros he said he was suspicious of tournament organisers who wanted to speed up the game in an attempt to increase spectator appeal. He reckoned faster time limits would undermine the integrity of chess – forcing players to cut corners and reducing that all-important search for the truth of a position – without greatly expanding its audience. 'There is a danger that we will lose the support of people who see chess as a traditional, intellectual, royal game,' he said. 'We have to preserve our niche.'

According to Sutovsky, there were around 1,500 active grandmasters in the world, playing competitively and earning a living from chess. But of that 1,500, he said only 200 earned their living exclusively from playing – the rest relied on coaching and writing. Many of those 200, he admitted, were far from wealthy. The top 20 earned well; those lower down the list struggled, but Sutovsky said that was their choice because if they wished they could coach. 'Coaching is a hard job and it's not to everybody's liking,' he explained. 'Playing is much more fun.' But surely playing is tough, I suggested; the pressure must be enormous. 'That's the fun of it,' he said. Spoken like a true competitor.

Sutovsky was number 17 in the world in 2004; when we met he was down to 60. He put the decline down to his other responsibilities – the presidency of the ACP, a wife and two children – and to the chess player's mortal enemy, age. 'It takes away a bit of energy,' he said. 'I'm also not sure now what my motivation is in chess, and that can be a problem. I can't say I have any target other than to win any tournament I participate in. I can't say that my aim is to be in the top ten in the world, because that isn't realistic, and to be top 20, which is realistic, is not a good motivation for someone who has been really high in the past.' He said such a target now would be a burden rather than an inspiration.

He learned to play chess at the age of four, and there was never much doubt it would be his life. He was born in Baku, also the birthplace of Garry Kasparov, and for a while the two lived in the same street. 'When I was six years old Kasparov would move pieces with me,' Sutovsky recalled. 'I was kids' champion of the Soviet Union, and even though I went to university and got an economics degree I never doubted that I would be a professional chess player. My passion for chess was always too serious to consider switching to something else. I just loved it.'

Sutovsky is steeped in the history of chess and says he could tell you who played in every world championship match and what the result was. But, as Stuart Conquest had pointed out to me back in Bristol, that is changing: many players, who now rely on computers rather than books, are becoming ahistorical. 'I was talking to one of the very top players, rated 2780 or something like that,' Sutovsky recalled, 'and he didn't know which year Fischer–Spassky was played. I couldn't believe it, but that doesn't prevent him being a great player. For me, though, chess is more than just a branch of sport. I am conscious of the heritage of chess and think we have to preserve the memory of those who allowed chess to reach its peak – all the champions of the past and even some of the great players who didn't become world champion. We have to build on the skeletons of these great players of the past. Traditions are not always respected in chess today, but I care passionately about them.' If chess forgets its past, it becomes a mere pastime.

FILE B
Art and War on the Road to Torquay

'Chess is the most elaborate waste of human intelligence outside of an advertising agency'
— *Raymond Chandler, novelist*

B1: LUZHIN AND LUNACY

'Are chess players mad?' I asked Emil Sutovsky when I cornered him in the restaurant of the Caleta Hotel in Gibraltar. Sutovsky clearly isn't, but what about the rest? He admitted some were a little eccentric, but said the link between madness and genius in chess players was exaggerated: 'The image has been encouraged by books such as Nabokov's *The Luzhin Defense* and by people such as Bobby Fischer, who was a bit crazy. But look at the top guys today – Carlsen, Anand, Aronian – they are absolutely normal. The mad chess player is a cliché; it's almost part of the mythology of the game.' Nevertheless the media and the public latch on to eccentric chess players; they need to believe in the myth of the crazed genius. Doc Saunders felt strongly about this. He reckoned the media fed off this myth – or perhaps near-myth – of the mad chess player. We journalists got interested in chess only when a player had a back story, preferably one tinged by insanity. In that sense Fischer was the template of what the chess player should be, and the danger was that, because no one else would ever be quite that unhinged, so chess would never again generate headlines quite that big.

As Sutovsky said, Vladimir Nabokov has to take some degree of responsibility for this. His chess prodigy, the St Petersburg-born Aleksandr Ivanovich Luzhin, is a withdrawn child who comes alive only when he discovers chess. From an early age Luzhin is attracted by patterns, mathematical puzzles, jigsaws and Sherlock Holmes novels. He is clumsy, anti-social, uncouth, unwashed and, as an adult, chain-smokes. Reading the book, one is drawn inescapably to the conclusion that he has a mental problem – Asperger's, autism, obsessive-compulsive disorder, perhaps allied to psychological problems relating to his difficult relationship with his father, whose grave he can never bring himself to visit. It describes a life which is not untypical of quite a few chess players: the logical problem-solving demanded of a chess game makes sense; the messier challenges of life don't.

In the novel, Nabokov draws many parallels between chess and music. Early on a violinist speaks of his love of chess to Luzhin's father: 'What a game, what a game … Combinations like melodies. You know I can simply *hear* the moves … The game of the gods. Infinite possibilities.' When he first sees the game being played, Luzhin looks for 'those harmonious patterns the musician had spoken of'. His spatial genius and problem-solving abilities mean he locates them easily, and he becomes a world-renowned player, but has a nervous breakdown while playing his arch-rival, the expansive Italian Turati, marries a woman who tries to remove chess from his life, and in the end kills himself. Chess is both the source of his problems – his endless, exhausting striving for those perfect harmonies – but also the only thing that sustains him. He has no interest in anything beyond the board.

The portrait of Luzhin is significant because others have taken it at face value. The philosopher George Steiner, who covered the Fischer–Spassky match in Iceland in 1972 for the *New Yorker* and published the resulting essay as a short book called *The Sporting Scene: White Knights of Reykjavik*, wrote that Nabokov 'comes as near as anyone has' to capturing the paranoia and unreality inherent in chess. There are many references in Nabokov's book to the dangerous absurdity of devoting your life to chess. Luzhin's manager and 'chess father', the controlling Valentinov, is said to have 'showed him [Luzhin] to wealthy people as an amusing monster'; early in their relationship, Luzhin's wife-to-be describes him as 'the most unfathomable of men, a man who occupied himself with a spectral art'; and her mother deems Luzhin's profession 'trivial, absurd … The existence of such professions was explicable only in terms of these accursed modern times, by the modern urge to make senseless records … It seemed to her that in former times, in the Russia of her youth, a man occupying himself exclusively with chess would have been an unthinkable phenomenon.' Steiner takes his cue from this to suggest not just that chess is ultimately pointless, but that devoting formidable mental attributes to such a pastime was almost guaranteed to lead to insanity.

'What needs emphasis,' writes Steiner, 'is the plain fact that a chess genius is a human being who focuses vast, little-understood mental gifts and labours on an ultimately trivial human enterprise. Almost inevitably, this focus produces pathological symptoms of nervous stress and unreality.' Naturally, Steiner had the irascible, unpredictable, at times out-of-control Fischer uppermost in his mind, though he might have asked himself why Fischer rather than the courteous, worldly Boris Spassky should be the archetype. But he was not merely thinking about Fischer; he believed the game itself encouraged madness. 'Whatever Fischer's idiosyncrasies,' says Steiner, 'there are abundant impulses to paranoia and unreality in chess itself, in the violence and *autistic* passion of the game.' I have emphasised that word 'autistic'. Steiner seems to be using it non-medically, to suggest a pathological absorption in the game, but many would now extend that to suggest that a high percentage of chess players – especially very good ones – are on the autistic spectrum. Steiner argues that chess can drive players mad, or at least make them even less inclined to parley with 'normal' society. Luzhin, and through him Fischer, becomes the archetype of all chess experts – men who exist only on the 64 squares.

Arthur Koestler, who admitted he was a 'passionate duffer' where chess was concerned, reported on the Fischer–Spassky match for *The Sunday Times*. He was struck by the double-sidedness of chess, calling it the 'perfect paradigm for both the glory and the bloodiness of the human mind. On the one hand, an exercise in pure imagination happily married to logic, staged as a ballet of symbolic figures on a mosaic of 64 squares; on the other hand, a gladiatorial contest. This dichotomy is perhaps the main secret of the game's astonishingly long history.'

Martin Amis, another passionate chess duffer who wrote a long essay previewing the 1986 world championship match between Garry Kasparov and Anatoly Karpov in *The Observer*, suggests that Fischer – the man who, in his view, made modern chess – 'shows that supreme chess genius can ally itself with the paltriest human material'. He emphasises the paranoia and bitterness at the heart of the battles between Karpov and Viktor Korchnoi in the 1970s and Karpov and Kasparov in the 1980s, but he does not build a case against chess in the way that Steiner does, because he is above all in awe of the genius of grandmasters. 'Nowhere in sport, perhaps nowhere in human activity,' he writes, 'is the gap between the tryer and the expert so astronomical. Oh, I have thrown 180 at darts – twice in a lifetime. On the snooker table I have brought off violent pots that would have jerked them to their feet in the Sheffield Crucible. As for tennis, I need hardly hype my crosscourt backhand "dink", which is so widely feared in the parks of North Kensington. But my chances of a chess brilliancy are the "chances" of a lab chimp and a typewriter producing *King Lear*.'

One of the most nuanced of the literary tourists who have explored the landscape of chess is the novelist Julian Barnes. In 1993, when he was writing a regular letter from London for the *New Yorker*, he went to cover the world championship match between

Kasparov and Nigel Short. His report is anthologised in a book of his missives under the chapter heading 'TDF: The World Chess Championship'. Barnes was already interested in chess – in 1988 he had published an essay called 'Playing Chess with Arthur Koestler', an intriguing meeting of two passionate duffers – and his analysis is alert. He, too, comments on the game's combination of 'violence and intellectuality', a combination that explains why chess is neither pure art not science but a unique mixture of both. He picks up on the sexual imagery favoured by Short, which is where the TDF in the headline comes from: 'Trap. Dominate. Fuck.' Unlike some occasional observers, Barnes pays chess the courtesy of treating it seriously. He is intrigued by the strange theatre of the absurd, the long pauses in the 'action', the way that Channel 4's ambitious real-time coverage of the match 'wandered into quasi-philosophical problems of being and nothingness' during periods when nothing at all was happening. But it is not *ridiculous*. Not quite. It is a legitimate mental endeavour. And he grasps the key point – that you are searching for a sort of truth. He likens a chess game to a courtroom in which the two parties contest their competing truths – a brilliant metaphor. It is that search for the truth of a position that makes chess worthwhile. It is because Barnes sees this that he doesn't descend to easy mockery. 'Chess is, famously, an activity entirely unrelated to the rest of life,' he writes. 'From this springs its fragile profundity.' This cleverly turns Steiner's argument that chess is a trivial pursuit for the neurotic on its head, and the phrase 'fragile profundity' perfectly encapsulates the fact that chess is both a ludicrous waste of time and a subject of infinite fascination and beauty, depending on what you choose to see.

Chess – or at least the mental state of its participants – has been ill served by novels about the game. If *The Luzhin Defense* (or *The Defense* as it was called when published in English for the first time in 1964) and the film version made in 2000 are the key texts that define the game in the popular imagination, not far behind is Stefan Zweig's *Chess Story* (another book with an alternative title – *The Royal Game*). Zweig's novella pits two chess stereotypes against each other: the youthful world champion Mirko Czentovic, an idiot savant who has taken the chess world by storm despite being unable to write his own name, and Dr B, a victim of Nazi oppression who taught himself to play to grandmaster level by endlessly analysing games in a chess manual to keep himself occupied while in detention. Neither figure is especially believable – many players have learned to play in prison, notably the author John Healy, but none has reached master standard. But perhaps I am being too literal: the novella ends with the two – who some critics have argued represent the new and the old Europe, intolerance and civility – pitted against each other in a dramatic match on board a ship sailing from New York to Buenos Aires, with the wily Czentovic winning out by reducing Dr B to the state of chess-related mania that had afflicted him in his cell.

Zweig's unnamed narrator – whom we should not perhaps confuse with Zweig himself – expresses his sceptical view of chess in the opening pages of the book: 'I have always been interested in any kind of monomaniac obsessed by a single idea, for the more a man restricts himself the closer he is, conversely, to infinity; characters like this, apparently remote from reality, are like termites using their own material to build a remarkable and unique small-scale version of the world.' The narrator seeks out Czentovic because he is unable to 'imagine a form of cerebral activity revolving exclusively, for a whole lifetime, around a space consisting of 64 black and white squares'. Without endorsing the narrator's disregard for that choice – or the book's Nabokovian implication that love of, and excellence in, chess are never far from mania – this is a legitimate question: should anyone, especially clever minds that could achieve great things in maths and physics and the upper reaches of logic, devote a lifetime to repositioning wooden chessmen? It was a question often asked of Emanuel Lasker, not least by his friend Albert Einstein, who disagreed with the view that chess was a game beautiful enough to waste your life for.

Zweig's narrator pinpoints the great paradoxes of chess. 'Are we not guilty of offensive disparagement in calling chess a game?' he asks. 'Is it not also a science and an art?' In a winding sentence that contains arguments for and against chess, he accepts that it has been 'shown to be more durable in its entity and existence than all books and works of art' and is 'the only game that belongs to all nations and all eras'. But at the same time – and the putdown is more powerful than the praise – it is 'limited to a geometrically fixed space', represents 'thought that leads nowhere', and is a form of 'mathematics calculating nothing; art without works of art; architecture without substance'. This idea of 'thought that leads nowhere' – a world that, brilliant though it may be on its own terms, has no influence on the world beyond – is endlessly repeated by critics of chess. William Hazlitt put it most succinctly in his essay 'The Indian Jugglers', published in 1821: 'A great chess player is not a great man, for he leaves the world as he found it; no act terminating in itself constitutes greatness.' A talent for a specific endeavour does not amount to genius. Ten thousand hours devoted to mastering chess would, in Hazlitt's view, in the end be wasted. Chess expertise – like juggling or walking on a tightrope – is a knack, no more, no less. The very thing that attracts some players – the hermetically sealed nature of chess, its freedom from the challenges and compromises of the world beyond – repels critics of the game.

The third of the triumvirate of novels that offer a genius-next-to-madness view of chess is *Carl Haffner's Love of the Draw*, written by the Austrian Thomas Glavinic, published in German in 1998 and in English the following year. It is based on the life of the Austrian player Carl Schlechter, who drew a world championship match with Emanuel Lasker in 1910 – a match which, but for a blunder in a winning position in the final game, Schlechter would have won. By virtue of drawing the match, Lasker kept his world title, and Schlechter missed his shot at achieving imperishable fame.

Glavinic, one of the strongest chess players in his age group in Austria as a junior, knows the world about which he writes well, and paints Schlechter as a modest, sensitive, immensely civilised, perpetually impoverished man who happens to be wonderful at chess. Glavinic's narrator suggests that the blunder that costs Schlechter (called Haffner in the book) the world title is self-induced: he is scared of the implications of winning the title, yet also feels he has to prove himself by winning the final game, in which a draw – usually his favourite result – would have been sufficient to win the match. Schlechter/Haffner commits a form of suicide at the board and forgoes his chance to cement himself in chess history as the third world champion. Thereafter, Lasker avoids a rematch, and eight years later Schlechter/Haffner dies of starvation and pneumonia.

In the book, one senses Glavinic's love of the game – he paints the scenes in the Vienna and Berlin chess clubs in which the world championship takes place very well. But he also finds room for a female character, Anna, who seems insignificant to the plot (unless perhaps she is in love with Haffner, or with the idea of someone so unassuming and ego-free) and is included essentially to act as a chorus asking why the Viennese players who idolise him are so obsessed by chess: 'Anna marvelled anew every day at the ability of these men to regard a chessboard as the sole reality. They were as singleminded as children. Their emotions were dominated by chess, and chess alone … "It's a game," thought Anna. "When all is said and done, it's just a game. There's no divine message in a game of chess. I don't understand these people.'" Again, to an outsider, the chess world is portrayed as strange, esoteric, impenetrable.

These novels take a partial truth about chess – and some of the people who play it – and make it universal. The 1925 Soviet film *Chess Fever* – which uses footage of several contemporary grandmasters, including the then world champion José Raúl Capablanca, Frank Marshall and Richard Réti, and may have influenced Nabokov – makes the same point: that a mania for chess can tip you over the edge; that, in the case of the film, excessive love for the game will even make you forget your betrothed. The problem for chess is that this has become the standard view of chess players, and the media want all their grandmasters to be maniacs. While there are undoubtedly players who embody the monomania, marginalisation, even madness that Luzhin, Dr B and Haffner exhibit, they are in the minority. For every Wilhelm Steinitz (who ended his days in an asylum) and Bobby Fischer, there is a Boris Spassky, a Vladimir Kramnik or a Viswanathan Anand – to name three former world champions who embody modesty, sanity and charm. But the outside world is not interested in sane chess players, which is why the death of Fischer in 2008 was front-page news and every world title match since has barely merited a paragraph. One crazed, dead chess player is worth a dozen rational, living ones. And for that Nabokov and Zweig must take much of the blame.

B2: WIMBLEDON WOE

The day after I got back from Gibraltar I went straight into another tournament – the Imperial College Chess Congress. This time I played in the 'Major' – division two, a step up from Chester and about the same standard as Gibraltar. The first two days went sublimely: a win against a player graded 138 and two fighting draws against opponents in the high 150s. By now I felt I was getting a feel for tournament play: long-drawn-out battles in which sheer willpower counted for a great deal. But after a fortnight of continuous chess I was drained and on the final day I collapsed, losing both games. John Saunders had identified a stamina problem when I'd suffered my last-round fiasco in Gibraltar, and here it was even worse.

I'd played OK in the morning against a player graded 147 who exhibited steely determination – a young, pallid, emotionless assassin. Playing black, I outmanoeuvred him in the middle game, but his superior endgame technique, a rush of blood by me when I glimpsed a win, and my seemingly obligatory time trouble combined to undermine what should have been a drawn position. The frustration and exhaustion of that defeat meant I could barely function in the fifth and final game. I hallucinated at one point, thinking my opponent's king was on c1 rather than b1, made a further miscalculation a few moves later, and succumbed in 20-odd moves. The avuncular old codger I was playing looked at me with a mixture of sorrow and contempt. I fear I had subconsciously been playing with the aim of being home in time for dinner. I succeeded with time to spare.

Generally, though, I was content. I'd scored 2/5, but in a stronger category than at Chester. My FIDE rating at Imperial was around 1700; my ECF grade performance across the three tournaments in which I had played in rapid succession was in the mid-140s – almost 20 points above my official grade. I felt I was playing better chess, though clearly I had problems seeing competitions through to the end. Some of the games had also thrown up deficiencies in the endgame, the phase of the game which, though technical, fiddly and unglamorous, is the one where most chess games are decided. Learn to love the endgame, as Arthur Winser had sagely told the young Stuart Conquest. Teaching myself to grind out endgame wins would be crucial if I really wanted to make progress.

The other nagging area I needed to address was the opening. On the white side I had switched from e4 openings to d4 – I'd felt that my opponents had systems, such as the Sicilian Defence, worked out against e4 – and was now winning a reasonable percentage of games. Black remained more of a problem. I was not satisfied with the Scandinavian, which was too passive. What to play against e4 remained an issue. As the Dutch grandmaster Hein Donner, a noted chess commentator as well as a very fine player, once remarked: 'I don't like this move. And they know it.' He had managed to become a GM, he was drily suggesting, without really knowing how to respond to the most frequent opening move in chess. I had dabbled with the Sicilian, but failed to grasp it. The theory attached to its many variations was, as Nigel Short once said to me, a 'vast ocean', and it was proving too much for my navigational abilities. I had toyed with the Caro–Kann, where black responds to pawn to e4 with pawn to c6, but in online games often got crushed in the face of a kingside attack, so quickly dropped it. I was all at sea and still lacking a compass.

Ultimately I wanted to play many more openings, to be able to turn my hand to more or less anything. That was in part because I felt a proper all-round player should be able to command a large number of openings, but also because it would keep me fresh and interested, forcing me to solve the problems posed by each different system. It might initially mean a decline in my results as I left the comfort zone of openings I had played many times, but in the long term there should be benefits. The downside was that there were scores of openings – my edition of *Batsford's Modern Chess Openings* runs to 708 pages – and just looking at the densely printed notation made my eyes glaze over. There were 114 pages on the Sicilian Defence alone. When, if ever, would I have the time and the energy to study these? I was a sucker for buying opening books, falling into the trap mentioned by Doc Saunders of believing that parting with money for a book and then letting it gather dust on the shelf would somehow make me a better player. *Flank Openings, The Two Knights' Defence, Play the King's Indian, How to Play the English Opening* (still unconsulted despite my shattering defeat against the system in a league game), *The Dynamic Réti, Starting Out: The Modern Defence* (another system I had toyed with, then dropped), *The Scotch Game Explained,* even *4 ... Qh4 in the Scotch Game,* by Lev Gutman. The last of those emphasised the hopelessness of my cause: an entire book devoted to analysing what followed after black's fourth move in one particular opening system. This wasn't an ocean; it was a universe. Where on earth should I begin?

After the tournament at Imperial there was a lull. I carried on playing the odd league game for Surbiton and turned out for Surrey against Middlesex in an under-160 match, but my appearances were infrequent and I got a high percentage of dull draws. A spark had gone out of my play. It was almost as if, after that month of solid chess that started with Chester when I began to learn to put the game at the centre of my life, I found it difficult to go back to being a part-time chess player. It didn't help that my other club, Kingston, had been evicted from their old home in the cold but convenient Quaker Hall in the centre of the town – it was due for redevelopment – and had taken refuge in a room at a 24-hour Asda hypermarket on the A3. I see chess as a game which, ideally, should be played under chandeliers in Mittel-European cafés, and the idea of playing in a supermarket and being interrupted by klaxons signalling that Mrs Snoggins was needed on Till 96 was anathema. So for a while I refused to play there. I have my pride.

In the spring the Felce Cup began again. This time, instead of playing children, I was up against two wizened old blokes who looked as if they might have been contemporaries of Steinitz and Lasker, and a young Frenchman who played well but had chronic problems with the time control, often losing on time in perfectly good positions. In the opening game of the competition I had a slight edge, but it was my first competitive encounter in almost a month and, after an hour and a half's play, I was having difficulty concentrating, so agreed a draw. It was a pathetic thing to do, but my opponent was graded 139 (the highest-graded player in my section of the competition) and once again I rationalised it as being a way of getting on the scoreboard. But in my heart I knew that my feeble first-round draw was becoming as ingrained as my disastrous last-round collapse, and if I wanted to progress both had to be eliminated.

My next cup game was against a solid player with whom I'd drawn before in a league match, the captain of Wimbledon's third team, graded 128 but better than that (captains of teams tend to be better than their grades suggest because their own play suffers from having administrative responsibilities). I was playing white and told myself I had to win. For the first 20 moves I was doing precisely that. I built up a huge space advantage – a key concept in chess, meaning you have greater freedom of manoeuvre, are controlling more squares and calling all the shots. A victory should have been routine, but instead of playing simple chess and consolidating my advantage I tried to play a fancy combination to land a knockout blow. All I succeeded in doing was knocking myself out with a series of errors that left me a piece down. I was psychologically wrecked and so lost track of the final phase of the game that I didn't even realise I was a piece down and offered my opponent a draw. He must have thought I was mad. Anyway, he shrugged off my suggestion with a contemptuous bark of 'No.' Later, he said he couldn't understand why I had given up a piece. 'I thought you must have had a rush of blood,' he said. As I walked back to Wimbledon station afterwards I once more questioned whether I could ever really make any progress. I had got so tired in the third hour of the game, misunderstood the position so profoundly, blundered so badly and then not even clocked that I had lost a piece. It felt as if I was back to square one and my snowy triumph in Chester counted for nothing.

B3: DONNER AND BLITZEN

 When John Saunders looked at my abysmal Wimbledon game, he diagnosed extreme lack of patience, inability to use my time properly – the old problem of not realising when the crisis had come and failing to use as much time as necessary to find the optimal move – and a tendency to oscillate wildly between euphoria and despair. 'Play patiently and without emotion,' he said. 'Treat it as what it is – a game of chess.' He noticed how, after my opponent had played a game-changing knight move which I'd failed to foresee, my recording of the moves had disintegrated: I'd lost track of the game; I was incapable of re-setting myself for the struggle. Just as I tended to overreact when things were going well and assume victory was now a formality, so when the tide turned I exaggerated my weakness, too, became confused and lost the capacity to fight on. He held up Michael Adams, the highest-rated British player of all time, as a role model because of his patience and coolness. 'Compare pictures of him at the beginning and the end of a game and he looks the same,' said Saunders. No matter how tense the struggle, he never gets flustered, never panics, just plays his own game in his own way and at his own pace. Adams is known as 'the Spider' because he slowly, inexorably, creates a web in which he traps and then strangles his opponent. It is the opposite of my headstrong, over-emotional, let's-get-it-over-with-as-quickly-as-possible style.

As we played through the Wimbledon game, I showed Saunders the point at which I thought the position was winning. 'It's strong, but it's not winning,' he said. 'Try not to think, "I've got a won position." There's no such thing as a won position – a human player's capacity to cock things up is infinite.' He cited another of Hein Donner's wry observations: 'I love all positions. Give me a difficult positional game, I'll play it. Give me a bad position, I'll defend it. Openings, endgames, complicated positions, and dull, drawn positions, I love them all and will give them my best efforts. But totally winning positions I cannot stand.' I later played through the game which prompted Donner's self-lacerating analysis. He was the "exchange" (rook for knight) up, with a clear win, but managed to blow it. 'It was not the first time this happened to me,' he complained. 'Always reaching winning positions, never winning.'

Donner played for the Netherlands in 11 Olympiads and won the national title three times in the 1950s, but is best remembered as a witty, waspish writer on the game, and many chess players name *The King*, a collection of Donner's journalistic commentaries edited by Tim Krabbé and Max Pam, as their favourite all-time chess book. I started dipping into *The King* to see if Donner's love-hate relationship with this most frustrating of games could teach me anything. I was still looking for heroes, talismans to guide me on this quest, and Donner seemed to fit the bill – an engaging Virgil to my Dante in the divine comedy of the 64 squares. There was something about his peculiarly Dutch brand of humour that appealed to me. It seemed the only sensible way to approach both life and chess.

He was first and foremost a provocateur. In their introduction to *The King*, Krabbé and Pam recall that in 1968 Donner was sacked by one newspaper when he donated a prize he had won in a tournament to the Viet Cong – on the strict understanding that they used the money to buy machine guns and not medical supplies. Everything about Donner was outwardly confrontational.

He loved to make ludicrous, absolutist statements. 'However painful it may be, we must not shrink from the truth,' he wrote in one essay. 'Women cannot play chess. They are hopeless at it and, if you ask me, they will never learn.' Donner didn't believe computers could play chess either.

For years he mocked Dutch IM Lodewijk Prins, with whom he had had an early falling-out. When Prins won the Dutch title in 1965, Donner called him 'the worst chess player in the world' and said he could barely distinguish a bishop from a knight. When Donner was not selected for the Olympiad in Malta in 1980, he was furious and wrote a piece imagining that the plane carrying the team, the selection committee and the chess journalists who had endorsed the selection had crashed and all the passengers had died lingering deaths. 'It was a humorous piece,' wrote fellow Dutch GM Hans Ree after Donner's death, 'but it nevertheless revealed the real bitterness of someone who felt undervalued and who at the same time feared that he had indeed lost much of his previous strength.' According to Ree, Donner became even more aggressive after he became ill in the early 1980s, with Donner blaming Ree for his exclusion from another Olympiad team. 'We'd often quarrelled before and thoroughly enjoyed it,' wrote Ree, 'but now it was different. At the artists' club where we were both members, we avoided each other. Hein had always been difficult, but in the period before his last stroke he became absolutely impossible.'

So, hero or monster? Krabbé and Max Pam give Donner the benefit of any doubt. 'This is not the place for an explanation of "the phenomenon Donner",' they write in their introduction to *The King*, 'but there is no doubt that Dutch chess life would have been less lively and less passionate without him.' They suggest that most of his provocations were done for outrageous effect, and that the main target of his attacks was himself. 'Even his most furious fits of anger always had an element of truth in them,' they argue, and 'his vinegary, ironic bombast made such wonderful reading.'

Chess subscribes to Sayre's law, which states that 'in any dispute the intensity of feeling is inversely proportional to the value of the issues at stake'. It is a circumscribed world filled with mighty egos; feuds go on for decades; the viciousness of chess blogs and forums is remarkable. In this world where, in truth, nothing is really at stake, the passions aroused are extraordinary. There may be an element of displacement here: it is a game, but a game that comes to mean more than life itself. Winning and losing mean nothing, but they seem to mean everything because they are the yardstick by which we judge ourselves. Donner was the supreme protagonist in these Lilliputian conflicts.

In the end, though, we forgive him everything because of the way he dealt with the stroke that ended his playing career in 1983. It came just in time, he joked, 'because when you are 56 you do not play chess as well as you did when you were 26'. (It was discouraging to read this at exactly the age of 56.) Ree, who was now reconciled with his fellow GM, visited Donner regularly in the nursing home in which he was confined to a wheelchair. 'Once I saw a game in the magazine *Schachwoche*, in which a computer had beaten the American international master Edward Formanek,' wrote Ree. 'I thought I'd tease him a bit by showing him that particular game. He couldn't walk any more, could hardly read or talk, so the fact that I still felt I could tease him tells you what strength of character he had.' Donner died in 1988, at the age of 61, but carried on writing to the end, though forced to type with one finger. 'My world has become very small now,' he wrote in one of his final pieces, 'but a chess player is used to that.'

B4: HOME SWEET HOME

 My next encounter after my disaster in Wimbledon was a rapidplay game against a child. Youthful opponents had so far proved problematic for me, but this game proved distressingly easy. I had turned up to offer moral support to the inaugural Kings Place Chess Festival in central London, they had been a player short in the final round, I offered to fill in, and beat the poor kid easily. It was my first win in ages, so that was something, but it was distressing too. I realised that at the end of a tough day's chess this was the last thing the boy needed as he sat there twitching nervously. I considered throwing the game or at least offering him a draw, but thought he'd realise what I was doing and think he was being patronised. It was a hopeless situation either way, so I just carried on beating him up. At least it taught him that chess can be cruel sometimes. We started analysing the game afterwards, but his dad thought he was getting tired and took him home. I hoped he wasn't too traumatised.

Children enjoy chess – the visceral nature of the battle, the killing of the pieces – but, prodigies excepted, they find thinking ahead hard. If they see any sort of plausible move, they will play it. They find the tree of analysis, the need to think three or four moves ahead in several lines, difficult to grasp. Doc Saunders, who was with me at the Kings Place tournament, said it was a mistake to set young children loose on proper games immediately. They just play random moves and chalk up blunder-riddled wins or losses against other children playing equally randomly. Teach them the principles first – it's a good idea to have just the pawns or a few pieces on the board initially so they can grasp the elements of the game rather than trying to understand everything at once – and let them start playing once they have a basic grounding.

After the Kings Place excursion, where the young English grandmaster Gawain Jones won £1,000 for winning the Open, I thought it might make for a poetic experience to return to Newport, the place of my birth, to play in the South Wales summer congress. The event was being held at Rougemont, a private school on the northern edge of the bruised, battered, committedly comprehensive town. Newport used to style itself the 'home of the mole wrench' – the sign making this bold claim was the first thing you would see as the train pulled into the station – but now that most of the heavy industry which used to define the place has departed, it is no longer clear what it is home to: teenage pregnancy, drugs, crime, all the social problems that come with poverty and post-industrialism. When I got to Rougemont, I told one of the organisers of the congress it was the first tournament I had played in Newport for 38 years – since my third place in a junior competition in the mid-1970s. I expected him to be impressed, moved even, but all he said was, 'I don't think they want to hear you call this area Newport.' Being the home of the mole wrench was, it seemed, not enough to generate positive associations. The Celtic Manor Hotel, the golf resort to the east of Newport which staged the 2010 Ryder Cup, likes to say it is in the Usk Valley. This bit of Newport evidently felt the same way.

I had taken a bye (which allowed me a free half-point) in the first round, played on Friday evening, so my first game was on Saturday morning. I was staying with my parents, who acted as if the intervening 38 years had never happened, making me sandwiches and giving me a Thermos flask of tea to see me through the rigours of the day. My first opponent had a relatively low grade and played like it, giving up a pawn for nothing in the opening and then losing a piece in the middle game. The game was to all intents over and it irritated me that he insisted on playing on. I don't know if it was boredom, fury, tiredness or simple incompetence but, as we approached the endgame, I then committed the mother of all blunders and gave him his piece back. We were now level on material and he was in a position where he could endlessly check my king with his queen if he wished – a draw by perpetual check. He offered me a draw instead, trying to mask his relief and disbelief at the mistake I had made, and I had to accept. I had thrown away an absolutely won position and felt ridiculous. It was another moment of crisis in what was becoming a worryingly recurrent pattern. I seemed to be becoming more, not less, blunder-prone.

I fled the school, taking the bus back to Newport town centre, where I sat beside the murky waters of the River Usk, bolted my sandwiches, and tried not to burst into tears. This was the most ridiculous failure I had yet had to endure, and it would be difficult to recover. So much for the poetry of my return. Feeling the need to pay some penance, I forced myself to walk the three miles back to the school for the afternoon session, in which I faced one of the highest-rated players in my section. I had about half an hour to kill before the game began, so sat on a bench in the playground, enjoying the sunshine and the views of the surrounding hills. The older players sat at tables outside the hall playing through their games, while some of the younger ones had a kickabout. It was like being at a Christian fellowship weekend, or some cult gathering – a world entire unto itself; a small world, as Donner said at the end of his life, but a strangely satisfying one.

As usual the congress was populated by 12-year-olds and men over 60, though with fewer retired accountants than you encountered on the circuit in the south-east of England. 'We've skipped a couple of generations,' one sixtysomething said to me later as he explained that the cohort of players in which he grew up had been meeting each other over the board for more than 40 years, with few players emerging to challenge them in recent decades. The Fischer boom of the 1970s, I said knowingly. But he had a more prosaic explanation – the building of the motorways in the 1960s. 'Suddenly we could get to Preston to play a congress there,' he said. 'It doesn't sound much, but it was very exciting when previously you had to play a match against the neighbouring village.' British chess history instantly rewritten. It also struck me that the replacement of steam engines by less enticing diesels at the same time took the romance out of trainspotting, and may have diverted more boys of a certain age and mental outlook into chess, though I had been devoted to both, a nerdy double-whammy.

I didn't know how to approach my afternoon game, in which I was both out-rated and playing black. Should I have some fun or try to tough it out? In the event I did both. My opponent was a thin, pale man who smelt of cigarettes. At the end of our four-and-a-half-hour tussle, he said, 'I'm glad that's over; I was dying for a fag.' We had both been down to our last two minutes on the clock and were utterly spent. I had plucked a lucky saving move from nowhere to avoid going the exchange (rook for minor piece) down, and eventually managed to win the game. Had I lost, having spent most of the game pressing, I don't think I could have answered for the consequences. The turbid waters of the Usk might have looked quite appealing. The game was full of errors and might-have-beens, but I was feeling more philosophical about all the missed opportunities. In the morning I had drawn when I should have won; in the afternoon I had won when I should have lost. Some say chess is an art; others see it as a science; what no one can dispute is that it is a dogfight, a Darwinian struggle to stay alive. A very Newportonian thought.

B5: WHY DO WE DO IT?

 In the middle of one of my later games at the Newport Congress – I had two draws on the Sunday, one against an old lag (and decent player), the other against a scary junior being watched over by his two proud, eager parents – I suddenly asked myself whether I was really enjoying playing. I had the same thought as I watched the deciding game in my section, in which a 17-year-old was playing a crop-haired, middle-aged man to decide who would take first place. Both were down to their last few seconds, the youngster was shaking, and almost every move they made was an error, a rook mislaid here, a bishop casually tossed away there. Eventually the crop-haired man lost on time – he took it very well, far better than I would have – and the 17-year-old had his prize. But the youth looked drained, shell-shocked, incapable of feeling any pleasure at his victory. Why did we put ourselves through this?

I'd had similar thoughts after that earlier game at Newport where I threw away a rook with what may have been the most ridiculous move in the history of chess. Why was I here making a fool of myself? What was the point? 'Playing chess is a vale of tears,' said John Saunders during one of our training sessions as we examined an especially egregious, error-riddled game I had played. 'This teaches us a very valuable lesson. It doesn't matter what you do, how you play or how you change your approach to the game. Chess is just a bitch that bites you in the arse.' Saunders was expressing, albeit less elegantly, a view propounded by H. G. Wells, in an essay entitled 'Concerning Chess' in 1901: 'It is the most absorbing of occupations, the least satisfying of desires, an aimless excrescence upon life. It annihilates a man.'

Siegbert Tarrasch, the best player in the world (though never world champion) in the 1890s before the arrival of Emanuel Lasker, took a rosier view. 'Chess, like love, like music, has the power to make men happy,' he wrote in the preface to *The Game of Chess*, the book summing up his thinking about the game, which he published in 1931, three years before his death. But is that really true? Doesn't the pain always outweigh the pleasure? Aren't we ultimately doomed to fall short of the perfection which those damned computer programs now allow us to glimpse? Saunders drew my attention to a blog by the English grandmaster Danny Gormally which encapsulated the nightmares chess can induce. 'I played a game a couple of days ago where I lost from a rook up,' wrote Gormally. 'At the end of the game I completely lost my rag and started screaming, which was quite embarrassing in hindsight. Really I was angry at myself. Other players in the tournament, including my opponent, saw this meltdown and must have thought, "What a nutter." Increasingly I'm suffering from poor emotional control. You'd think I'd get calmer as I get older, but at times I even feel I'm teetering on the brink of madness.'

Donner, my new if flawed guide in this minatory world, is good on the pain and paranoia chess can induce. Writing about the great Fischer–Spassky world championship match in 1972 and the beginnings of the Russian's disintegration, he poured scorn on the idea that chess was one of the least demanding of pursuits. 'What comes dramatically to the fore in this match,' he wrote, 'is that chess is a tough sport. What seems so easy at first sight – "Can you imagine a lazier sport?" I heard someone say – in fact puts a greater pressure on the players than any other branch of [physical] sports. To sit immovably still for five hours on end, in a condition of semi-consciousness, under the heavy burden of a possible mistake – all this opens the door wide to serious distress.' Donner was capable of his own meltdowns – or at least liked to immortalise his reactions to losses in a suitably mock-heroic manner. 'After I resigned this game with perfect self-control, and solemnly shook hands with my opponent in the best of Anglo-Saxon traditions,' he wrote, after losing to his old foe Hans Ree, also in 1972, 'I rushed home, where I threw myself on to my bed, howling and screaming, and pulled the blankets over my face. For three days and three nights the Erinyes were after me. Then I got up, dressed, kissed my wife and considered the situation.'

A chess win offers a high that is almost sexual – that moment of release after sitting at the board for four hours plus. But do the highs make up for the lows? Saunders didn't think so. 'The pain of defeat is greater than the joy of victory, at least for a pessimist like me,' he insisted, which may be one reason why he retired from competitive play in his fifties to concentrate on writing about the game. He found it even harder to derive satisfaction from playing once computer programs became all-seeing, because they would spot the flaws even in games you thought you had won well.

David Spanier, another journalist (and hapless amateur) who fell in love with chess and wrote a book about it, mentions Tarrasch's famous quote in his first chapter. Significantly, that chapter is about motivation – the why question that was bothering me too as I struggled to make progress. It seemed to be a question that concerned amateurs and latecomers more than the pros, who had played since they were five and for whom it had become a way of life, as natural as breathing. Someone like Emil Sutovsky could eulogise upon the game's beauty and heritage, but for most it was enough that they excelled at it. Their prowess was its own justification, while we strugglers needed to try to rationalise its appeal.

Spanier's explanation for the game's enduring appeal was simple: 'Chess is a substitute for life itself ... Over the board all the dramas and colours of living are continually being played out in imagination. [It has] something like the effect of a gently powerful, pervasively consuming, hallucinatory drug.' Edward Lasker, a five-times US champion who was a contemporary of the great Emanuel and claimed to be a distant relative, also likens chess to a drug in his affectionate survey of the game's history and culture, *The Adventure of Chess*. 'A single exposure is apt to make an addict of anyone with a sense of adventure,' he writes, 'and I know of no reliable antidote.' Robert Desjarlais, a chess-loving American anthropologist, is another who uses the drug analogy, in his book *Counterplay*: 'Chess gets a hold on some people, like a virus or a drug. Just as the chemical properties of heroin directly and immediately affect the central nervous system, so chess can lock into certain pathways of the mind, and it doesn't easily let go.'

Desjarlais, though, doesn't stop there. His mission is to examine this peculiar passion, the reasons we become addicted. He reckons there is no single explanation to the question 'Why bother?' 'For some, chess is a hobby picked up along the way,' he writes, 'while for others it's a cathedral of truth and beauty. There's a score of interlocking reasons why people stick with the game. The attractions often relate to the drama that each game promises, the competitive challenge in pitting one's skills against another's, the intricate complexity that comes with any chess position, the rewarding intellectual conversation that takes place between two minds during a game, how focused concentration can take a person into a domain of pure thought removed from the hassles of everyday life, the way chess enables people to know their mind better, the pleasures of learning and participating in the conceptual history of modern chess, the camaraderie to be found at chess clubs, the thrill of accomplishing something creative at the board, and the way in which truth and beauty – and perhaps a measure of wisdom – can be found in chess. It's a swirl of deeply felt intensities that cut through the lives of chess players.'

I liked the fact that truth and beauty were not the dominant characteristics in Desjarlais's list, because for the amateur – me and the other under-150s playing error-riddled, time-troubled games at Newport – they were likely to be some way down the pecking order of reasons we persisted with this often infuriating game. When I began this odyssey, truth and beauty were in the forefront of my mind – I wanted to grasp the truth of a position and create something beautiful. Now, increasingly, I just wanted to win; to improve my grade; to become a better player. Of course, one does that by understanding more about chess, by getting closer to the truth. But I had also come to see that strength of character, calmness under pressure, the sheer will to win were all just as important, maybe even more important at the amateur level, where errors abound. 'The winner of the game is the player who makes the next-to-last mistake,' said Savielly Tartakower, a Polish grandmaster from the first half of the 20th century and the game's greatest aphorist. Kill or be killed. To hell with truth.

The romantics would disagree. 'Chess is a form of intellectual productiveness, therein lies its peculiar charm,' wrote Tarrasch. In the early decades of the 20th century, chess was seen as a beautiful, rarefied pursuit akin to philosophy and the arts. The French artist Marcel Duchamp loved the game so much there were frequent rumours that he planned to forgo art to concentrate on chess – he was an excellent player, good enough to play for France in Olympiads and to get a draw in a strong tournament in 1929 against Tartakower, a result that pleased Duchamp so much he framed his scoresheet. Francis M. Naumann, co-author of *Marcel Duchamp: The Art of Chess*, suggests that both were fundamental to his life: 'Not only was the theme of chess an ever-present motif in his work – from his earliest paintings to works of his final decade – but on more than one occasion he buried coded messages in his art that could be fully comprehended only by proficient players of the game.' 'While all artists are not chess players,' said Duchamp, 'all chess players are artists.'

There is, though, a conflict at the heart of chess, one that even Duchamp, who did not disguise the inherent violence of the game, recognised. Chess aspires to the condition of art, with beautiful ideas and aesthetically pleasing combinations, but it is also a base struggle to impose your will on the other player. Albert Einstein expresses the conflicting notions of chess as art and chess as war in the foreword he wrote to Jacques Hannak's biography of Lasker, published in 1952. 'I am no chess player myself [and] have always disliked the fierce competitive spirit embodied in that highly intellectual game,' writes Einstein. He said he detected a 'tragic note' in Lasker's personality, and ascribed it to Lasker having to devote his life to chess, on which he depended for his livelihood, when he should have been concentrating his great mental powers on more serious pursuits.

Donner addressed the question of whether chess was a profound endeavour or a complete waste of time in a column published in 1959. He imagines world champions, once they have reached the summit, asking themselves: 'What purpose has all this energy served? Has there been a point in all this strenuous effort?' Lasker, he says, quit the game for ten years; Capablanca preferred dominoes; Alekhine took to drink. But all these, in Donner's view, were more legitimate than the then world champion Mikhail Botvinnik's rationalisation of chess as a branch of art. 'A chess player produces nothing, creates nothing,' argues Donner. 'He only has one aim: the destruction of his opponent. This may be done in a very artistic way. But there is something strange about those perfect games in which deep strategies or brilliant combinations secure victory. They are published all over the world and are included in textbooks, these games that are "all of a piece", but in fact they are not chess games at all, they are monologues. A real chess game can only be experienced by two people. Nothing can be said about it. Nothing comes of it.'

According to Donner, 'The whole point of the game [is] to *prevent* [my emphasis] an artistic performance.' Garry Kasparov makes the same point. 'The highest art of the chess player,' he says, 'lies in not allowing your opponent to show you what he can do.' Always the other player is there trying to wreck your masterpiece. Chess, Donner insists, is a struggle, a fight to the death. 'When one of the two players has imposed his will on the other and can at last begin to be freely creative, the game is over. That is the moment when, among masters, the opponent resigns. That is why chess is not art. No, chess cannot be compared with anything. Many things can be compared with chess, but chess is only chess.'

B6: END OF THE WEALD

It was, to be frank, a competition too far. I had been looking to get one more weekend tournament in before the British championships in Torquay at the beginning of August, and settled on the Weald Congress in Sussex. I had been warned it would be full of underrated juniors – this is a prosperous area with aspirational parents and talented, driven children – and so it proved. I managed only one of the two days and was reduced to a quivering wreck by the end of it. I should have known it wasn't going to be my day from the very beginning. The tournament was being played at a prep school near Crawley. I was sitting on the grass waiting for it to begin when a small Chinese boy kicked a football at me. I had been making notes with a pen that had a very fine point, and the impact of the ball somehow pushed the nib of the pen into my finger, puncturing it. The boy's mother apologised as my hand bled over my notepad, but the boy looked singularly unchastened. I should have gone home at that point. It was a portent.

The hundred-strong event, broken down into four sections, was being played in the school sports hall, as many chess events are. It is a deadening setting for this noble activity. My opponent in the first round didn't turn up, so I won the game by default. My opponent in the second game was a boy who spent the entire game sniffing, rocking back and forth, and when it was my move wandering round the hall. He had a very low grade and, in theory, I should have been able to win easily, but he played perfectly sensible chess, I failed to make any headway, and after about two and a half hours we agreed a draw.

That was OK. I now had 1.5/2 and was reasonably well placed, but the next game – against another of these precocious, self-confident 12-year-olds – was painful. I was on the run for most of the game, managed to get back to equality, then lost a crucial central pawn as we headed for the endgame. With my position disintegrating I started to fall apart too, playing abysmal moves and rapidly going down to defeat. The boy looked annoyingly pleased to have won, and went off to celebrate with his father, leaving me (once again) to tell the organisers that I would not be making the trek to Crawley the following day for further ritual humiliation (obviously, I didn't put it quite like that – I invented a pressing engagement). It had been a dismal day in which I didn't feel I'd played a single interesting or imaginative move. My concentration was poor; my will to win was low. In that grotesque final game, even after going a pawn down, I should have been able to keep the battle going for a while, but I crumbled. It wasn't quite Bournemouth – I had developed a bit of mental resilience since that early setback – but it was close.

My last two games in the Felce were also a disaster. I had rallied in the middle of the competition and at one point even thought I might have a chance of qualifying for the finals. But then it all fell apart: I lost a game against the young Frenchman, who played a very nice sacrifice and then beat me in a time scramble, and made a dreadful error in another game that cost me a bishop and the game. I seemed to be going backwards. I could work out one of the reasons for my multiple failures myself. I was trying to play too fast: I was still playing a lot of "blitz" – games with very tight time controls – online, and it was affecting the tempo at which I played proper games. I had to play less blitz, and learn to spend time digging for the truth of a position. I thought I could play quickly and creatively but I couldn't; I was just playing superficially.

In my final game in the Felce I still had 40 minutes left on the clock – 40 minutes I could have used to find better moves than the nonsense I ended up playing.

I hadn't experienced a run of defeats like this before – defeats against children and old blokes; defeats where I messed up positionally or tactically, where I blew it in the middle game or the endgame. The entire ship was leaking; I didn't have enough fingers to plug the holes. At around this time I read John Williams' novel *Stoner*, in which his protagonist, studying English literature at a university in the American Midwest, is inspired to pursue a teaching career when confronted with Shakespeare's 73rd sonnet: 'That time of year thou mayst in me behold/When yellow leaves, or none, or few, do hang/Upon those boughs which shake against the cold,/Bare ruin'd choirs where late the sweet birds sang.' This passage in the novel resonated with me because I, too, have often tried to grasp Shakespeare's sonnets, and usually failed. They are so complex, so many-sided, so playful both in the language and the identities of the lovers being described. Usually I give up and pass on to the next one, satisfied just to hear the sound of the words and not worrying too much about the meaning. It struck me that each of these sonnets is the literary equivalent of a chess position, and that to penetrate its meaning you had to look and look again and keep looking until your eyes hurt. That is what makes a great critic and that, too, is what makes a great chess player: an unwillingness ever to be satisfied with the apparent meaning; a desire to grasp this thing completely; to truly understand it. I was a superficial critic and a superficial chess player because I was too lazy to dig and dig and dig. Perhaps it was too late to remake myself, to unlearn five decades of drifting along, getting by with a certain wit and native intelligence. The indolence might by now be ingrained. My play over the past fortnight made me fear that this quest was going to end in failure – that, unlike William Stoner, I would not have the doggedness and determination to crack the code.

I needed some moral support, and happily Doc Saunders was on hand to provide it. When I played through the games with him, they somehow seemed less bad than I had thought at the time. We decided the 12-year-old who beat me in the Weald Congress was already a strong player. He had a rapidplay grade of 143, which suggested he was going to be seriously good by the time he was in his mid-teens. Saunders also drew encouragement from my game against an experienced old hand called Dai James (the man with the theory about motorways revolutionising British chess) in the South Wales summer congress. He knew James from his own playing days and reckoned he was a capable player, with a grade of 175 in his prime. Getting a draw against him was a good result. The more I thought about it, the more I realised I had enjoyed playing the game against James, and as a result played better (though cause and effect are of course difficult to untangle). I played the game organically, didn't try to force the issue, and liked the way it went from a highly tactical opening to a very strategic middle and endgame. I had applied myself properly and felt I knew what I was doing. It must have helped that I had nothing to lose. He was the highest-rated player in my part of the tournament; I was already on 2/3 when I played him, so defeat wouldn't have been the end of the world; and I was able to play a smooth, thoughtful, engaged game. Proper chess.

Impulsiveness remained my biggest problem. Saunders told me to take my time – to check my analysis over and over, try to judge which were the critical positions and use as much time as necessary to resolve them. There's no point in being ahead on the clock if you are losing the game. In several of the defeats I had suffered I had had a lot of time left. I couldn't claim time pressure had caused me to blunder. It was sheer laziness. I was guessing when I should have been calculating. 'Chess is all about objectivity,' said Saunders. Or, as Emanuel Lasker put it in a famous formulation, 'Lies and hypocrisy do not survive for long on the chessboard. The creative combination lays bare the presumption of a lie, while the merciless fact, culminating in a checkmate, contradicts the hypocrite.'

Mikhail Botvinnik, three-times world champion, stern logician and founder of the Soviet school of chess analysis, could not understand why chess lovers doted on the chancers of the game. 'It is peculiar but a fact nevertheless,' he complained, 'that the gamblers in chess have enthusiastic followers.' The roundheads, he argued, would generally beat the cavaliers. My approach was one of hit-and-hope. Or, as Saunders described it, 'the art of coarse chess': 'It's a crude, "I can't analyse this position properly, this move feels right and I should get lucky."' It might work playing online blitz – Botvinnik also hated blitz, saying, when asked whether he ever played it, 'Yes, I have played a blitz game once. It was on a train, in 1929' – but it will rarely work in chess played at classical time controls where good players will find the best move. Play coolly, slowly, and try to treat all positions with equanimity were the doctor's orders: 'You're too emotionally involved with your games.' This was an implied criticism of my extreme disappointment at losing to the 12-year-old, and perhaps of my failure to turn up for the second day of the Weald Congress. It was a feeble, taking-my-ball-away response to defeat. Stay and fight; get over the defeat; try, like Magnus Carlsen, to react to defeat (admittedly a rarer occurrence in his chess life than mine) by being even more tigerish in the next game.

So what to do? 'You've got to do some book work,' said Saunders, eyeing my shelves of unread books. Don't just admire them, read the damn things. Learn some theory; find some new openings; then try to be more objective when analysing; don't make rash, impulsive moves; don't be ruled by emotion. 'Maybe I've just got a brain problem,' I said, as I reflected on the rash of tactical blunders that had cost me several games in the preceding weeks. 'That's a thought,' said Saunders. 'Let's get you a replacement brain.'

B7: A RISING STAR

I had hoped to meet grandmaster Gawain Jones at the London Classic at the end of 2012. He had become British champion the previous summer, reached a FIDE rating of 2650, and broken into the world top 100. That's super-strong, stratospheric to most of us, and yet at the elite event in London – an all-play-all with eight of the world's strongest players – he struggled, managing only three draws and five defeats. He had told me he was too focused on the tournament and too knackered to meet at the Classic, where he was competing for the first time, but I eventually caught up with him in the spring of the following year in a trendy pub in Shepherd's Bush, west London, close to where he lived.

Jones contradicts all the grandmaster clichés. He is friendly, relaxed, well adjusted, painfully normal. When I arrived, he was sitting next to the pub fire drinking a pint and reading a fat fantasy novel. Just another ordinary twentysomething bloke, except that he's an outrageously good chess player. Whereas he had come last in the London Classic, less than a month later he had won the New Year tournament at Hastings – the first British player to win the title outright for 15 years. At Hastings he had comfortably eased away from a field of 'average' grandmasters, whereas in London he had been the little guy picked on by the super-GM bullies. In chess, everything is relative; everyone is someone else's bunny – quite a reassuring thought when you've just been hammered in a game. His contrasting fortunes demonstrated the vast gulf between grandmasters rated 2550 and those rated

2750-plus – so vast, in fact, that there probably needs to be a new super-GM title, awarded when you reach, say, 2700.

He explained that against the very strongest players the smallest inaccuracy – a mistake so infinitesimal that only super-GMs would even know it was a mistake – would invariably be punished. Sometimes when you lose to a top grandmaster, it's not even clear where you went wrong. You have been knifed, but the blade has been inserted without leaving a mark. 'You have to have total focus, total concentration when you play these guys,' he said, adding that because his opponents were so strong he played more slowly than usual, double- and triple-checking his over-the-board analysis, and fell into time trouble. 'Generally I was coping until time trouble, and then I just couldn't keep up. I knew what was going wrong, but it's hard to change it. When I'm playing a 2500 grandmaster, I know that even if I make a small mistake they'll give me a chance to get back into the game. I'm generally a very tricky player, I like to attack, I'm very tenacious and I don't give up. When I play a 2500 player I can even play something slightly suspicious to get them out of their comfort zone. But against the top guys I know I have to play perfectly or I'll get taken apart.'

He said that at the Classic the other players saw him as the whipping-boy and went all out to win, producing games that lasted six, seven, almost eight hours. Jones recommended running to build up stamina for these long games. 'It's important to be fit. You need the stamina to stay focused for seven hours without dipping too much in performance.' He reckoned Magnus Carlsen, who won the Classic, was the most tenacious player of all time: 'He gets to an equal endgame, where most people would agree a draw, and then keeps on going until his opponent makes a slip after six hours, which he pounces on. In general his moves aren't fantastic. He sees things very fast, of course, and he plays very tricky openings, but mainly it's his endurance. You know that you can never drop your guard.'

Jones believed he was capable of getting his rating over 2700, which would propel him into the world top 50 and bring both more invites to elite tournaments and more money. The first prize at Hastings was £2,000 – for ten days' hard slog. By contrast, Carlsen picked up 50,000 euros for winning the London Classic. At that point, Jones preferred not to spend time teaching chess or writing books about the game – the traditional earners for chess pros. He just wanted to play; to get as good as he could. The downside was that he wasn't earning much – just £19,000 in the year previous to our meeting. Less than the average salary in the UK – for one of the greatest young chess talents in the country. It wouldn't keep a footballer in chewing gum.

Much of his income came from playing league chess. He played for several clubs in the UK, plus teams in Germany, Iceland and Italy – like most active GMs, he lived out of a suitcase. The clubs paid him a small fee each time he played for them: 'You need these leagues because if you're playing in tournaments where you always rely on prize money, it's just too stressful. A lot of players you see have this problem when they're playing opens [as opposed to invitation-only tournaments]. They get to the last round and they might be second equal, and they know that a draw will guarantee them maybe £400; a loss will get zero; and if they win they'll get £2,000. They go, "Well, if I get zero I can't afford to eat, I can't afford to pay the mortgage, so I just need to agree a quick draw." You see it all the time in these opens, and then people criticise them for not playing fighting chess, but you have to understand the pressures.'

It has become far tougher to be a professional chess player over the past 20 years. Chess is now much stronger and more competitive globally, in part because of the emergence of very strong players from China, India and other parts of Asia, but at the same time the game has contracted in the UK and prizes have become smaller. The UK experienced a chess boom in the wake of Bobby Fischer's triumph in the world championship in 1972; the generation of players produced by that boom – notably Nigel Short, Jon Speelman and John Nunn – carried the British game through the 1980s. But since then the supply of top players has started to dry up, England have fallen from the top two or three in the world league to a place among the also-rans (at the 2014 chess Olympiad the English team came a distant 28th), and tournaments offering big prizes have become fewer in number. It is very hard even for a 2600-rated grandmaster to make a decent living – hence their need to teach, write books, commentate, do anything to earn a few quid. Hence, too, their need to economise at all times: sleeping on sofas in friends' houses; sharing hotel rooms with fellow GMs when away playing at tournaments; and making two or three visits to the hotel breakfast buffet. A grandmaster never knows where his next meal is coming from, so makes sure to eat multiple fried breakfasts when staying at a B&B. Beans, sausage, bacon and fried eggs are the ultimate GM food. Except at the Carlsen/Anand/Kramnik super-GM level, where it's muesli and orange juice in plush hotels paid for by the tournament organisers. It isn't just in playing strength that there's a great divide; the differences in their way of life are also stark.

Jones's reason for not earning easy money by coaching weaker players interested me. As well as the fact that you are spending time helping others get better when you should be working on your own game, he said that teaching chess compromises the grandmaster mentally: 'When you're coaching, you lose the natural flow of how you're thinking. You try to bring your thought process down to their level. You say, "You've got to think about this position. What pieces are *en prise* [in danger of being taken]? What kind of moves might you be thinking about?" Whereas when you play your own game, all these thoughts are subconscious.' Grandmasters don't need to think about how they do it, they just do it, and Jones reckoned you should be wary of looking too deeply at the nuts and bolts of how you play. At this rarefied level it's hard to break chess down into component parts, and Jones admitted he would struggle to tell weak players how they could improve their chess. In the grandmaster's world everything fits together in one beautiful, organic system of chessness. Good moves just are. This is a beautiful thought, but also rather depressing for the novice.

Jones admitted that if he was having a bad tournament, it was tough to motivate himself and prepare properly: 'You sit there and you just want the tournament to be over.' What was striking was how the emotions at play were the same for grandmasters as they were for us players at the other end of the food chain. In chess only the ratings are different; the mental side of the game is the same, though the pros have the additional pressure of needing to earn enough to eat (and drink). But if you define yourself in terms of your performance on the board, coping with defeat is difficult no matter how good or bad you are as a player. Strength and weakness then become a question of psychology. 'When you're a professional chess player, you're always going to have a bad result,' said Jones, 'and how you cope with that differs from player to player. Someone said that Magnus [Carlsen] was always most dangerous after he'd just lost. But someone like [Vasily] Ivanchuk, if he's just lost, will probably feel disillusioned and play far weaker than he normally plays. It's very important how you survive defeats.'

I asked Jones how long he would carry on. At the back of my mind lurked the question facing every grandmaster: what happens when you turn 40 and the only way is down? How do you avoid the weekends in dreary edge-of-town hotels playing for a couple of hundred quid? In terms of the career arc, chess is similar to boxing. The only difference is that the beatings you take are psychological rather than physical. 'I enjoy playing,' he said. 'I've always enjoyed playing. I remember a couple of years ago I was having a terrible tournament, but in the last round I played a game I really enjoyed. I said to myself, "Oh, it's time to play some chess now." I like winning. If I get to the point where I lose more games than I win, then I will probably start thinking about moving on.'

B8: MIRACLE IN TORQUAY

Towards the end of July the new English Chess Federation half-yearly grades were issued. I had edged up from 128 to 132, a tiny improvement that reflected my good performances in the early part of the year, especially in Chester. My last five games – four ugly defeats and a draw against a lowly rated youngster – had, thank goodness, come too late for inclusion in the official half-yearly assessment. Buoyed by the crisis session with Saunders, I intended to get back on the horse immediately. I toyed with the idea of going to Riga to play a week-long event for players with a FIDE rating of 2150 or below, but decided that was a bit too ambitious and, in any case, a return budget flight cost more than £200. So, instead of the delights of Latvia, I opted for the British championships in Torquay – not the main event, which was populated by grandmasters and international masters, but the under-160 championship.

Just before I went to Torquay I read a blog by American chess journalist and keen amateur player Tim Hanke on the Chess Improver website that struck a chord. 'Without exception,' he wrote, 'whenever I have spent a few weeks studying hard, and then played in a few tournaments, my game has shown noticeable improvement … The biggest obstacle to chess improvement is what I might almost call a non-chess factor: maintaining your focus on chess for a sustained period of time – weeks, months, years, however long it takes to reach your chess goals.'

In that fortnight when I'd played three tournaments in a row – a serious, tough game every day – I felt I had been making some improvement. Then what passes for normal life resumed and the improvement stalled. 'Chess usually must take a distant back seat to other more pressing issues, for all of us except perhaps a few monomaniacs or a special few whose lives have been arranged around the issue of chess improvement,' continued Hanke. He argued that youngsters made rapid progress not just because of the 'plasticity' of their brains, but because they had fewer distractions. 'When you get older, and you have been exposed to the wide world and its many facets, it will forever after be harder for you to shut yourself in your room and limit your focus to the 64 squares ... Bobby Fischer himself instinctively understood the threat to his concentration posed by the world beyond chess. He once famously demanded of a hotel clerk, "Give me a room without a view."'

I couldn't quite match Fischer's steely determination. When I checked into the Gleneagles Hotel in Torquay, I insisted on a view of Babbacombe Bay. The hotel's claim to fame was that it had been the inspiration for the TV series *Fawlty Towers*. It had cleverly turned the Fawlty association into a selling point: the reception was adorned with photographs from the series and you could have a G&T in Basil's Bar. I was attracted by its heritage, but even more persuasive was the fact that, at £65 a night, it was the cheapest room I could find in Torquay at the height of the summer season.

Despite my recent travails I arrived in Torquay with a renewed sense of purpose. My session with Saunders had cheered me up. 'Be patient, resolute, implacable, accurate, clinical' – that's what I told myself on the train down to the West Country. It was the hundredth edition of the championships – the event was founded in 1904 but not staged during the First and Second World Wars, or in several years between the wars because of clashes with various international tournaments – and the central event and all the satellite competitions, organised by age and level of ability, had attracted more than a thousand entrants. The congress scene, it seemed, was booming, especially among all those highly competitive retired accountants. The championships were being played at the Riviera Centre, a huge concrete leisure and conference venue near the esplanade. It was functional but faceless – rather like the event itself. The British chess championships ought to be a great showcase for the sport, but it is largely ignored. 'World's eyes on Torquay as championship starts' crowed the optimistic headline of a preview article from the *Western Morning News* pinned up in the foyer at the Riviera Centre. If only. The truth was that, though the games would be followed by aficionados online, the wider public, preoccupied with such trifles as Wimbledon and the Ashes, was as blasé as ever.

The centenary of the championships should have been the opportunity for trumpet-blowing, and the English Chess Federation had laid on some modest celebrations, but it was all very low key. As ever, cash was at the heart of the problem. A shortage of sponsorship money meant Britain's two best-known players, Michael Adams and Nigel Short, were not playing. A top prize of £5,000 hadn't been enough to tempt them – they would normally expect 'conditions' such as free accommodation and meals, as well as some sort of financial guarantee in the form of appearance money. Adams was playing at a prestigious invitation event in Dortmund, which he won – one of the all-time great tournament victories by a British player; Short had just won a big tournament in Canada. Another British star, Luke McShane, was also missing. McShane, who was in his late twenties, had taken a job in the City and was playing chess on a part-time basis, making him the world's strongest amateur. Their absence left my new chum Gawain Jones, the reigning champion, as favourite to retain the title.

In the under-160 section I would be facing players who on paper were a good deal stronger than me. My fear was they would also be stronger on the board. Even with my new, improved grade of 132, I would be one of the half-dozen weakest players in the 50-strong field. Saunders thought I would be doing well to get one point from the five games; I worried that I would get zero. When I arrived in Torquay, in a moment of madness I also entered the afternoon open tournament, which included several players with a rating above 2000. I thought that, since I was there, I might as well play as much chess as possible, but that meant potentially up to ten hours a day – a four-hour game in the under-160 section in the morning and a six-hour game in the Open in the afternoon. This was going to be a hell of a week.

The suitcase I took to Torquay contained very few clothes, but I packed a stack of instructional texts. Naturally, these would be largely ignored. When you have just played two exhausting games, the last thing you want to do – or at least the last thing I wanted to do – is study a book on opening theory. No doubt this was one reason my progress was so slow – chess fever had yet to afflict me. All I was fit to do after my two games was go back to my room, listen to the screech of the seagulls and stare vacantly across the bay. Torquay was wet in the early part of the week – wet as only the West Country can be – and I felt sorry for the anoraked holidaymakers, especially the little girl who was playing golf with her parents on the pitch-and-putt course next to the Riviera Centre. Her mother, who had clearly never played golf before, played three air shots before connecting with the ball and sending it shooting sideways into her daughter's shin. 'What sort of God allows that to happen?' I thought to myself. 'Isn't it enough to rain on their holiday?'

I started rather better than the woman pitch-and-putter, drawing my first game in the under-160 against a congress regular graded 150. But the afternoon game in the Open provided an instant reality check. I was up against a Lancastrian graded 170-plus who quickly took control of the game and dominated throughout. I tried to get some counterplay, but couldn't land a blow and endured three and a half hours of torture before resigning. It made me aware, if I needed a reminder, that the gulf between a grade of 150 and one of 175 was huge. An ECF grade of 175, equivalent to a FIDE rating of more than 2000, is the level at which true expertise begins. From where I sat it looked a lot more distant than the little yachts bobbing up and down in Babbacombe Bay. That loss on the first day of the Open meant my last seven games had produced five defeats and two draws, with a grade across those games of about 95, a truly awful performance and a trend I was desperate to reverse.

In between the morning and afternoon games I grabbed a few minutes with Brendan O'Gorman, a mad-keen congress player I had first encountered at Chester. O'Gorman plays several hundred graded games a year – at Chester he had told me his total was the third highest on the English Chess Federation list – and I liked the fact he referred to the group of weekend congress regulars as 'the Barmy Army'. There was, indeed, something crazy about subjecting yourself to this trial week in, week out. How did he do it? 'I don't find it a strain,' he told me in his lovely Irish brogue. 'Perhaps I don't commit myself to chess as much as some players do.' (This seemed unlikely given the number of games he played a year and his beard-stroking intensity at the chessboard.) O'Gorman was sceptical about my strategy of playing chess in intensive bursts. 'I'm not sure it's wise to suddenly concentrate your chess in that way with two games a day,' he said. 'I think you'll struggle a bit in the afternoons. You'll be tired.' He did offer a couple of practical suggestions: 'Try to avoid making mistakes more than killing yourself finding the knockout combination which is going to win all the games. Most games at amateur level are lost by blunders, so if you can avoid them you should be OK. Pace yourself and try to relax.' Should I be enjoying it? He laughed. 'If I do very badly I don't enjoy it,' he admitted. 'If I do well, it's great. Because I don't commit totally I'm not suicidal, but it's a high-risk holiday.'

O'Gorman also offered some interesting general reflections on the congress scene. He said the biggest problem – especially in the UK compared with, say, Holland, where he also played – was the absence of players aged between 20 and 50. In the UK it was predominantly juniors and greybeards. Too many players who should be in their chess-playing prime had given up the game, just as I had after university. What about the absence of women? Wasn't that an even bigger problem? He reckoned that was a lost cause. 'Chess appeals to a kind of male, autistic mentality that women don't have, or fewer women have,' he said. 'Women are more sociable than men, and chess is at base a rather anti-social game. The periphery, the before and after, can be social, but the game itself involves being silent for hours.' And women don't like being silent? 'I'm not saying that as a criticism,' he added hurriedly. 'It's more a positive than a negative. They're just more sociable creatures.'

My high-risk holiday improved considerably after the first day, along with the weather, which made dowdy Torquay look almost beautiful if you squinted, looked seawards and avoided the grim bars in the high street. I was so pleased for the holidaymakers – all the elderly couples and working-class families having a safe, unchallenging holiday. I hoped the little girl on the golf course had forgotten her bruises. I quickly forgot my loss to the player graded 177, thanks to a draw and a win (admittedly against a weakish player) on the second day, and then a draw and another win on the third day. That latter victory was a watershed moment, because it came against a player with an ECF grade of 170 and a FIDE rating of 1930 (see Game 3 on p382). More importantly, I really felt that I could play, winning in 19 moves with a fierce and well-calculated attack. OK, my opponent's play was lacklustre and gave me a big advantage in development, but for once I exploited it to the full and didn't get too excited as I pressed home my advantage. Clinical, emotionless, unerring, all those things I'd vowed to be on the way down to Torquay. It was the greatest thrill I had ever experienced at the chessboard, and I emerged from the Riviera Centre walking on air.

I had been staying in touch with John Saunders back in London to let him know how things were going, and he sent me some warm words when I talked him through the game. 'It all panned out like a dream,' he emailed. 'After his twelfth move you found the computer's first-choice moves on each of your last seven moves! Perfection!' This worried me slightly, because accusations of cheating using chess apps on mobiles were increasingly prevalent, and I wondered if someone might think my absurdly frequent trips to the toilet as I became excited during the game were to consult one – how else to explain a shock win against a player with a grade of 170? But, reader, I promise you – it was all above board.

I was on the way. 'I was delighted with what you said about not allowing yourself to get excited as you sensed victory,' Saunders told me. 'You are developing very good chess sense. So many games have been thrown away due to emotional turmoil, and it is essential to maintain your concentration until the scoresheets have been signed.' He also gave me my instructions for the rest of the week: 'Don't allow today's excitement to affect you. Elation is as big an enemy as depression. Once the game starts, concentrate only on the next move and forget tournament position, grade and all that nonsense – there's plenty of time to think about that after the tournament. One move at a time – your opponent's as well as your own. Imagine the calm composure of Mickey Adams or Mark Hebden at the board. Monitor your emotions and try to maintain an even keel. Stay in the moment. Zen and the art of chess.'

I tried to be Zen-like throughout the tournament, thinking of nothing but chess, not allowing any other aspects of my life to distract me, abjuring alcohol (mostly anyway), and trying not to eat pasty and chips – standard fare at the Riviera Centre – every day. I relied on supermarket sandwiches and even tried sushi one evening, hoping it would boost my brain power (it didn't). In the evening, if I had enough mental strength left, I played through a few games from the British championship proper – won by young grandmaster David Howell with Jones, Hebden and Stephen Gordon joint second – as they were posted online and then went to bed early. The main thing was that I was enjoying the challenge: being in this enclosed world, trying to forget about normal life, playing long, slow games and aiming to do my absolute best.

After the setbacks in the Weald and the Felce I felt I had to some extent redeemed myself. I was constantly reminded of the weakness of my opening theory (though Saunders insisted I shouldn't get hung up on this), and knew I had a huge amount of work to do. I played one middle-aged obsessive who said he competed in 50 congresses a year, had won more than 200 tournaments in his career, clocked up more than 300 graded games in one year, and studied chess for four or five hours a day. ('Why do you do it?' I asked him, incredulously. 'I love chess,' he replied with touching simplicity.) Somehow I got a draw despite him getting a huge advantage in the opening because he knew the line – the King's Indian Defence – so well. I went the exchange down – giving up rook for bishop – but fought back to force a draw, which pleased me almost as much as my triumph against the player graded 170.

My final games in Torquay went less well: I drew with a 12-year-old (graded 152) whom I would have beaten if I had calculated properly in a modestly complicated position; I was thoroughly outplayed by a 14-year-old graded 177 (one of the huge number of excellent, highly motivated juniors from migrant families playing in Torquay – they are the future of British chess); and I lost to a committed thirtysomething from the Lake District whose chilly manner at the board, rapid speed of play – he seemed almost contemptuous of the moves I was making – and sound tactical awareness were too much for me. I didn't do much wrong, but he still beat me easily – the mark of a good player. Nevertheless, I was enthused and emboldened by my week by the sea. Torquay, despite your horrible bars and amusement arcades, I salute you.

FILE C
The Battles of Hastings

'Every chess player should have a hobby'
— *Savielly Tartakower, grandmaster,*
writer and aphorist from chess's golden age
in the first half of the 20th century

C1: THE WALL

My excitement at the end of Torquay may have been rather overdone. OK, I had made some progress: my grade across the two tournaments was around 147; I felt I was becoming more battle-hardened. But the reality was that overall I had scored less than 50 per cent and had succumbed fairly tamely to three decent players. I hadn't been humiliated or even unduly embarrassed. That was the source of my end-of-tournament euphoria. Simple relief. But when the league season resumed, Clark Kent had not been transformed into a chess superman. I lost my first game against a player graded 133, my only excuse being I had been drafted in late having not touched a chess piece for almost a month; got three draws against mid-140s, playing soundly in each of the games; beat a 126 who played very poorly; and then won against a man graded 129 who made a point of telling me he was blind in his left eye. He was extremely odd in many respects, humming, berating himself loudly when he blundered away a knight, and refusing to resign despite being a queen and bishop down by the end. He even wanted to adjourn, to force us to resume the following week, but I refused and kept him playing until after 11pm, when he finally gave up on the point of checkmate. It was good to win, but I knew my play had been lacklustre after he had gifted me a piece. The only really big development was that I had started to wear glasses to play – first for online encounters where the screen tired my eyes, then over the board. I tried to convince myself it was helping, especially in longer games, but they gave me a different sense of space and I wondered whether they might make me even more prone to

error. So far I had played six games in them without making any monumental blunders, so I persevered.

Doc Saunders looked at my batch of early-season games and pronounced them insipid. He said it was hard to gauge anything from the wins because the opposition was so weak. As for the draws, he accused me of excessive passivity. 'You're getting boring,' he said. 'It's a very worrying thing.' Ironically he thought my best game was the one I'd lost. I suggested I'd been marking time, and he agreed, arguing that I was too willing to settle for draws against 140s. 'One part of your brain is saying, "I'm going to be a grandmaster." The other side is saying, "I've drawn with a 145, I'm not a bad player." You're doing what we all do, which is to find your level.'

I pleaded guilty to being overly obsessed by my grade. 'You're demonstrating all the sad symptoms of the club chess player,' he said, remembering his own grade-obsessed days. 'You are what you are at the moment,' he added, gnomically. 'That's the difficulty.' I had hit the wall identified by Andrew Soltis in *What It Takes to Become a Chess Master*, that point when something dramatic needed to change for me to reach the next level. I realised that I might need to deconstruct my game and suffer some pain as a result in order to improve in the long term. But was I willing to suffer that aggro? Saunders had doubts about my d4 openings with white, arguing they were too strategic and positional. 'To me the whole opening is wrong unless you are a super-grandmaster,' he said. 'That's where I'm heading, I deadpanned. 'But you ought to think about the intermediate steps between you and Aronian first,' he suggested. I was, though, reluctant to change something that seemed to be working – my two most recent wins had come playing d4 and I felt very happy playing it online, too. At least my d4 repertoire with white was effective in beating up elderly men with grades in the 120s. In the kingdom of the one-eyed the man with the new spectacles is king.

The games I showed Saunders were so dull that we quickly passed over the moves in favour of the way you make a move. 'I can tell a good player from the way they move the pieces, and particularly the way they make a capture,' he said. There was more to the game than just playing chess; you had to embody it, looking at home at the board and instilling fear in your opponent. Vasily Smyslov, the Soviet world champion of the late 1950s, was noted for the way he almost screwed his pieces on to the squares to which he was moving them, as if to emphasise that he had decided this was their natural place and they would remain there always. The 'Smyslov screw' entered chess lore. Conversely, said Saunders, some players would feign uncertainty to give their opponents a false sense of security. These were deep psychological waters. Even the way you placed your knights might have a deeper meaning: should they be facing forwards at the start of the game to emphasise attacking intent or be placed sideways to suggest a more defensive mentality? I felt my at-the-board style was OK – I had adopted GM Joe Gallagher's approach of getting close to it, as if to claim ownership, and liked to let my hands hover above the pieces for a few seconds before swooping to make a move – but I vowed to pay greater attention to this aspect of the game. One day the 'Moss meander' might be recalled with the same awe as the 'Smyslov screw'.

A few days after meeting Saunders I had an evening of pub chess with Julian Way, a 180-plus graded player who captained Kingston's first team. Way had been an exceptionally strong junior player – he had had a FIDE rating of around 2300 at the age of 17, the level at which you are awarded the title of FIDE master – but he suffered a breakdown at university and it took him a long time to recover. When he resumed playing chess in his late thirties, his strength had greatly diminished and his grade was barely better than mine was when I set out on my chequered journey. But it had climbed inexorably and he was now close to where he had been almost 30 years previously. It was a wonderful story and one I hoped might have some lessons for me in how to make that jump from a grade of 130 to one of ... well, I wasn't sure: 150, 170, beyond, I could never quite decide.

Way has an admirable approach to the game. 'One of the great things about chess,' he told me, as we sat and played in a noisy pub, 'is that if you can retain and stimulate your interest, that for me is the catalyst to improvement.' He said he had no set opening repertoire; he played everything because he had to challenge himself. 'If you're bored, how are you going to improve? Some players have a very consistent opening repertoire because they want to win every game. I'm not bothered if I play a few games with an opening I don't understand and lose, because I feel I've learned something.' He believed anything was possible if you kept your love for the game and avoided getting stuck in a rut. 'Motivation is integral to improvement. If you're grappling with the issues of the chessboard, your rating will rise without you even having to think about it.' He had had an exceptional season and reached a grade of 200 when we had our session in the pub, but said he hadn't made a conscious effort to get there; it just happened because he was playing interesting, imaginative, committed chess. Obsessing about your grade was probably the surest way of *not* reaching your target. What mattered was trying to play good chess; the results – and the consequent rise up the ratings – would look after themselves.

Way's advice was to be pragmatic and don't try to force it. 'Put your pieces on good squares [squares where they control space and exert pressure],' he kept repeating. Do that and you will give yourself a chance of winning. 'If you go into a game thinking you've lost, you've lost,' he said. 'When I sit down against a grandmaster rated 2550 I try to remember that, if I put my pieces on good squares, there's not much that even he can do about it.' His thinking reminded me of what the young Dutch grandmaster Anish Giri had said a few months earlier after winning a game against the fast-rising American star Fabiano Caruana. 'I made some good, healthy moves and the position played itself,' said Giri. 'I love this kind of game, when it just goes naturally and all you need to do is listen to the position.' Listen to the position – what a glorious phrase. Nabokov, who saw chess as being closely allied to music, would surely approve.

'You don't need to put a ceiling on your chess improvement,' Way insisted. 'The sky's the limit. What you do need to realise is that you can't jump a step.' He suggested buying instructional DVDs, which he said he watched while cooking. He made them sound much more palatable than hefty books on obscure opening lines and rook endings. Way's other piece of advice was to play more positionally. Instead of launching opportunistic sorties, he said you should take a more strategic view. 'In a lot of the games I was losing I had got my pieces on bad squares,' he said, 'but recently I've been keeping my pieces very central, keeping them well defended, trying to think in a coherent, coordinated way rather than play reactively.' His advice echoed that of Chris Briscoe, one of the leading Surbiton players, who had made a significant advance in his late thirties by adopting a more positional style. Briscoe told me he had put on 100 FIDE rating points very quickly by playing a more thoughtful, strategic game, but now felt that having reached 2250 – very strong but still 150 points short of an IM title – he had got as far as he could and was concentrating on teaching rather than playing. As Soltis said, everyone comes up against a wall at some point. Where, ultimately, would mine be?

C2: BACK TO THE ROCK

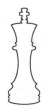Soon after my evening with Way I decided to go back
to Gibraltar to spend a weekend with Stuart Conquest,
my long-distance grandmaster guru. Partly I wanted to
get a chess boost, but the weather was a factor too – a
chance to escape the onset of an English winter and
enjoy the year's last rays of Mediterranean sun. Conquest had by
now left his home in northern Spain and was based permanently
on the Rock, as a kind of chess ambassador. As well as organising
the annual tournament in which I had played the previous
January, he was trying to extend Gibraltar's international profile
with junior tournaments. One of his duties was coaching
children, and I saw him in action at a lunchtime lesson for a
group at the Loreto convent school. I had tried to teach chess to
children myself at a school in north London, and knew how
hard it was – the kids used to end up crying and hurling bishops
at each other. Loreto being a Catholic institution, there was a
good deal more respect for bishops; in fact, better behaviour
all round.

After the coaching session we went to Conquest's flat
overlooking Rosia Bay, where Nelson's body was supposedly
brought ashore after his death at the Battle of Trafalgar in 1805.
The flat has stunning views across the Strait of Gibraltar to Tangier
and the sunsets are extraordinary. Conquest, the great bohemian,
seemed to have landed on his feet. Over the board the bohemianism
disappears and he has what Saunders calls 'a glint of steel'.
Once, he had set us both a puzzle in a pub and wouldn't let us
off the hook until we'd had a proper stab at solving it. Here he

set me a puzzle and refused to give me the answer until I had solved it, even though it took me three-quarters of an hour. Chess, he was trying to tell me, wasn't easy. He didn't become British champion and a GM rated 2600 just by being an artist of the chessboard; he could scrap too when he needed to.

What was unquestionably true, though, was that he loved the game, and it was that love which had driven him to the top. Whenever I met him in Gibraltar, he was always carrying a small book of chess puzzles, so he could solve one while he was sitting in a bar or waiting to cross the border into Spain. He had largely stopped playing competitive chess, but the game was still at the centre of his life. He told me that he never felt he was playing a person when he was at the board: 'I never had that Fischer thing of wanting to crush the other guy's ego – that alpha male, hunt, kill, drag-it-back-to-the-cave thing. Winning was nice, of course, but it wasn't really all that important to me.' The challenge was more abstract than that: an exploration of possibilities, as if he were playing against chess history itself. He said he often got into time trouble because he chose to lose himself in the beauty and aesthetic challenge of chess rather than tell himself to make a move, any move. He was seeking perfection rather than adopting a pragmatic, clinical, results-based approach.

I asked him how he knew when he was playing well. 'Every so often I'd get something that was almost like a chemical release in the brain during the game,' he told me. 'It was a total high, a chess trip, pure chess thought. You would have a realisation of it at the same time as it was happening, and everything made sense. It wasn't even that I had seen some incredibly deep combination; it was just the thrill of being there at that moment, playing chess, probably at a moment of great tension and pressure.' He called it a 'superconsciousness of the artistry of chess', a moment when he found himself entirely at one with the beauty of the game. He made it sound wonderfully mystical.

Conquest's flat had chess books scattered over every surface; this was a working library. He also had large framed photographs of all the world champions on the walls. There was an old Indian chess set on the terrace and a more functional one in the living area. He had chosen to surround himself with the trappings of chess, to live in and through the game. Compared to Conquest, I was just a chess tourist. His refusal to play online blitz spoke of the same love for the game's deeper purposes: 'The reasons I play chess – the way I perceive the game, the challenges of it, the pleasure of finding a nice idea, executing it, and the cut-and-thrust of the game – are lost completely in online blitz. It just comes down to results – trying to flag someone [win on time], for example. I'd sooner resign the game. Trying to flag someone when you're X pieces down, and he's got ten seconds left and you've got 12, or trying to get your Internet Chess Club rating up to 3000. I never got into any of that stuff.' This was gloriously purist – the chess player as true artist. Duchamp would have been proud of Conquest's approach.

Conquest looked at my recent games and, echoing Saunders, pronounced them routine, lacking verve and imagination. 'Nigel Short would call them flaccid,' he said. Why turn up for a game of chess, travel all the way to Torquay indeed, and then accept a draw on the 24th move – as I had in one game I showed him – when there was huge potential still left in the game? We played through a few of the games and in one he demonstrated how, with a single bold stroke, I could have lit a fuse under the position, provoked tension, danger, excitement, all the things I fearfully shied away from. What became obvious as we talked was that I was more intent on not losing than on trying to win. I was playing the percentages, which made for tedious chess. I was also being lazy, refusing to let my mind embrace all the possibilities. 'Why should the first move you see be the best move?' he said. As we went through games, he showed me the complexity that existed in even seemingly simple positions. 'There's hardly such a thing as a boring game of chess,' he insisted. 'There are always little wrinkles and things that suddenly present themselves. Maybe it's just a one-move shot where you have a chance to do something slightly off the run of the mill. If it's playable, (a) you have to spot it and (b) you need the balls to do it. Maybe it will work, maybe it won't, but at least you will be putting the guy under pressure.' I had to get my opponents out of their comfort zone, force them to play unorthodox, asymmetrical chess.

'Seize the moment!' said Conquest, in a sudden outburst of something akin to poetry. 'You'll never have this position again in your life. Here you are, you're playing chess in the 100th British championships [we were looking at one of my dull – or, as I had thought at the time, honourable – Torquay draws]. There should be a sense of place, a sense of time, a sense of responsibility to the game, if you like. This is the joy of playing chess. What are we doing here? This is a very special moment in your life. This is it. You can play a great move here. See it, look at it and, if it looks interesting, play it. If it doesn't work out and you lose, so what? Show a bit of spunk!' As well as getting my opponents out of their comfort zone, I needed to get out of my own comfort zone.

C3: ANGST IN ASDA

I felt this latest meeting with Conquest was a potential watershed. He had shown me the light: embrace truth and beauty; forget the base pursuits of murdering your opponent and chasing rating points. Play for the right reasons and glory will follow. Inevitably, in my first game after my return from sun-kissed Gibraltar to cold, unwelcoming Kingston, it didn't work out that way. I had finally succumbed to the allure of Asda and agreed to play a game there for Kingston, one of my two league teams, against Redhill. I'd been playing for Kingston for about ten years without ever really feeling attached to them. Whereas my other club, Surbiton, met at a large, rambling detached house that doubled as a day centre for the elderly, Kingston stumbled from crisis to crisis with too few players and now no real home. The club met weekly for matches against other teams in the Surrey and Thames Valley leagues – Ashtead, Crystal Palace, Ealing, Harrow, Maidenhead, Meadhurst, Wimbledon, Wallington. The leagues have no geographical rhyme or reason. How can Harrow be in the Thames Valley? Does Meadhurst really exist? Saunders' theory was that the composition of the leagues reflected railway timetables in around 1932. These clubs are hangovers from a time when chess was thriving and every community had a club. Back then there was little else to do and men – it was invariably men then, too – were looking for a way of filling dark winter evenings. Chess, like fishing and pigeon fancying, is a great form of structured time-wasting.

Television, computer games and the demise of the world in which everyone finished work at 5pm were gradually bringing down the curtain on club chess. The old blokes who had played since the 1950s still attended, along with the eager young juniors, but it was hard for people in jobs to play regularly, and numbers were falling – though Surbiton was bucking the trend thanks to the efforts of a wonderful 70-year-old called Paul Durrant, who had been devoted to chess all his life and filled the club with energy, enthusiasm and something close to love. He had perfected what a chess club should be: competitive and match-oriented but also warm and able to embrace players of all ages and standards. Elsewhere club chess was in gentle decline. Hammersmith in west London still had a club, for example – a tiny group of men playing in a grim little community hall – but once there had been a thriving Hammersmith chess league. Many clubs have closed or amalgamated, but a disparate group hangs on, under the auspices of their historic leagues, playing for grand trophies donated by long-forgotten benefactors. Kingston had 15 or so regular players, all but one of whom were men. Mostly they were past 50, had played chess all their lives and weren't going to stop now. They had grown up in that post-war period when it was part of their school life, and the game had then become an integral part of their adulthood too. They got the habit in the days before television, and it never left them. Even the ones who took breaks to marry and have children eventually came back. Chess had them for life, and for some the board really was their world, perhaps even their salvation.

Asda's café, where the games were being played, was thankfully closed to the public by the time we started. I was up against a player graded 160 who annoyed me by his habit of invading my space by stretching his legs out under the table. He played slowly and fell hopelessly behind on time. I was gradually building a better position and had a huge time advantage, so as we neared the time control, felt it was inevitable I would win (oh, Donner!). A victory over a 160 would be my second best win ever, and I was convinced it was in the bag. As the time control approached, however, he started to speed up, banging his hand down on his clock and stopping recording his moves, as is sometimes allowed when you have less than five minutes left. I was still playing at a leisurely speed, convinced I had more than enough time to secure victory. My advantage was getting bigger, and I felt sure he would resign at any moment. But he didn't: he carried on, played ever wilder moves, drew me into a time scramble, and set me a series of problems that ate into my time. I lost control of the position and, worse, lost track of the time, so that my flag fell as I was about to make my 35th move – the point at which the time control is reached and another hour added to the clock. I had lost on time – a game I had spent the past hour believing I had won. He had somehow made ten moves in a minute and suckered me into defeat. I was devastated, hardly able to speak or think coherently. I never wanted to see the inside of an Asda store again.

The chess world championship was taking place when I played this appalling game. Magnus Carlsen was giving the reigning champ Viswanathan Anand a beating, and the latter had just lost a crucial game with a terrible blunder that virtually guaranteed Carlsen would become the title holder – at 22 the joint youngest player, with the great Garry Kasparov, to become world champion. After Anand's defeat, Jonathan Rowson tweeted, 'An unpublished draft of *Dante's Inferno* includes a circle of hell where you learn how it feels to lose an important chess game.' Later he wrote, 'The degree of pain is not comparable, but just as men will never "get" what it feels like to give birth, non-chess players will never know the unique torment and anguish that flow from such a defeat.'

Rowson had summed up precisely the way I felt after losing the Asda game.

I believed that somehow I had been cheated. I *deserved* to win that game. My opponent may have been nominally a 160, but I had played the better chess. Natural justice demanded that I should be the victor. I wanted to make some sort of protest. Did he stop recording his moves too soon? Did the five-minute rule really apply in these circumstances? Should we have made an effort to reconstruct the game afterwards – neither of us was scoring by the end – rather than offer a frosty (on my part) handshake and disappear into the night? I made myself look ridiculous by moaning about the injustice to anyone who would listen. 'When you win you say little, when you lose you say less' – an old sporting maxim which contains a great deal of wisdom. I should have taken it on the chin, but I seemed incapable of doing so. I had a terrible, sleepless 24 hours, until gradually some sort of sanity reasserted itself. Another maxim helped me get through. 'In sport you don't get what you deserve,' I heard former England rugby player Brian Moore say while commentating on Wales' rugby match with South Africa a few days later. You had to find a way to win, not think you would get there by divine right.

C4: MEN BEHAVING BADLY

 I had behaved very badly after my defeat at Asda, trying to find grounds for an appeal against the result, moaning to the team captain and getting him to complain to the opposing captain about our mutual failure to reconstruct the game at the end. It was all useless and desperately undignified. Within a few days of getting back from Gibraltar, I was already ignoring what my Zen master had told me: play with grace; worship beauty; exist in that glorious, unique moment; put petty concerns aside. Chess etiquette had never been my strong point. I remembered a 'friendly' game I had played years earlier against a young woman who, in her teens, had been British girls' champion. I had been winning, but eventually blundered in time trouble, handing her victory. Afterwards I couldn't bring myself to speak to her, and packed away the pieces with surly resignation. It was pathetic. As well as becoming a better player I needed to learn how to become a more gracious one.

My interest in what might be called the moral aspect of the game was heightened by an incident I witnessed at Surbiton a week after my Asda meltdown. It was a first-team match between Surbiton and another very strong team in the Surrey League. There was a dispute on one of the boards over the way a player was recording moves when his opponent was in a time scramble. The player in time trouble accused him of not recording moves as they were being played but doing it in batches, enabling the player with extra time to gain valuable seconds. It was an absurdly abstruse point, yet it almost led to a fight, with the player being accused of gamesmanship getting increasingly agitated. His face became so red I feared for his health. The captains had to be called in to arbitrate, and eventually the matter was settled, but it disturbed me. Was this supposed to be an evening of pleasurable mental activity in which we toyed lightly with the beauties of chess, or the sort of Dantesque hell Rowson had alluded to when he wrote about Anand losing his world title? Was Saunders right that in chess the pain generally outweighed the pleasure?

In *The Adventure of Chess* Edward Lasker reflected amusingly on chess etiquette. As well as being remembered for his writing, Edward Lasker's name lives on because of a famous game he played against two-times British champion Sir George Thomas in 1912 which has been endlessly anthologised. Lasker sacrifices his queen and then chases Thomas's king from one side of the board to the other before delivering a delightfully throwaway *coup de grâce* – a classic of the golden age. Thomas, the consummate English amateur (as well as being a very good chess player, he won numerous badminton titles, reached the semi-finals of the men's doubles at Wimbledon in 1911, and was a dab hand at hockey), congratulated his opponent on winning this game. Many players would have been mortified to have been humiliated in this manner – the king hunt was a ferocious one and the game lasted just 18 moves – but Thomas remembered his manners. 'That was very nice,' Lasker later recalled him saying. Had the victory been chalked up against a Berlin amateur, said Lasker, the response would have been, 'You were lucky.'

There is a section at the back of *The Adventure of Chess* called 'How to Behave at the Chessboard'. It is really a series of tips on how not to behave at the chessboard: feel free to hum or sing during the game; tap the table; yawn or look at your watch when it is your opponent's turn to move; if playing an inexperienced player, show your contempt for him by strolling round the hall inspecting the other games, as if they hold a greater challenge for you than your own; and while watching two experts analysing a game, offer your own random observations on the position. 'By adhering steadily to the hints thrown out above,' writes Lasker, ambiguously, 'I think I can promise that their practice will, in a short time, obtain for you a reputation of no ordinary kind in the chess circles you frequent.' I dreaded to think what my own reputation was. At the board I hummed, rocked, tapped and sighed deeply and repeatedly; I sank into red-faced bewilderment if my position began to disintegrate; I drank water, tea or Coke (but never, unlike some more laid-back players, alcohol); I ate apples, bananas, Twixs, Penguins and occasionally sandwiches and pork pies – I may as well have brought a hamper, tablecloth and folding chair; and I went to the toilet at absurdly frequent intervals. I must have been a nightmare to play against.

Lasker says in a footnote that these tips were 'condensed from suggestions made by Captain H. A. Kennedy, one of the leading players of England about 100 years ago'. He was, though, being a little disingenuous. In reality he had lifted six paragraphs word for word from an essay with the baroque title 'A Fasciculus of Chess Wrinkles', which was collected with Kennedy's other chess writings in a book called *Waifs and Strays, Chiefly from the Chessboard*. 'When you have lost a game or games, never be guilty of the preposterous silliness of allowing that you are fairly mastered by the more expert skill of your antagonist,' advised Kennedy. 'There are many ways of accounting for such a mishap, without having occasion to resort to an admission so humiliating to your self-esteem. You may conjure up a bad headache for the nonce. You have been in weak health lately. Your mind was otherwise occupied. You wanted sufficient excitement – a capital excuse, as it implies your opponent's force being so inferior to your own that you could not muster interest enough to take the trouble to beat him.'

How familiar all this was, especially online, where you can accuse your opponent of using a chess computer to find moves, or of boring you to defeat. How many times had I allowed my time to expire rather than make the move that would have doomed me to defeat, believing that by wasting my vanquisher's time I was somehow winning a small victory of my own? In searching to renew myself morally through chess I was starting from a very low base. Somehow I needed to hate losing – all good competitors need to feel that anguish – while learning how to lose well. I needed to emulate Sir George rather than the dragon.

Hugh Alexander Kennedy, to give him his full name, felt like a real find, a Victorian precursor of Donner: an expert player devoted to chess but who recognised the madness in that devotion; and a witty writer able to pierce the absurdities of the game. In another of the essays in *Waifs and Strays* he reflects on the difficulties posed by treating triumph and disaster as impostors: 'I do not know whether it is more difficult to win gracefully at chess, or to lose without giving way to an undue exhibition of pique and disappointment. Both are hard matters to compass, and to effect them requires a natural generosity of mind and evenness of disposition which but few possess ... I have known persons, whose suavity of disposition nothing else could touch, display over the chessboard the most strange and painful irascibility.' Kennedy tells the story of an old clergyman playing a game on a 'beautiful new Chinese set of delicately carved ivory' which he had just been given as a present. The clergyman had been winning the game throughout, but blundered and lost, causing him to sweep the pieces from the table and trample them underfoot before bursting into tears. In chess, man's true nature expressed itself. 'The chessboard,' wrote Kennedy, 'is a mirror in which the broad features, and no less the minuter traits, that make up individual character are distinctly and visibly shown.'

One of Kennedy's earliest recollections was of his parents playing chess, and the experience was a painful one. 'The two used to quarrel like cat and dog over the game,' he writes. Thanks to his early experiences, he knew exactly where he stood in the art v fight-to-the-death debate: 'A game of chess is essentially an argument. The board and men are accessories to the argument: that is, they are the outward symbols of the language in which it is carried on. But they are by no means necessary to it. Indeed, I have heard of a saying among the Hungarians, who are fond of chess and in the habit of contesting games while riding on horseback, that the board and men only spoil the play.'

Kennedy, who was an officer in the Madras Native Infantry, played a great deal in India – there doesn't appear to have been much soldiering to do – and represented Madras in a correspondence match (with moves being posted back and forth) against Hyderabad. 'I used to examine my positions sitting in a tub of water, cooled with saltpetre,' he recalls, 'with a scooped-out pumpkin on my head by way of refrigerant to the brain, a method which I strongly recommend to the notice of all who engage in chess by correspondence in torrid climates.' His love of the game sustained him after he left the army, and he reminisces about playing in the famous chess divan in the Strand, a coffee house which became the home of English chess in the 19th century, quoting a couplet from the 15th-century poet John Skelton's 'Vppon A Deedman's Hed': 'Our days be datyd/To be checkmatyd' – an epitaph that should surely adorn every chess player's grave.

C5: NOT QUITE A CLASSIC

 While the near-fight was taking place in the first-team match at Surbiton, I was finishing off a rather pleasant game in the internal Surbiton under-150 championship. It was an easy win against a man who was very nice but had a very low grade. I played OK, but when I looked at the game on my computer I realised I had still missed a great deal. Nonetheless I was satisfied: a win was a win, and at least I had felt in control throughout. I had tried to see the game holistically – to develop a narrative in which I could see where the game was going from beginning to end; opening, middle game and endgame should flow seamlessly into each other, and here they did, more or less. It helped me put the Asda nightmare behind me.

Great challenges lay ahead. I had booked to play a weekender at the London Classic – the event in which I had made faltering progress the previous year. I had also signed up to play in the New Year congress at Hastings, and was contemplating playing in a big tournament at the annual chess festival at Wijk aan Zee, a small town on the Netherlands' North Sea coast that everyone warned me would be freezing in January. I had come to a key point in my journey. I felt I knew what was required to be a complete chess player – energy, imagination, respect for the game and my opponent, a will to win but, above all, a will to play well and truthfully – but could I put these things into practice in the heat of battle? I bought a new scorebook to mark my symbolic fresh beginning. I would obliterate the old games, the old me, the Asda nightmare, all the nightmares thus far. I would put these down to experience and start afresh.

The Classic started like a dream. In the first game I beat a woman in her mid-sixties who had come all the way from Switzerland to play. She exerted some initial pressure and things looked ominous after 20 moves, but I managed to turn it round, grabbed a pawn and won the endgame. The second game was even better: I gambited a pawn playing my usual Scandinavian as black (I still hadn't managed to find an alternative to white's pawn to e4), had the initiative throughout and won nicely despite being three pawns down at one stage. In round three I was on top board and feeling extremely pleased with life. Vishy Anand, fresh from losing his world title to Magnus Carlsen, and Vladimir Kramnik, another former world champion, were playing in the elite event. Just to be playing at the same venue as two former world champions was inspiring.

There were 500 competitors playing at the Classic, with everyone except the GMs in the elite tournament (who had their own auditorium) gathered in one big hall at Olympia. I recognised quite a few of my rivals and now really felt I was on the circuit. Each day I would celebrate the end of the session by having a hot dog with onions and lashings of ketchup. Truly I was living the dream – if, again, not quite living up to Carrera's dietary diktats. It couldn't last, of course. In round three I blundered in the opening and spent the entire game playing catch-up to a canny old bloke who always kept his nose in front. I was desperately close to getting a draw, but went wrong again in time trouble and lost. That was the end of my interest in the £200 first prize. The only consolation was that my laconic, hard-nosed opponent himself went down to his arch-rival in what turned into a grudge match in the next round. On the Sunday, free of any pressure, I managed two draws to end on a respectable 3/5.

My performance across the three days was again equivalent to an ECF grade of around 147 – exactly the same as at Torquay. Not bad, considering my official grade was 132, but confirmation that any substantial progress had stalled. I was having terrible trouble beating players graded above 140. My style was just too one-dimensional to beat anyone with a bit of nous. I tried to follow Conquest's instructions to play with more flair, and felt there was a bit more energy and imagination in my play, but it was still a struggle. Doc Saunders, who was acting as press officer at the Classic, laughed when I said I hadn't made that elusive leap to the next level. 'I'm not surprised, with the amount of work you do,' he said. Naturally, he meant the amount of work I didn't do.

We were talking close to the bookstall, and if I'd had any money I would happily have bought some more books to sit on my shelves. It struck me how self-helpish some of them sounded – *Pump Up Your Rating* by Axel Smith, the chess equivalent of *Lose 12 Stone in a Fortnight* or *Perfect Abs Now!* These books promised instant progress, but, as the Doc liked to point out, the only real progress came with long-term slog. There were no quick fixes.

I also had the pleasure of analysing a game with Gawain Jones as it was being played. Jones had been knocked out at the group stage of the elite tournament, but had stuck around to help with the commentary. It was mesmerising to try to follow his speed of thought and the way he took in everything that was happening on the board in one breath. He seemed to see everything at lightning speed and without having to break the analysis down into its constituent parts. 'It's easier when you don't have the pressure of actually playing,' he said, modestly. It was a privilege to get that sort of insight into the grandmaster mind, but also depressing. How could we mere mortals ever approach that combination of technical know-how, strategic vision and speed of thought? It was another world. Planet Chess.

C6: THE ROCKY ROAD TO GRANDMASTER

 While at the Classic, I made a point of meeting Will Taylor, who was playing in the Open – a nine-round tournament for the ultra-committed. Three years earlier, Taylor, a 24-year-old who had recently graduated in physics and chemistry from Durham University, had embarked on a project similar to my own. He had decided, from an almost equally low base – though with youth and a mathematically inclined brain on his side – that he wanted to be a grandmaster, and set up a blog called 'Road to Grandmaster'. Naturally I wanted to talk to him to pick up tips. Taylor set out on his journey in September 2010 and was so confident he would succeed that he staked £200 with bookmakers William Hill at odds of 25-1. At 21 he was already a little late to launch his quest, though not quite as late as me, and William Hill's odds were by no means generous. His FIDE rating was around 1860 when he began and getting to 2250 should certainly have been within his compass, but reaching 2500 and winning his five grand from the bookies was going to be tough. When I met him, he was up to a rating of 2017 – a gain of 150 points in three years, which was good (I would have killed for it) but not earth-shattering.

From his blog I learned that he had worked like a demon initially, putting in up to seven hours' chess study a day. How he fitted in his degree *and* – that rarity among chess players – a regular girlfriend, God only knows. I was impressed by his commitment (which put my feeble efforts to shame), but, a year into his quest, he seemed to have suffered something of a crisis and posed himself a troubling question on his blog: 'Given that, despite many hours of hard work, my progress is not all that could be desired, is it clear that I do not have the innate talent required to become an excellent chess player?' His answer sounded less than emphatic: 'I'm not yet prepared to accept that as the only explanation.'

Almost two years into his mission he reached the conclusion that he was operating on too broad a front and needed to 'study just one thing intensively and repetitively'. However, after that impressive call to arms, there was a sudden diminution in his enthusiasm: the entries became shorter, he admitted that 'chess is currently not my top priority', took a year off to study Mandarin in China and, when he returned, seemed to have abandoned his project, or at least put it on hold. The road to GM had reached a cul-de-sac.

So what had happened? He was clearly still playing chess – here he was, after all, playing with the big boys at the Classic while I was swimming in the shallow end – but on his website he appeared to have given up on becoming a GM and settled for having reached the level of 'expert' (equivalent to a FIDE rating of around 2000). 'I've now returned from my year in China, but the future of my project to become a grandmaster is still uncertain,' he had written in August 2013. 'In order to study chess it is absolutely necessary to be alive, and in order to remain alive for any length of time access to food, water and shelter is useful. The acquisition of these requires money, so it is to the generation of said money that I now turn my attention. It is my hope that at some point in the future I will once again be able to dedicate a significant amount of time and energy to chess, but that point is not now.' I needed to find out why Taylor's early optimism had turned to ashes.

We had arranged to meet near the arbiter's table at the Classic. I told him to look for someone who was old and world-weary; he replied that I should look for someone who was young and world-weary. He told me he had played the game since the age of 11 and been reasonably strong in his teens, but only when he was at university did he settle on his pursuit of chess excellence. 'I was a respectable club player but obviously a very long way from being a grandmaster,' he said. Nevertheless he thought he had a chance. 'I believed I could make significant progress and that it was possible to make it. Odds of about 100-1 would have been more realistic, but the bet wasn't the point really. It was a way of giving myself some motivation and getting myself a following online. I thought that would motivate me too. It turned out to be quite fun, but also quite stressful.' He said following the road to GM in public added to the pressure. 'I was thinking about it during the games, and at times it was affecting my chess negatively. I played one disastrous tournament in Sunningdale [Berkshire] where I repeatedly threw away equal positions by doing unwarranted exchange sacs [giving up a rook for knight or bishop] because I was thinking I had to try to win. I felt I needed to make progress, and to do that I had to win games.'

Taylor reckoned he had made progress, but admitted his work ethic had diminished since that initial 50-hours-a-week burst. 'I decided to try to salvage my degree. I also became obsessed with finding the right way to study and the right things to study, and that meant I kept chopping and changing. I spent a lot of time thinking about the right approach and less time actually studying.' It sounded like the way I used to revise for exams, with about 85 per cent of my time spent drawing up elaborate revision schedules using multi-coloured marker pens, leaving almost no time for revision. 'I've got a lot of books and very few of them I've finished,' he said, 'which is obviously not good.'

Taylor thought the only way to improve was to adopt the sort of 'deliberate practice' recommended by Malcolm Gladwell. 'You have to work hard on some technical aspect and really practise that until you master it.' Playing through the odd grandmaster game without really understanding what's going on and clocking up hour after hour of random blitz online will not do the trick. He also advised me to look through all my games and try to identify my style and pick openings appropriate to that style, though he admitted he was struggling to do it himself: 'I still don't really know what sort of player I am. The way I described it to my new team captain a week ago was that in quiet, boring positions I play speculatively and try to liven things up by playing dubious moves, and in wild attacking positions I get scared and try to shut things down. It was said jokingly, but I think it's true.'

Taylor said he still believed he could make it to grandmaster. 'I haven't changed my opinion about that. But you do need to dedicate a lot of time to it – at least 10,000 hours – and at the moment I'm looking for a job and can't do that. You also have to want to dedicate that time, and I'm not entirely sure I do. I still really want to improve, but there are other things in life, and whether I'd want to put in all the work to go all the way I'm not entirely sure. I like the game, but playing against strong players and beating them at long time controls is extraordinarily hard work. I hadn't really played in open tournaments before – I'd mostly played in majors – and it's really punishing.' He was right – competitive chess against good players saps mind and body. The day after the London Classic, which for me had meant 20 hours of chess spread over three days, I felt not just exhausted but physically ill. There was nothing else I expended as much effort and concentration on; nothing I found so stressful and frustrating.

Taylor said he had not abandoned his quest, but admitted it was on hold until his life was more settled. 'If I suddenly shoot up to 2200 I might start writing about it again, but when I do I'll relaunch it with a slash through the grand of "grandmaster" and put "FIDE" instead, and if I make FIDE master [which requires a rating of at least 2300] then I'll make it road to IM, then GM.' Everest can only be conquered in stages. I asked if he had any advice for me in my own quest. 'Well, what is your quest, exactly?' he said pointedly. 'Is it to become a grandmaster? If it is, then I'd say give up being a journalist and dedicate all of your time to chess.' I told him I hoped to get to 150 at least. He was reassuring. 'That should be very achievable.' I boasted about my chess doc and my grandmaster guru in Gibraltar, sherpas on the long climb that lay ahead. 'I don't think it just rubs off,' he said. 'You only get there with hard work.'

C7: COLD COMFORTS

When I subjected my games at the Classic to the merciless gaze of the computer, I realised I had been fortunate to score 3/5. Objectively I should have lost both the games I won, though ironically I had good drawing chances in the game I lost. If my opponents had played properly, it could easily have been one out of five, with just a couple of draws to show for my exhausting efforts. Doc Saunders was, however, more upbeat: 'Computers play to a rating of 3000. They are Magnus Carlsen-plus. Of course they will see things you don't. The thing to think about is your style of play. You are an initiative player.' What he meant was that I needed to be the one making the running. He liked my play in game two where I'd given up pawns for an attack. 'That game was amazing,' he said. 'The computer didn't understand it.' He then paid me the biggest compliment in the 18 months we'd been working together: 'You're a chess player now. You used to be somebody who played chess. Now you are a real chess player.' It was a satisfying moment, even if he did swiftly qualify his praise. 'You can see things coming and have the fear of a chess player. You do think about what the other guy is doing. If anything the pendulum has swung back too far the other way, and there's a danger that you will become too inhibited.' Play your natural game; don't be scared to inject some anarchy into positions; enjoy your chess. Like Conquest, he was preaching a doctrine of freedom and fearlessness.

A couple of weeks after the London Classic I played in the opening four-round weekender of the annual Hastings tournament which, having first taken place in 1895, likes to style itself 'the oldest chess tournament in the world'. Venerable it certainly was, and it could summon up a certain vintage charm – some of the players looked as if they had probably played in the inaugural event – but its glory days were long past. I had always wanted to play at Hastings. It used to be one of the world's great tournaments and its list of winners reads like a who's who of chess – Rubinstein, Euwe, Tartakower, Alekhine, Marshall, Capablanca, Bronstein, Paul Keres, Botvinnik, Tal, Spassky, Smyslov, Karpov, Korchnoi. In its heyday it was an all-play-all premier to which only the very greatest players were invited, but for the past ten years shortage of money had forced that format to be replaced by an open in which anyone willing to pay the entrance fee could play. This year a dozen grandmasters from the UK and overseas had turned up to fight for the prize but, in truth, they were not names that could compete with the participants of even 20 years ago. The venue had lost its glory too: the tournament used to be played in the ballroom on the pier, but the pier burned down in 2010 and the sports centre in which the event now took place was a charmless substitute. The pier, the town, the tournament: all had declined in concert from the golden age between the wars when Hastings had a touch of panache.

In the main tournament a hundred players were doing battle over ten days for a top prize of £2,000. Once again I avoided the stars and played in a satellite event. I had vowed to play in the Masters one day, but not quite yet. I arrived on Friday afternoon to allow plenty of time to acclimatise ahead of the early start on Saturday, but boredom in the evening – Hastings out of season is desperately dreary – prompted a glass of wine in a grotty pub and a vast meal in one of those unchanging Indian restaurants where lonely men eat biryanis and drink lager and the staff outnumber the customers. I went to bed early, but woke soon after 4am and then spent three hours listening to the cricket coverage on Radio 4 – it was the Melbourne Test and there was a brief hope that England might raise themselves from abject humiliation. That hope was extinguished in the three hours when I should have been sleeping. The result of this un-Carrera-like behaviour was that I was facing my first game in the tournament having had too much curry and Kingfisher and too little sleep.

It was cold and wet and the sea was roaring as I walked along the front and up to the sports centre. Nigel Short had told me that playing at Hastings had been a formative experience for him as a teenager. He'd stayed in a dingy hotel in a room with a window that wouldn't close, and he was freezing for the entire ten days. My room was cold, too, but at least I only had to stay for a weekend. I decided that if I returned to play the following year, I would splash out on a hotel that was warm, inviting and offered breakfast.

Despite my sleeplessness I managed a draw in my first-round game against a delightful old Hastings regular whose love of chess was clearly undimmed after all his years there. After we had agreed a draw I asked him whether he wanted to analyse the game – the traditional post-mortem – and he most certainly did, spending a good 40 minutes examining every possibility we could see, though when I looked at the game later with the aid of a computer I realised there was one key line that neither of us saw which would have produced a win for me. I had played in a cavalier manner, grabbing material and allowing a huge attack on my uncastled king, which was more than adequate compensation for him. In the end, after a great deal of violence, we sued for peace, and in an odd way I was satisfied. He was part of the fabric of the place and should be bowed down to.

Round two was a grim struggle against a capable player graded 141. I was under pressure throughout, but defended well and hung on for a draw, ignoring the headache and sense of ennui produced by my restless night. But my opening as black was excruciatingly dull. It made it too easy for white to develop. I determined never to play so tediously again. At no point did I cause my opponent the slightest discomfort. My whole approach, especially with the black pieces, had to change. There had to be more dynamism, danger, drama. I realised, too, that my approach to this tournament had been feeble. I was here just to make up the numbers, with no real strategy for winning it. In a four-rounder you would almost certainly need to win all your games to win the tournament, so why had I agreed a draw in my first game? Yes, there had been a possibility I might succumb to his attack, but in objective terms I'd still had a slight edge. I was forgetting Stuart Conquest's first lesson – respect chess by exhausting all the possibilities offered by a game – and here in the town where he grew up and learned to play chess. Sacrilege.

The next day I was feeling a little better. England had been marmalised in Melbourne, so there was nothing to stop me getting seven hours' sleep. My sympathy for the plight of the teenage Short, facing a chilly, lonely ten-day struggle, increased by the hour. What a battle chess is, physical, mental, emotional, psychological. What resilience and self-belief you needed to succeed. I woke early and went for a walk on the beach. The storms had abated and it was a gorgeous, still morning, a pallid sun just rising above the calm of the English Channel. As I admired the view, a large wave rose up the shingle bank on which I was standing. I tried to flee but was too late: it caught me and soaked my trousers. I retired to a café to dry out. The owner looked at me pityingly as, wet through, I counted out the pennies for my sausage and eggs. 'Don't worry, that's enough,' he said, as I reached £5.70, but I insisted on digging out the extra 10p. Once again, back in the chess bubble, I was living up to the battered stereotype – shabby, dysfunctional, short of money, likely to be hit by a wave.

Despite the damp trousers, my game that morning started well. I even experienced a Conquest-like moment when I was lost in pure thought – lost yet, as he had said, aware of being lost, almost able to stand back and celebrate the lostness. In an age devoted to the cult of the instant, this felt rather beautiful: 50 blokes, a few youths and the odd woman absorbed for four hours in abstruse thoughts about knight manoeuvres.

By move 30 I was a piece up and, despite a few technical issues because my doubled pawns gave my opponent some counterplay, it was a clear win. Unfortunately, what had happened at Asda happened again. I allowed my opponent's time trouble to infect me, an ailment first diagnosed by Doc Saunders. Despite being a piece down and short of time, he created complications, I froze, couldn't think straight, missed an easy tactic that would have won the game, half-realised I'd missed it, got bothered by the growing number of people standing nearby to watch the game, and by the fact that the arbiter, scenting that the clock was going to be a factor, was marking down the moves as we approached the 40-move control when we would get an extra 20 minutes. I noticed I had 17 seconds to play my 40th move and then somehow forgot about it. As I was lifting my rook to play something, anything, the arbiter announced in a loud voice, 'The flag has fallen' (metaphorically, in fact, as it was a digital clock) and that was that. Once again I had lost a game I should have won. I was about to say 'deserved to win', but there was no 'deserved' about it. After going a piece up, my play had been atrocious, my thinking became hopelessly fuzzy, and what I got I deserved.

The realisation that the only person to blame was myself made me far more philosophical than after the Asda debacle. My opponent's sorrowful look and the fact that he seemed a nice chap also meant I spent only a few minutes, rather than an entire day, rueing the ludicrous end to a game in which, for the first three hours, I'd played well and thoughtfully. Another factor may have been that at the adjoining board I heard a man in his early seventies telling his opponent he had cancer. But here he was, playing his umpteenth tournament in this pinched, god-forsaken town, choosing to spend what was left of his life playing a game that had sustained him against opponents he had encountered so many times they had become friends. How could I feel angry in such circumstances if he wasn't?

Whatever the reason for my placidity, as I sat on the seafront in the wintry sunshine at lunchtime, I told myself it was only a game. The loss had wrecked my tournament, but I was alive and there would be other congresses where I would play well, where I would not lose from a position of strength because of some fear of throwing away my advantage, where I would win.

In the afternoon, with little but my usual mid-table mediocrity to play for, I played a speculative King's Indian Defence as black, an opening I barely knew. I played wildly, yet somehow conjured up a terrific tactic to win the game. I told myself that if I hadn't lost that insane game in the morning, I wouldn't have had the chance to play this marvellously satisfying game in the afternoon. God moves in mysterious ways and all that. Perhaps I was starting to go a bit mad.

C8: DON'T CALL ME A 'JOURNEYMAN' GM

At Hastings I had the chance to talk to grandmaster Keith Arkell, who for three decades had been a mainstay of the British chess circuit. He had won his game in the first round and was having a beer with some friends. Arkell interested me for two reasons. First, he was the archetypal English chess pro, in his fifties but fighting on, living mainly on his winnings, getting by on not very much, but still enthused by the game and working hard to get his rating back above the 2500 watershed – it had fallen in the past decade, but once you have the GM title you have it for life whatever happens to your rating. The other reason was that he had published a book called *Arkell's Odyssey* in which, as well as showing some of his best games, he explained what chess had meant to him, how it rescued him in his teens from feelings of social inadequacy, and how it sustained him financially when he knew that he would be incapable of dealing with the discipline of office life (he had managed one 'terrifying and claustrophobic' day working as a wages clerk in a battery factory soon after leaving school before fleeing). 'It helped me a lot with confidence after leaving school and getting respect from people,' he told me. 'I loved the chess environment. The people seemed similar to me.'

In the book Arkell is painfully honest about his early infatuations, the breakdown of his marriage to five-times British women's chess champion Susan Walker (better known now as Susan Lalić following her marriage to another GM, Bogdan Lalić), and the panic attacks which have periodically afflicted him. He describes one which occurred during a game at the British championship in 2000. 'When my attack came on,' he writes, 'I managed to get out of the building and into the open space of an adjacent playing field – far away from other people. I have always dealt with my attacks silently, resisting the urge to scream and shout. I wandered around aimlessly for 12 minutes or so until the problem – which is perhaps best described physiologically as a massive adrenaline rush – subsided. I then felt able to go back inside to continue the game.' A game he ended up winning.

Chess, with its tension and uncertainties, seems an unlikely resort for someone prone to anxiety, but in Arkell's case it has been his sanctuary, offering validation to a teenager with low self-esteem and now offering stability and security. At Hastings, where he has been competing for more than 30 years, he was friendly, relaxed and insisting that, despite his veteran status, he was still finding fresh challenges in chess. 'I look forward to playing tournaments,' he said. 'The travel, seeing who's going to be there, going out for a meal in the evening, and I enjoy the chess.' He reckoned he was playing tournament or club chess for about half the year, clocking up around 150 competitive games in that time.

After 35 years spent earning his living as a chess player he still believed he could improve: 'I tell myself that I haven't reached my potential yet. I feel I'm still underperforming. I play some positions well, but there are massive gaps. My theory is very bad and sometimes I get a bit lazy and don't prepare, so there are things I can do to get better.' Whether or not there is an element of self-deception in this – very few players are going to get better in their fifties – it is essential to believe it, or you really are just going through the motions as your competitive career winds down. Few chess players stand still: they are either heading up or down, and if you don't believe you are getting better the only way is down.

Arkell earned very little, but said he didn't crave possessions. He explained that if he had had children, he would have had to rethink and do a lot more coaching. Relying on over-the-board earnings, living in fairly basic accommodation, travelling constantly and staying in nondescript hotels is not a lifestyle that suits the married person, which is why so many chess pros are male, single, sometimes still living with their parents into their thirties, a bit dysfunctional, preferring to travel by public transport (many strong chess players have never learned to drive, either for economic or what appear to be cognitive reasons). 'You trade in being more wealthy for having a less restricted life,' he said. 'I like the freedom. I can't imagine having to get up at 8 o'clock and commute to the same office every day.'

It surprised me that Arkell didn't do more coaching, which is a much easier way of earning a living than slogging away for ten days against GMs from Georgia and Germany and IMs from Romania and Uzbekistan in the forlorn hope of winning a couple of thousand pounds. 'It doesn't interest me,' he said. 'I don't seek pupils and I wouldn't want more than the three or four that I have. I could earn a lot of money by teaching, but I enjoy playing too much.'

Arkell's peak rating was around 2550 in the 1990s. It had dipped since then, but he argued that was the inevitable result of playing in open tournaments against juniors whose ratings have yet to catch up with their talent. I asked him if his drift down the ratings worried him: 'I find it frustrating. I wouldn't care if nobody else cared, but I realise that people do care. If someone says, "Arkell's a weak GM," because I've got a weak GM's rating, that irritates me. It hurts my pride. For that reason I want to at least get it back to 2500 or 2520,' which he did, indeed, achieve soon after we met.

I asked him the question every veteran chess player must face up to – how long could he carry on in this ultra-competitive world full of youthful, fearless calculating machines? 'I don't know,' he said. 'My style is built to last. It's not hard work. I'm not frantically analysing long variations. I can name players who burned themselves out ten or 15 years ago because they put so much energy into their games. You can't play at that level of intensity for 40 years.' He bracketed himself with Mark Hebden, another veteran English grandmaster and almost an exact contemporary of Arkell, and said both had learned how to pace their careers. Some have called him and Hebden 'journeymen' GMs, but that is a term Arkell both rejects and resents. 'I'm one of the 12 or so best players in the country,' he said simply. The grandmaster title still means something, and he remembers whooping for joy when he made it in 1995. He retained his dignity when he won the game with which he qualified for the title, then ran into an adjoining field and emitted a scream of delight. 'There were a few animals looking at me,' he recalled.

Like Nigel Short, he didn't go to university, opting at the age of 17 for the life of the professional chess player despite, unlike Short, being no prodigy. He was a strong player who reckoned he could get a lot better, and that proved to be the case. But how could he take that gamble? 'It was all part of my fear of normal life,' he said. 'I think I was running away from normal stuff. I was afraid of doing something normal, so I said, "I'll just do this and see what happens." I had no idea I'd end up as a GM 18 years later.' Arkell, like many players, found himself on the board: 'The rules were clear, I could slowly become better, people made me feel good about what I was doing, and there was nothing to stop me.'

FILE D
Going Dutch

'There is no remorse like a remorse of chess. It is a curse upon man. There is no happiness in chess'

– H. G. Wells

D1: CHAMP OR CHIMP?

 As 2014 began I was convinced I was on the verge of a breakthrough. The Conquest view of chess had conquered me. I was a man reborn, with an urgent desire to be a better person and to play beautiful chess. Online I was now playing quite differently, embracing complexity, trying to make leaps of the imagination, not worrying overmuch if I dropped points, just trying to play interesting, vivid chess. I was also encouraged when, looking at my FIDE rating (which now stood at a just-about-respectable 1706), I was rated as 971st among active players in the UK. I had made the top 1,000. I was ignoring the fact that many higher-graded British players than me did not have FIDE ratings (I was only number 4,157 according to the English Chess Federation stats), but who cares about such pedantry? I could claim to be in the domestic top 1,000, and only international lawyers and prize bores could prove otherwise. In FIDE world terms I was ranked 72,382, which sounded less impressive until you remembered that was out of about seven billion (we will ignore the fact that most of them have no idea how to play chess). I wasn't Magnus Carlsen, but I wasn't completely useless either. I felt I knew one end of a bishop from the other, and the statistics proved it.

A few days after getting back from Hastings I analysed the games I had played there with Michael Healey, a young man John Saunders had told me was a good player – he was rated 2100 but his recent results were in the 2300 class – with an interesting view of chess. I had met him briefly at the London Classic, where he had won one weekender and come second in another, and he had struck me as highly intelligent – he had studied classics at Oxford, worked in a bookshop part-time (he was an avid reader and was immersed in Yevgeny Zamyatin's dystopian novel *We* when I introduced myself), and taught chess. Like so many young male chess players, he seemed a bit directionless. The game gave him a focus. As a junior he was one of the top five players in the country – his contemporaries included David Howell and Gawain Jones, the UK's two leading young grandmasters – but he went to an academic school, found it hard to combine exam work with chess study (an old conundrum), his progress stalled and he fell out of love with the game. Only at university did he fall back in love with the 64 squares, and this time it was the real thing.

Healey was quite complimentary about my games, but said I was impatient and too inclined to trade off pieces if I had a small advantage. 'If your opponent has a bad piece, don't trade it off, make him suffer,' he said. Don't stop playing ambitiously when you have your nose in front, he told me: 'That's when your opponent will play his best chess, because he has nothing to lose.' I realised that, when I had the edge in a game, I had to take a step back and take a strategic look at the position. How could I finish this off? What tactical tricks might my opponent have? What was my gameplan? The game was not won. It was not even half-won. Some chess games had to be won half a dozen times as your Rasputin-like opponent wriggled on the point of death. I had to learn to expect that and play accordingly. Put all thoughts that the gentlemanly thing would have been for him to resign out of my mind. Chess is not a game for gentlemen; it is a game for hired assassins.

Healey's most useful tip was one he said he had taken from Botvinnik: that you should use your own time to look at tactics and your opponent's time to think about strategy. Calculate when it was your own move, but try to do some big-picture stuff when it was your opponent's turn. He thought I was pretty good tactically, but far less astute strategically at finding moves that denied my opponent space and laying long-term plans that would eventually allow for tactical blows to be landed. I was not a subtle chess player. My horizon was three or four moves, and I had no long-term sense of how the game might unfold and what the pivotal points in the position were. By separating the two types of thinking, I thought I might be able to make progress. Encouragingly, Healey reckoned I could get to a grade of 160 or 170, though the comment was a little double-edged. 'I've known a lot of bad 160s and 170s,' he said. Still, I would settle for being a bad 170, the point at which I could almost claim to be a chess expert.

My early results after Hastings did not entirely justify Healey's optimism. I was on the defensive in a couple of games with reasonable players. I got draws in both, but was lucky to survive. I then played one of those pesky juniors – this was in a lowly league game for Surbiton – and, though I had all the pressure, couldn't put him away. When I played the game through on the computer, I realised I'd missed a winning knight tactic and felt irritated. But when I emailed the game to Doc Saunders, he was in emollient mood: 'The key lesson to take away from this game is not to let post-game computer analysis depress you.' He said he had also missed the key knight manoeuvre, and another tactical trick later which would have given me a material advantage. 'I may have spotted them under match conditions,' he said, 'but I couldn't guarantee that. So don't beat yourself up for missing them. Neither tactic was simple.'

'Don't beat yourself up. It's only a game. Get things in perspective.' These were all lessons hammered into me a few days after my disappointment against the junior by Professor Steve Peters, a psychiatrist who had become famous as adviser to the all-conquering British cycling team. He was also credited with making snooker player Ronnie O'Sullivan and footballer Craig Bellamy more focused and less impetuous, and I hoped he could show me the light too. I attended a talk he gave based on his book *The Chimp Paradox*, in which he outlined his theory that our minds are a potentially conflicting combination of chimp and human, and that to get the best out of both you have to program another bit of your brain to override the chimp's excesses. The chimp part of you will always be seeking sex, territory, success and power, but often it paid to be a little more circumspect. Much of what he said made sense. My inner chimp had screwed up a good deal of my life and it was time to get him under control.

After his presentation, we got the chance to talk and, with the help of a tatty magnetic chess set, I tried to explain some of my failings and showed him the knight move I'd missed, suggesting that my oversight arose in part because I thought the game was already won and it hardly mattered where I put the knight. 'That's your inner chimp,' he said. 'One part of you rationally knows you have to pause and make sure of your analysis, but another part of you wants to move impulsively because you have assumed the game is won. When you get to a point where you are about to impulsively jump, that impulse should be the warning to have a new autopilot which tells you to stop.' Pause, go through the analysis again, try to look further ahead. And never make assumptions. Machines play very good chess, and machines do not make assumptions. We were back to merciless objectivity.

I realised that what I tended to do was analyse scenario A and then, when moving on to analyse scenario B, do the latter analysis with the assumptions from scenario A still in my head. Peters said I had to 'park' the first part of the analysis and look at the second, third, fourth possibilities with no baggage from what had gone before. Again he blamed the chimp: 'You're saying to me that, "I, as a human, want to park something up and move on," but your chimp is saying, "No, you can't do that."' The chimp is keen to get on with it, secure the win, but his impulsiveness makes the win less likely and has to be resisted. The successful chess player needs to combine the will to win of the chimp and the rationality of the human – an echo, I realised later, of Alekhine's beast of prey and monk. I tried to blame my own laziness for not getting to the truth of the position, but Peters said that wasn't the reason. 'You're not lazy,' he insisted. 'I'm not allowing your chimp to say that. It's such a negative thing to say. I know you're not lazy because you've condemned that, which means it isn't you.'

I also told Peters how ambivalent I was about the result of my game with the junior: part of me was disappointed only to draw after dominating the game, but another part of me was pleased he'd got the draw he wanted after a not-very-pleasant two and half hours of squirming defence. Was that a weakness? He said I was conflicted between wanting to win and wanting to reward the kid in some way. 'Your chimp has got compassionate, but that's dumb. If you had prepared before you went in, you wouldn't be in this dilemma. If you give him a draw on compassionate, emotional grounds, you've taught him that, if he pouts enough and shows distress, people will be compassionate and give way. It's not a good lesson to learn in life. Two things: it's passive aggression, and it's not going to happen with everyone and then he's going to get very annoyed. You're giving him a lot of information which is misinformation.' In trying to be encouraging I was being exactly the opposite.

Peters is a Yorkshireman and prides himself on his plain speaking – as he now proved: 'What you're telling me is, "My chimp is very compassionate, it's very impulsive, it's a very healthy little chimp." It's just not very suitable for playing chess.' This was not what I wanted to hear. 'Compassion is not helpful in a chess game and neither is impulsiveness, so you have to pre-empt all this by building an autopilot that blocks both. You have to learn what your chimp is like and then deal with it accordingly.' You can't eliminate him, nor would you want to, because he's supplying a lot of dynamism, but you have to control him and harness his energies. A chimp does not generally become a champ.

Peters' other main argument was that the key to succeeding in sport – and indeed in life – was happiness. This was pure Carrera: you had to have conquered your anxieties before you could express yourself. The game had to mean everything and nothing. You had to play as if your life depended on it, but know that in the end the result was of no significance. 'When you're playing chess, you are personalising the game,' Peters told me. 'You are letting yourself and your ability be judged by the result. If I play chess, I say it's just my mind having a bit of fun, so there's no pressure because I don't know what my mind is going to do. I've dissociated myself from it. The result doesn't touch me. I'm different from my mind. It's not me.'

So should I beat myself up over missing the key knight move? Peters wrote down the word 'should' pointedly. 'That's your starting point,' he said. '"I should, I should." As soon as you bring that word in you have guilt. You are telling yourself, "I must achieve." I "must", I "should", all those words induce guilt. You've immediately put it into the realm of success and failure. But watch …' He crossed out 'should' and wrote down 'could'. 'It's gone. It's all gone. The pressure's gone. It must never be so important that it defines you. Get a life!' Peters has had a very successful career as a veteran athlete – he is in his sixties and still running – but he says that, while his chimp is very competitive, the human part of his brain knows that it means nothing. He has dissociated himself from the idea that it means anything, and that frees him to do well.

It struck me that Peters was giving a psychological underpinning to the Conquest view: the game was a beautiful, mentally taxing pursuit in which you were competing not against another player but against your own limitations, and in the context of every game ever played. You defined the game; the game did not define you. England's annihilation in the Ashes series in Australia in 2013–14 had been attributed in part to their loss of freedom. They were playing with fear rather than joy. To be a winner you had to realise that winning and losing meant nothing. It was a delightful paradox and one I felt could set me free.

D2: A BUS RIDE TO WIJK

Meeting Michael Healey and spending a couple of hours on the couch with Steve Peters were part of my build-up to playing in the great annual chess festival in the Dutch North Sea town of Wijk aan Zee in the second half of January, my most ambitious tournament foray so far, a nine-round event with one long-play game a day in which I would encounter players rated with a FIDE rating of around 1800. I was suffering with a bad hip (the legacy of an old riding accident), which worried me – chess demands such a focus that a physical ailment makes it almost impossible to play well. As part of my joy-through-chess programme, I was also experimenting with some new, more adventurous openings, including the King's Indian Defence against d4, and realised that could backfire. But there could be no going back: chess would henceforth be my servant, not my master; a way of expressing myself but not of defining myself. Peters had laughed when I said I was around the 4,000th strongest active chess player in the UK. His response was: Who cares? Free yourself from such status symbols. You are more than a number in a chess database.

I was going to chess-loving Holland for a fortnight and, as usual, packing was a problem. All I could fit in my case were 14 pairs of socks and underpants once I'd packed a dozen chess books: a biography of Max Euwe, the revered Dutch world champion (number five in the golden line) who beat the mighty Alexander Alekhine to win the title in 1935 but was beaten by him in the return bout in 1937; the writings of Donner; books by Hans Ree and Genna Sosonko, two grandmasters I hoped to meet in Amsterdam or Wijk; and opening books on the King's Indian and the Scandinavian (I had been carrying the latter around since Gibraltar the previous January). There was barely room for any other clothes. There was a danger I would smell by the end of the fortnight.

When the bus I was on got to Wijk on a grey afternoon I was a bit lost. A young man had heard me say the name of my hotel to the bus driver and pointed at an attractive dark-haired woman. 'Follow her,' he told me, 'she's staying in the same hotel.' Happily she was willing to be followed, and guided me to the place that was to be home for the next fortnight. As we talked on the short walk to the isolated, beachside hotel, it emerged she was married to Jan Timman, the veteran Dutch player who in 1993 played for the FIDE world championship against Anatoly Karpov. She told me she'd had to go back to Amsterdam, three-quarters of an hour away by train, because their cat was ill. Timman looked pretty ill, too, when I saw him come back to the hotel half an hour later, having been beaten by Yu Yangyi, one of the numerous Chinese *wunderkinder* rapidly climbing the world chess ladder. These wannabes are no respecters of ageing legends.

My first evening in Wijk, a cold, windy, sleepy seaside town which for a fortnight every January becomes chess heaven (it optimistically styles itself the 'chess capital of the world'), was spent playing blitz in a bar. More bald, middle-aged, ultra-competitive accountants, but at least this time they were Dutch and French. It was great to be in a place where chess was taken for granted as an activity central to one's life, with chess sets placed on the tables of the bars and the hotel in which I was staying. Maybe I could challenge Timman to a game. Or perhaps his wife would be a better bet – she had told me she had a FIDE rating of 1850. The hotel had also extended its breakfast hours until midday to cater for the late hours kept by pro chess players, who try to peak for games that tend to be played from about 2pm on. For these two weeks everything would revolve around chess. It was the 76th edition of the event and I was proud to be playing in it.

One of the shops in the square next to the church had a window display of large, ornamental chess sets. Chess had put Wijk on the map – the tournament began in neighbouring Beverwijk in 1938, migrating here in 1968 – and the town was repaying its debt. The morning after I arrived I stumbled on the showing of a documentary about the history of the tournament. I was too late for the film – it was in Dutch, so maybe this was not such a loss – but I spoke afterwards to Bert Kistjes, a former hotelier in the town and keen supporter of the tournament who had been instrumental in sustaining it. Kistjes, a typically friendly, baggy middle-aged Dutchman with a hangdog look and a walrus moustache, explained that chess was very popular in the local Hoogovens steel factory in the 1930s. The Dutch player Max Euwe had shocked the chess world in 1935 by beating Alekhine to win the world title – the modest Euwe said that even he had not expected to win – and his victory had triggered a boom in Holland in which the steelworkers had been caught up. They organised a tournament in 1938 for themselves but invited along Euwe, who had lost the title in his rematch with Alekhine in 1937, and other leading Dutch players. Thus was born the concept of an elite event being played alongside a tournament for the rest of us.

The festival combined two grandmaster groups – 12 'Masters' (2700-plus players) and 14 'Challengers' (international up-and-comers, a handful of Dutch titled players and Timman, the sixtysomething hero of Holland, now in gentle decline) – with a variety of amateur tournaments. I was playing in the biggest of the amateur events – more than 600 competitors divided into nine categories according to rating. I would be in level five, slap bang in the middle, Mr Average, as ever. The appealing aspect of the event was that everyone played in the same room, with the superstars – Lev Aronian, Hikaru Nakamura, Fabiano Caruana, Boris Gelfand, Sergey Karjakin – at one end and the throng of amateurs arrayed across the large hall.

A chess store had been set up in the centre of town for the duration of the tournament. I got talking to the man running it, 70-year-old Kaarlo Schepel, who insisted on giving me a coffee and telling me his life story – a surefire strategy to sell me even more chess books. He had been born in Beverwijk and always loved chess. He had been a merchant seaman, used to study the game at sea – he stressed that he was an autodidact – and became a strong player. He ended up in Hong Kong running an export business, writing a column on chess for the *South China Morning Post* for 14 years and even representing Hong Kong in the biennial Olympiad in 1990, before returning to Holland to set up his chess business. He told me a funny story about Hein Donner, who alongside Euwe is one of the two presiding spirits of Dutch chess: Euwe the upright, earnest, immensely hard-working former world champion; Donner the hard-drinking, chain-smoking, larger-than-life bad boy of Dutch chess who became the country's second grandmaster – Euwe had been the first – in 1959.

As a boy, Schepel told me, he had operated the demonstration boards at the Hoogovens tournament, as it was then called, and one day he was talking to Donner. Donner told him he had had too much to drink the previous night, and had needed to have a pee on the way back to his hotel. But as he was peeing a policeman suddenly appeared, and insisted on booking him for urinating in a public place. 'But I am three-times Dutch chess champion,'

Donner had protested. The policeman was unmoved. 'And my father is chairman of the supreme court.' The policeman was still unmoved. 'Well,' said Donner, 'if you are going to book me whatever I say, why don't you at least leave me to have a piss in peace.' Schepel's anecdote brought Donner to life for me more than all the tributes to him I had read.

I had arrived a few days before my own tournament started so I could watch some of the master tournament. I also hoped to get a feel for why the Dutch love chess and write so well about the game – the highly respected magazine *New in Chess*, co-edited by Timman, is published in Holland, and the same company produces many excellent (if expensive) chess books. One of the rounds of the Masters was being held at the Rijksmuseum in Amsterdam – a way of evangelising on behalf of the game – and I went along, though as the audience shuffled and bobbed up and down restlessly it convinced me that chess is always likely to struggle as a spectator sport. In what other activity can you leave for a couple of hours, have lunch, take in the history of western art then return to find the positions much as they were when you left? The high spot came in the loo at the museum – peeing was becoming the theme of my stay, indeed of my entire chess odyssey – where I had the pleasure of taking a piss not just next to Aronian (my old friend from the London Classic, and someone who seemed to need to empty his bladder as often as I did when I played) but former world title challenger Boris Gelfand too, who was using the urinal on the other side. It was a magical moment and I was convinced it would have an osmotic effect. I would piss group five.

While I was in Amsterdam, I visited the Max Euwe Centre – a chess museum and library set up to commemorate the former world champion and FIDE president, who died in 1981. It is on the first floor of an office block just off Max Euweplein, a square also dedicated to Holland's chess god. (Donner, too, has not been forgotten – he has a bridge nearby named after him.) There is a giant chessboard next to the entrance to the museum and I liked the fact that whatever the weather it was in constant use, mainly by down-at-heel elderly men who rarely seemed to move far from the square. I stood in the rain watching them, cigarettes drooping from their mouths and lost in concentration, as they shuffled the giant pieces around with their feet. A few bemused tourists looked on, alongside a man with a beard who had two small children in a carrier attached to a bicycle. The children, too, watched with fascination: what was this strange game with these odd knight manoeuvres? I had the same feeling watching the grandmasters at the Rijksmuseum.

Eddy Sibbing, manager at the Max Euwe Centre, gave me a guided tour and explained that it was Euwe who created the enduring popularity of chess in Holland. 'Until the emergence of Euwe, Paris and London were the great chess cities,' he said. 'And it was because of him, and later on his writings, that Holland became a real chess country.' In 1935, the year in which Euwe became world champion, the number of members of the Dutch Chess Federation quadrupled from 3,000 to 12,000. The game became firmly planted in the Dutch soil, and by the 1960s there were more than 600 chess clubs across the country. A decade later, in the wake of the Fischer–Spassky match, there were 34,000 active tournament players. That's now down to 20,000 and the number of clubs is diminishing too, but the rate of decline is slower than in other countries. As well as the Max Euwe Centre and the well-used giant chess set outside, Amsterdam boasts a couple of chess cafés. Happily this is still a city and a country in love with chess.

'Euwe was one of the strongest players in the world until the 1950s,' said Sibbing. He had been Dutch champion at the age of 20, became world champion at 34, and remained at the top for another 20 years. Euwe was an amateur when he won the world championship, a teacher of mathematics who built his chess career around his job. After winning the world championship he was given an extra two days' holiday by the city of Amsterdam. He was playing league chess at 80 when, according to his biographer Alexander Münninghoff, he was still rated above 2300. Critics often say Euwe was the weakest of the 16 world champions, and he held the title for only two years, but it was still a fantastic career – as player, writer and, in the 1970s, as a well-meaning, incorruptible president of FIDE. At the end of his biography, in an emotional summing up, Münninghoff argues that, far from being one of the less celebrated world champions, Euwe, for his multiple achievements in these different spheres, should be hailed as one of the ten greatest figures in chess history. Spending a fortnight in a country that still gives chess a place in public life, who was I to disagree? Chess max.

D3: THE ELEGIST

 While I was in Amsterdam, I met Genna Sosonko, a grandmaster and one of the most evocative writers on chess. Sosonko was born in 1943 in Siberia (where his parents had moved because of the German invasion) and grew up in Leningrad, but he emigrated in 1972 at the age of 29, eventually settling in Holland. In a beautifully written series of books he has memorialised that era from the 1940s to the 1980s when, with the interruption of only the inimitable Bobby Fischer, the Soviet Union dominated world chess. Having spent almost 30 years inside the system before breaking free from it, he had a unique perspective, allied to sharp intelligence and the perceptiveness of the natural writer. An afternoon in his company was guaranteed to be illuminating.

Sosonko said he learned to play chess at the age of eight or nine. 'We were so poor,' he told me, 'that my mother used a cardboard chessboard and bits of paper with the names of the pieces written [on]. Even now I remember those pieces of paper.' His family – mother, sister and grandmother; his parents had divorced early – lived in a single room in an apartment block shared with other families. In his books he has on several occasions pointed to the large number of chess champions who did not have fathers at home – Bobby Fischer and Garry Kasparov immediately spring to mind – and suggested that their chess trainers became surrogate fathers, adding to the intensity of the training programme. A characteristically brilliant observation.

Sosonko was not enthusiastic about the game at first and was keener on football, but then he had a six-week lay-off when he broke his arm, and he started to play chess instead. He progressed quickly, joined a Young Pioneers club in Leningrad and, at the age of 15, became the city's junior champion. From then on he was earmarked for a chess career. His trainer was the celebrated Vladimir Zak, who also trained Boris Spassky and Viktor Korchnoi. Trainers such as Zak were the foundation of the Soviet system. At an early stage masters tended to become either players or trainers, and that fairly rigid separation was crucial in cementing Soviet chess strength. Sosonko himself was recognised primarily as a trainer and became a fully fledged tournament player only after he left the Soviet Union. Chess was seen as more a science (or perhaps a secular religion) than a game and treated with great seriousness. Mikhail Botvinnik, who succeeded Alekhine as world champion in 1948, laid down the basis for the systematic study of chess theory which underpinned the Soviet system, and as a good Soviet citizen also emphasised that chess should be played for the greater glory of the motherland. In the Soviet era chess was always a political weapon, part of the cold war armoury, which was why Bobby Fischer's victory in 1972 was so sensational and, in the US and elsewhere in the west, greeted with extraordinary fervour.

Playing chess in the Soviet Union was a serious business, and Botvinnik's low opinion of blitz was shared by Zak. 'It was permitted to play blitz only once a week, on Sundays,' recalls Sosonko in *Russian Silhouettes*. 'Occasionally, permission was received also on a weekday, with the obligatory promise not to make any noise, a promise which, of course, was constantly broken. The guilty person would be chided, and in the event of a recurrence the clocks would altogether be taken away.' Sosonko told me the story of a Dutch journalist asking Botvinnik why he didn't play some blitz for fun after his retirement from serious competition. 'Young man,' he replied, with Sosonko acting as translator, 'I never played chess for pleasure.' That was the credo of the country whose chess philosophy he both embodied and propagated.

Sosonko studied economic geography at university but never had any job except chess. He told me he did look for work outside chess, but the fact that he was a Jew counted against it. Eventually he gave up and concentrated on chess. He explained why he was seen as a trainer rather than a competition player. 'When I was in my mid-twenties, I had a reputation as a chess theorist,' he said, 'and Mikhail Tal asked me to come to Riga to help him.' It was the start of a close relationship, and Sosonko's memoirs of Tal are perhaps his best pieces of writing. Tal, in Sosonko's portrait of him, is the archetype of the unworldly chess player: 'He was totally indifferent to any form of technology, and it goes without saying that he never entertained any thoughts of learning to drive. Only in the last period of his life did he acquire an electric razor, and the marks of its actions could be seen here and there on his face ... He did not like ties, and wore one only when circumstances demanded it. Needless to say, he never learned how to fasten one. And he never wore a watch. "What's that?! You've got something ticking on your arm!" For him, time in the accepted sense did not exist.'

Sosonko, who also helped Viktor Korchnoi, was well established as a trainer, but in his late twenties he applied to leave the Soviet Union: 'People now don't understand how difficult the decision to leave was. It was a very risky business, and you might have been sent to Siberia.' His request to emigrate was accepted, but it was three or four months before final approval came through, and in that time some former friends and colleagues cold-shouldered him. But he was determined to go: 'I understood that my life was not full. I desperately wanted to be free.' That freedom meant that he had to leave his mother, and after he left in 1972 he never saw her again. But she put no pressure on him to stay. Indeed, it was a regulation that parents had to give their permission for their child to leave. His mother did that willingly: 'She understood that for me this was an opportunity. She also understood that she would never see me again.'

He went first to Israel, where he stayed a couple of months, and then moved on to Holland, where he made his home. When he left Israel he had a rail ticket – Amsterdam, Frankfurt, Paris. He didn't get further than Amsterdam. 'I still have the ticket,' he said. 'You never know.' He started playing in weekend tournaments and, whereas in the Soviet Union he had been cosseted by a salary as a trainer, now he faced the exigent life of the chess professional: 'I had to win' – to live and to eat. He not only won virtually all of these weekenders, but won the Dutch championship in 1973, and Wijk itself in 1977 and 1981. It was remarkably rapid progress for a player whose rating was only around 2350 when he arrived in Holland. He became an international master in 1974 and a grandmaster in 1976, but despite his achievements the Soviet Union declared him an un-person, and even when he won Wijk the chess press there refused to print his name.

What is interesting about his books is that, despite the hardship and the eventual bitter leave-taking, they are suffused with nostalgia for Soviet chess. He portrays a very masculine, closed world, filled with remarkable characters: men, often fitters and welders turned trainers and players, who were obsessed by cards and dominoes and games generally, wrapped up in a world of unreality which protected them from the grim reality of life in the Soviet Union and the complexity of their marital relations. In his memoir of Semyon Furman, a grandmaster best remembered as the trainer of Anatoly Karpov, he tells a funny, rather brutal story of Furman's wife and young son going out on a river in an inflatable dinghy as Furman himself sat playing cards: 'The wind got up and began carrying it away from the bank. When the situation became alarming, everyone grew anxious – "They are a long way off. We must do something." "Until this rubber is completed," said Furman, "no one is going anywhere."' In the topsy-turvy world of the Soviet Union, games mattered more than life itself.

Sometimes in his books Sosonko betrays the fact that some of what made chess wonderful has been lost. In an essay on Alexander Koblenz, Tal's original trainer, he concludes that 'the aura and the halo of the game itself have largely gone'. He believes computers have taken away some of its mystery; that they might even one day 'solve' chess – an apocalyptic view not shared by most mathematicians. Computers can solve a position with up to seven pieces on the board – they can determine the result with perfect play – but any more than that and the variables are too numerous. The old adage that there are more possible moves in a chess game than there are atoms in the universe still defeats them. Sosonko is right that something has been lost in the computer age, but he is surely too pessimistic. Chess in its present form is likely to last for at least another couple of generations.

He is a fund of marvellous stories and told me a very funny one about Korchnoi once playing in a simultaneous display in Cuba, which included Che Guevara as one of his opponents. 'Please make a draw against him,' the Russian team manager asked Korchnoi. 'He loves chess and will be very pleased.' 'Oh yes, very well,' the irascible Korchnoi replied. Later that day Korchnoi returned to the hotel after the simul. 'How did it go?' he was asked. 'I beat all of them!' said an exultant Korchnoi. 'But what about Che Guevara?' 'I beat Che Guevara as well,' said

Korchnoi. 'He doesn't understand anything in the Catalan [opening]!' A delightful tale that perfectly captures Korchnoi's combativeness.

Sosonko gave up playing once he believed his powers to be diminishing. Databases show he played very few games after 1997, when he was in his mid-fifties. Some players can carry on at a reduced level, needing chess in the way that they need oxygen. But Sosonko was not like that: it went against the grain to play at a level lower than he had once been capable of. Once he had stopped playing, Sosonko moved seamlessly to writing about the game, and it is his second career that will make the greater impression on chess history. As a player he was strong but not overwhelming; as a memorialist of the Soviet era he is unique. His style is elegiac, and he writes movingly about the travails of Soviet players who had to come to terms with the collapse of the Soviet Union. Players who once had a comfortable salary within the Soviet system now had to play big, highly competitive open tournaments and would eat only if they won a decent prize. The brave new world was a difficult, demanding one, and they had to face it in the latter part of their careers, when their powers were declining. It was a savage fate. Chess animated the lives of these great Soviet players, but in the end it abandoned them. 'Society does not regard chess as a profession,' writes Sosonko in *The Reliable Past*, 'and all the consequences for choosing it as such are borne by the player himself.'

D4: WELCOME TO CLASS 5B

 As well as peeing with grandmasters, I was also staying in the same hotel as them and would see them each morning at breakfast – the dreamy Timman, the sharp-as-a-tack Caruana, Gelfand in his black leisurewear. Surely this would rub off. You had to register at 11am on the day the tournament in which I was playing started, and I nervously joined the lengthy queue, which comprised the usual army of grizzled veterans and a smattering of youngsters. There was a sanatorium close to the playing hall, and it struck me that in a way both were attending to the sick. Who were all these strange men turning up for nine days of intense, convoluted chess under lowering skies in windswept Wijk? An additional problem was that I had spent too much money in Amsterdam and, more legitimately, in the chess store in Wijk, so was now trying to limit myself to ten euros a day, doing the GM trick of eating a triple breakfast and carrying off fruit to eat later, and buying bread, cheese and biscuits at the local supermarket.

An oddity of Wijk is that the 600 or so competitors in the amateur are not just split into nine categories according to rating, but those big groups are then further split into units of ten, so that you know straightaway who your opponents over the next nine days will be. I liked to think this was a throwback to the democratic steelworker days, when you knew the people you were playing with and played the game in the right spirit. There was not any money at stake either, unlike in weekenders in the UK, so there was no incentive for playing off a false rating, and perhaps less likelihood of the sort of ill feeling I had witnessed at too many events at home. These groups of ten would, I hoped, play as friends. Certainly the player sitting to my right was doing that: as well as shaking me by the hand and welcoming me to Holland (my playing card announced me as being from 'Engeland'), when he was mated he said, 'Nicely done,' to his opponent. The sporting English amateur Sir George Thomas would surely have approved. This was proper social chess.

I had never played at such long time controls: two hours each for the first 40 moves; then another hour plus a five-second increment per move for the rest of the game. Potentially these could be six-hour games. Nevertheless in my first game I and my opponent still managed to get into time trouble, each having to play moves 25 to 40 in about 12 minutes and making the 40-move control with seconds to spare. Not good for the middle-aged heart. My rival, who had a rating of 1830, was a sweet-natured man from Haarlem who bought me a cup of coffee. His fingers twitched nervously when he was about to make a move, which encouraged me, and I thought I detected a lack of assurance about the way he filled in the moves on his scoresheet. Despite these tics, after 15 moves I was in trouble, a new line I had recently learned in the Scandinavian proving a liability as he launched a big kingside assault. I was behind on development, my king was still in the centre, and both my queen and my white-squared bishop were running out of squares. He just needed to be patient and I would have wilted, but mercifully he thought he saw an instant tactic, overreached himself and lost a piece. It was far from over – as it panned out, I was only the exchange (rook for bishop) up – but for once I stayed cool, played sensibly and eventually forced a win. In a nice gesture he laid down his king and shook my hand. I had somehow made a winning start in Wijk and celebrated with a plate of chicken satay and chips in the café at the sports centre that was hosting the tournament. It cost a budget-busting 11.50 euros, plus two euros for a beer, but frankly I didn't care. I had won my first game, was not going to finish on nought, and could rarely remember when I had felt so relieved.

I called Doc Saunders to tell him the good news, and he counselled me to stay calm. 'Don't get too elated when you win; don't get too depressed when you lose,' he reminded me. I agreed to treat the two impostors of triumph and disaster just the same … tomorrow. I allowed myself the tiniest bit of elation that evening and skipped back to the hotel to study the grandmaster games from the afternoon. Aronian was leading the Masters group, but Gelfand was having a nightmare. A tale of two urinals. How do these pros do it? Week in, week out, they are in anonymous hotels, living and breathing chess with their coaches, their moves being pored over online by thousands of lesser players armed with computers. Gelfand had lost in 29 moves to 20-year-old Filipino-born grandmaster Wesley So that afternoon; the young Hungarian Richard Rapport had been annihilated by the Cuban Leinier Domínguez. They really must have taken Kipling's advice to heart to be able to cope with such setbacks. Especially Gelfand, who had lost to a player – admittedly a fast-rising star – 25 years his junior in facile fashion. As Sosonko says in his memoir of Botvinnik, 'In chess there applies the same cruel custom that existed for the inhabitants of Tierra del Fuego: as the young grow up they kill and eat the old.' Poor old Gelfand always looked hangdog, trudging around the hotel with his head bobbing as if it were too heavy for his body. I was determined to mask my elation if I saw him at breakfast the following morning.

Luckily I didn't run into Gelfand at breakfast, but I did meet the man I would be playing that afternoon, a computer programmer and part-time chess arbiter who had travelled from Milan to take part in the tournament. He was fascinating on how computers evaluate chess positions – a combination of strategic thinking and tactical calculation – and encouraging about the future of chess. Unlike Sosonko he didn't think computers would 'solve' chess any time soon, in the sense of being able to calculate a perfect winning line with many pieces still on the board. He also emphasised their limitations, and said there were still positions they failed to understand. Grandmasters may not be seen quite as reverentially as they once were, now that a free software package you can download from the internet can beat them, but computers aren't perfect and they haven't cracked the entire chess code yet, thank God.

My game against the programmer was a bit of a damp squib. For some reason I felt lacklustre, got slightly outplayed in the opening, got into a locked position where neither of us was making progress, and offered an early draw, which after ten minutes' contemplation he accepted. Stuart Conquest would have been disgusted – I could almost hear him saying, 'You go all the way to Holland and settle for a tedious 20-move draw ...' – but the way I rationalised it was that the Italian seemed a competent player, and at least by playing for only a couple of hours I was husbanding my resources for future battles. It also gave me a chance to talk to Colin Gilbert, Welsh champion in 1967 and now, aged 82, playing at the next table to me. He was a delightful, affable man who told me this was his tenth Wijk. 'I started up there,' he said, pointing to the tables where the top amateurs were playing, 'and now I'm down here.' His rating had fallen from 2200 in his prime to a more modest 1800, but he was clearly still besotted with the game and had a smooth win on the day we met. I admired these players whose love for chess had never faltered and who played in such an admirable spirit, treating it as an intellectual *jeu d'esprit* rather than a fight to the death. It *was* a fight to the death and I witnessed some terrifying time scrambles among the amateurs, but each of the losers took defeat with a shrug, a smile and a handshake. The atmosphere at Wijk, fuelled by bowls of the famous local pea soup, was warm, winning and rather wonderful.

D5: CHESS AS HUMAN COMEDY

 While I was staying in Holland, I got the chance to meet the other great Dutch writer on chess, Hans Ree, a grandmaster of the same vintage as Sosonko but one who takes a very different view of the game. Whereas Sosonko, when he felt himself to be in decline, gave up playing to concentrate on writing, Ree carried on – even now he plays some league chess and online blitz. What for Sosonko, in that Soviet way, was a profession has for Ree been a love affair. In many ways the contrast encapsulates the way chess has been seen in the east and the west: science v art, study v game, way of life v way of dodging life. In the Soviet Union chess was seen as a fitting subject for the academy; in the west it has been the preserve of the coffee house.

I asked Ree if his famous adage that chess was a game 'beautiful enough to waste your life for' was really how he saw it. 'It was a sort of joke of course,' he laughed, 'something I said on the spur of the moment to a writer who was doing some interviews for a book. I don't really think it's a wasted life. I am happy to have spent my life playing the game and writing about it.' In his book *My Chess* he makes it plain that, like many professional players, he initially saw the game as an escape from the workaday world: 'I remember exactly when I realised that I would be a professional chess player – while taking a shower in a hotel room in Lugano during the 1968 Olympiad. I was already earning money by playing chess, but up to then I had always thought that I would find a job as a mathematician. But suddenly I had an epiphany. It wasn't really necessary to get a job, was it? I liked mathematics, but I disliked getting up early to go to work.' There was, though, a sting in this tale of indolence: 'Later, Donner told me that you become a chess player in order not to have to work until, at some point, you realise that you are working harder than other people.'

Ree is witty, sardonic, slow moving, very Dutch. As with Donner, it is impossible to imagine him existing outside Amsterdam, this quiet, literary, free-thinking city which allows you to live any life you wish. Holland loves chess and it encourages good writing about chess; Ree embodies both. Donner showed that you could pretend to be writing about the game while in reality writing about life itself, and Ree – and Sosonko too – have carried on that tradition. They write about chess not as a technical exercise but as a way of life. They search for its true mainspring and meaning, wonder why it has endured. Ree is fascinated by the cultural impact of chess and has written several essays on Marcel Duchamp's love of the game. He finds the game beautiful, fulfilling, endlessly engaging. 'I know that I will never abandon chess and that chess will never abandon me,' he writes, movingly, in an essay called 'A Sunny Existence'.

Ree became a grandmaster in 1980 when he was in his mid-thirties. That is extremely late by today's standards, but there were far fewer GMs then. There has been not just ratings inflation but GM inflation, too, though Ree said standards have risen and the pool of professional players has become much bigger. At his peak he reached number 52 in the world and won the Dutch title four times – a worthy career but not one that brought him great riches. He started writing a chess column early and that was an essential part of his income. He is grateful for playing when he did. 'I have the feeling that my chess career played itself out in a golden age that is now gone,' he writes in *My Chess*. He recalls the large amount of space devoted to chess in the newspapers in the

1970s and 80s, and the amount of technical analysis he and other commentators were allowed to include. 'This would be unthinkable now,' he writes. One upside of that golden age was that, because there were fewer GMs, Ree got to play many of the greats, including eight world champions, something else that wouldn't happen now, when the elite – the world's top 20 or so players – tend to meet each other in closed events.

When I met Ree, I was keen to play up the contrast with Sosonko – the westerner v the Soviet-trained player, the GM who has carried on while his rating declined v the GM who could not accept increasing fallibility. I asked him if that contrast was legitimate. 'Genna always suffered when he played,' said Ree, cryptically. 'Everybody suffers when things go badly, but I carried on playing long after I realised I had declined. At first it was difficult to accept, but OK after a while – that is how it is. I can remember losing a tournament game in Amsterdam, and afterwards I had the feeling that I had really lost my touch, that I couldn't work out things any more. That was frightening, but I went on playing. It had gone and never came back.' The ability to work through long variations almost instinctively had gone, but the love of, perhaps even dependence on, the game remained and carried him along.

I asked Ree if chess was a game or a way of life, as it was in the Soviet Union. 'Treating it as a game and as a way of life are not contradictory,' he said. 'Think of Tal. Chess was his way of life completely, but he also had this playfulness. They are not such great contrasts. They are aspects which are both necessary. Botvinnik and Tal are extreme examples of the two types of player, but they are extremes and most people are somewhere in between.' One needed to study and take it seriously, yet at the end realise it meant nothing. Like life itself, which is perhaps why it appealed to Duchamp, who insisted 'there is no solution because there is no problem'. Life was not a puzzle to be solved or a dilemma to be fretted over. It just was, and should be celebrated as such. Similarly a game of chess meant everything while it was being played and nothing once it was concluded. We should love it, but, as Steve Peters had told me back in London, not allow success or failure at the board to define us. It was a game, brilliantly transient, deeply vacuous. Play as if your life depended on it, but, if you die, do so gracefully, graciously.

D6: IN THE SOUP

Round three at Wijk was a wake-up call. I was black and responded to pawn to d4 with the King's Indian Defence – where you allow white to occupy the centre and then hit back hard. Unfortunately my version of the KID proved to be useless, and I was soon in deep trouble and facing a huge attack on my queenside. There was no way I should have been able to survive, but I hung on gamely and found a tactic that got me back to equality just as we reached the 40-move control. I might even have had a slight advantage when my opponent offered me a draw, but I was so pleased to have escaped defeat I accepted. Again I could hear Conquest saying, 'No, no, no,' but I didn't want to stretch the patience of the chess gods too much. They had been kind to me in round one and kind to me again today, and I was content. I decided to give the KID a rest until I understood the theory a little better.

My poor diet was getting to me – scrambled egg in the hotel for breakfast, pea soup at the playing hall for lunch, supermarket fruit buns with ham and cheese for dinner – and I wondered about raising my ten-euros-a-day limit. So far, though, I hadn't found a cashpoint, so decided to stick with it. I felt that as a wannabe chess pro I should suffer for my calling. It meant that I spent even more time sleeping, so that the four or five hours' chess in the middle of the day and an hour of post-match analysis in the bar (I allowed myself one small beer a day) were pretty well my only daily activity, other than a brief walk on the beach in the morning and reading the chess books I had brought with me. Nevertheless I found it strangely satisfying: everything was geared to that one daily game and, since there was nothing else in my head and I had had plenty of sleep, I felt hardly any stress as I played. Even as I faced almost certain defeat with my useless KID, I was still trying to get counterplay and attempt some trickery; my will never weakened. Only as we neared the time control did I feel I was buckling, and then from nowhere I saw a sequence that got me back in the game. It was a lovely sensation: to peer into the abyss, to prepare to fall and, at the last moment, manage to pull back and survive.

In round four I was determined to make my move in the tournament. I was white; my opponent had managed only a draw and two defeats in his first three games; Carlsen-like, I would go all out for a win to stay in touch with the leaders. I even made sure I wore the red fleece – the lucky red fleece, as I now saw it – that I had worn for my opening-day win. I had an edge in the opening, made my opponent double his pawns (two pawns on the same file are usually a weakness as they are unable to defend each other), had a time advantage, and felt sure I could polish him off. But damn it, he hung on. We ended with opposite-coloured bishops and six pawns each, and the position proved easy for him to hold. So much for the lucky red fleece.

I felt, in retrospect, that my play had been rather insipid: just plain, boring, sound, un-tricksy chess which, even though he fretted his brow a lot and used oodles of time, didn't really challenge him. I had also failed to grasp the elementary point that opposite-coloured bishops made it well-nigh impossible for me to win unless he made some crass mistake. The doubled pawns counted for nothing. So my entire strategy had been misconceived. It wasn't a disaster – I still had 2.5 points out of a possible four – but I had played with a sort of tedious competence which depressed me. I also realised that it mattered to me that I was unbeaten in the tournament, and that such an attitude could be self-defeating, making the fear of defeat more powerful than the craving for victory. It was the occupational disease of old chess players who would no longer put themselves on the line. Negativity had to be resisted; the carapace of competence dispensed with. But maybe not yet; I really did want to go home from Wijk unbeaten.

Some hope. I lost in the next round, despite building up a massive position. I was convinced I was winning the game throughout and certainly had all the pressure but, as usual, I wasn't clinical enough, went wrong in time trouble and left my opponent with a winning endgame. He was an affable pharmacist – the Dutch players were far more civilised than their counterparts in the UK – but I did wish he would stop apologising for winning when he analysed the game over a beer. 'Don't worry about it,' I told him. 'It's kill or be killed.' This seemed to shock him – he was the player who, in round one, said 'nicely done' when his opponent produced a combination to mate him. Like many of his fellow countrymen, he seemed far too sweet-natured for chess.

The loss was a blow, especially when I virtually had the game won on at least two occasions. My undoing was imprecision, undue haste in key positions, a failure to analyse properly – the familiar enemies of promise. Now, instead of being joint leader of the group, as I would have been if I had won, I was languishing in mid-table. I tried to rationalise it. Once again I'd won a game I should have lost, then lost a game I should have won – a feature of so many of my tournaments. Swings and roundabouts. I was on 2.5/5 – the time-honoured 50 per cent. Respectability. It could have been worse. But it didn't work. I should have capitalised on my early luck in the tournament by winning this game. My new Italian computer-programmer friend also lost his game after a huge six-hour struggle. He said losing didn't bother him, which is why he reckoned he would never be a really good player. It did bother me, but after this loss I too doubted whether I would ever make it to expert level. In despair I called my wife. 'Maybe you should finish the book right here,' she said. 'Perhaps this is as good as you're going to get.' 'But I'm only halfway through,' I pleaded. 'Well, couldn't it be a shorter book?' she suggested, practical as ever.

In the evening I read more of Genna Sosonko's book, *Russian Silhouettes*. Having lived by playing the game, he understood perfectly the pressures it placed on you (one of the Dutchmen in my group had described a man at his club who had a heart attack at the board; my question, naturally, was whether his opponent had claimed a win). I found Sosonko's description of a typical game oddly reassuring. 'Time and again,' he writes, 'a game proceeds according to the following approximate pattern: slightly worse, clearly worse, a mistake by the opponent, joy, winning chances, time trouble, missed opportunities, draw. Such changes in mood and emotion occur both in professional and in amateur play, with the only difference that in the latter case these sharp peaks of ascents and descents can be seen several times.' It was reassuring to know that even grandmasters suffered these highs and lows. It is not, he concludes, a game that offers much hope of psychological stability. 'Giving the joy of creativity, and sometimes prizes and money,' Sosonko concludes, 'chess at the very highest level demands a trifle in return – the soul.'

D7: TEA WITH TIMMAN

Jan Timman's tournament had perked up by the time I got around to asking whether I could meet him to talk about his remarkable 40-year career. He was happy to meet, but preferred to do it on the Challengers' rest day. Luckily it was a rest day in my tournament too, so we could have a reasonably relaxed teatime chat. Only reasonably relaxed because Timman doesn't do super-relaxed, unlike Lev Aronian, who was leading the Masters tournament and used to appear at breakfast in his tracksuit after his morning run, laughing and looking as if he didn't have a care in the world. The heavily built, laconic, slightly nervous Timman seemed as if the world weighed on his shoulders. He looked like an angel, or perhaps a pop star, when he first came to prominence in his twenties – slim, long-haired, thick-lipped – but the sedentary chess lifestyle takes its toll. Unshaven when we met, even though it was mid-afternoon, he said that playing a tournament of this length was exhausting, but he was satisfied with his form – with 7/10 he was third and more than holding his own against players 30 years his junior.

He told me he had decided to become a professional chess player after he'd finished high school and chose not to go to university. His father was a professor of mathematics and was disturbed that his son was forgoing a conventional career for the uncertain world of professional chess. 'I don't know if I would do it now,' Timman admitted. 'You really have to work hard. But I didn't like the prospect of getting up early every morning. In general I like to be free, and that is what I still like.' Freedom – every chess player's mantra.

I asked him how he could justify devoting his life, energy and considerable intellect to chess. 'I don't know that I wanted to justify myself at that particular time,' he said. 'It was a different time, of course. I didn't really look for a career. People just liked to do what they wanted to.' He has never regretted his decision: 'What I regretted was not being more serious about the game at an earlier stage – to be more competitive, like Karpov. But then I didn't want to do that. I just wanted to have a good time. Later, when I was around 26, I became more serious about chess.' By then he was number four in the world, was winning big tournaments and realised he might have a shot at the world title. He said that by that time he was more settled as both a person and a player, and was better able to cope with the constant travelling.

Timman's rating was standing up remarkably well as he entered his sixties, and he told me he was playing better than he had a few years before. He said he took inspiration from the example of the great Russian player Viktor Korchnoi, who had possessed more energy, inspiration and determination at 70 than he'd had a decade before: 'I believe it is possible [to perform well] as you get older, but of course you have to focus. Sometimes older players get tired, but you can fight against that tendency.' Timman said it had been crucial to his continuing strength as a player that he had made computers central to his preparation – something players of his generation, who had grown up without them, tended to fight shy of: 'Many of the older players don't like them. Once I played in a match of old grandmasters against young players, and I noticed that many of the old legends, like Boris Spassky, didn't have computers. You see this reluctance. Only Korchnoi was modern. The other players from my generation didn't like this idea that you could just push some buttons and see what happened to your game. It's a strange idea, but I'm used to it now. Computers sharpen your tactical feel, and sometimes they entirely change your ideas about a position. You may feel a position is good for white or black, but the computer disagrees, and then it's interesting to see why. But the computer doesn't always give answers. Sometimes it does, but not always, and it's interesting to look for those answers. That can change your way of thinking.' He likes to work with a computer, but he points out that they are by no means infallible: 'There are some positions, such as rook endings, that I understand better than computers. The computer can be wrong.'

I asked Timman how he bounced back from the sort of defeat I witnessed on the day I arrived: 'You need a very tough fighting spirit. You have to learn to focus completely and forget about what has happened in previous games.' Timman has always had that fighter's reputation, which in part accounts for his longevity. In this tournament he had accidentally allowed a draw by repetition (if exactly the same position occurs three times in a game, a player can claim a draw) against a young Dutch player, and he admitted that had been a 'big blow' because he'd had a completely winning position. But he said he had recovered, which proved to him that his chess was in better shape than it had been a few years previously: 'Two years ago I didn't play well in Wijk aan Zee. Last year was already better, but I was tired towards the end. But this year I am satisfied, I have a better attitude to working on chess now, and my ideas and concentration are better.'

He has been playing top-level chess for more than 40 years, and I wondered if there was ever a time when the game bored him. 'Yes, sure,' he said, 'although I cannot imagine that now. In around 2000 I somehow didn't want to play, so I didn't do well.' He said some older players got bored; others could no longer cope with the pressure. But Timman came through his crisis, and rediscovered his passion for the game. 'There was a period when it no longer appealed to me, but then somehow that moment was over. It took a while. For a long time I was not so fond of playing, but it came back. I started to miss it.' He loves composing endgame studies – theoretical positions in which he can search for the truth beloved of GMs: 'It is the most fantastic work to do, because it is the very pure side of chess rather the competitive side.' An echo of Conquest here – that all-important curiosity and fascination with the boundless possibilities of a position. This, I realised, was the thing I would almost certainly never have, as well of course as the mathematical and spatial capacity to explore that vast universe. My chess was earthbound, whereas GMs of a certain stamp are forever shooting for the stars. Timman was a determined fighter, but he was also a deep thinker – chess, he pointed out, could be played 'with an opponent and without an opponent'.

He said he was optimistic about the future of the game and pleased that computers were no longer seen as competitors for humans. The era of man v machine matches in the 1990s and at the start of the new century had, he believed, been a distraction, and now that computers were demonstrably superior even to the very best GMs (tactically if not necessarily in terms of strategic vision) players could get back to the more interesting business of competing against each other. Timman did not share Sosonko's fears that computers would 'solve' chess. 'He will not live to see that, and neither will I. It will take 50 years.' And then? 'I'm not sure,' he said. 'I would probably be interested in that question if I was 20.'

D8: MELTDOWN

After my disappointment in round five, when I contrived to lose from a position of great strength, I bounced back with a wonderful win in round six, playing black against the only player who to that point was unbeaten. I saw a very nice tactic, it all worked beautifully and my opponent was mated on move 35 – a delightful mate with a knight (see Game 4 on p383). I reckoned it was the best game I had ever played, but oddly I didn't feel the need immediately to write about it, as I had with my round-five defeat. 'Happiness writes white,' as the French novelist Henry de Montherlant pointed out. It just is; it does not need to announce itself. 'You learn from your losses,' Garry Kasparov once told me, and now I knew exactly what he meant. When you lose, you can't get the game out of your head. You have put your hand in the fire and vow not to do it again. When you win, you simply tell yourself how brilliantly you played and don't give it another thought.

After my victory in round six I really thought I was in with a chance of winning my section of the tournament. I mapped it all out: use an aggressive e4 opening to beat the relatively weak player I was due to meet in round seven; study the English opening, which I noticed my round-eight opponent favoured, and outmanoeuvre him; and then play a steady d4 game against the tournament leader I was facing in the final round. None of it worked. I had the edge in round seven, but couldn't force the win and had to be satisfied with a draw. Again I swapped off material when I was a pawn up, but couldn't convert my advantage in the endgame; an old failing – not understanding that often a single extra pawn is not enough to win. Against the player who specialised in the English and despite (at last!) looking at the early games in Anatoly Karpov's book on the opening, it was I who was outmanoeuvred and easily beaten. Then, in my final game, came the greatest debacle of all – a game that once again made me doubt everything and wonder whether coming to Wijk had been worth the trouble.

I played confidently and powerfully to begin with, and established a commanding position. But, as usual, I couldn't calculate with sufficient precision, and my opponent kept finding get-out-of-jail moves. At one point his king was unable to castle because of my powerful white-squared bishop on c4 – a king can't castle across check – but he sacrificed a pawn to allow himself to castle, I played a few less-than-optimal moves, he gradually mobilised his pieces and started to fight back. The advantage see-sawed in the middle game, but I was sure I had the advantage in the endgame and turned down the offer of a draw. I was doing what Conquest had instructed me to do – play on, play to win, carry on so long as there is life in the position. There was just one problem: I pressed so hard that the advantage swung back to him. I lost a pawn to his predatory queen, he swapped queens and seemed to be marching his lone pawn to the eighth rank and queendom. I resigned. 'You know that position was drawn,' an incredulous spectator immediately said to me. And to my horror I immediately realised he was right. It would have been simple to exchange my final pawn for his and draw the game, but my head was so frazzled after six hours of chess and the snuffing out of my attempts to win that I had barely looked at the final position. I had just assumed he was on the point of breaking through. It was a devastating blow.

Naturally, the first thing the player (to whom I had just handed victory and the tournament) did was apologise. 'I'm really sorry, Stephen,' he said. But I don't think he was. He was a canny operator and had cleverly played the last few moves very quickly to accentuate my time trouble and not give me a chance to come to my senses. It wasn't so much that I felt bad for myself, though the defeat meant I would lose rating points as well as self-respect. What really irked me was that I felt I had let down the two players who would have shared victory in the group with my opponent. All three would have been tied on 6/9, and presumably all three would have been promoted to division four at Wijk next year. Now the player who had this fortunate, foolish success was left alone at the top of the leaderboard, and only he would be promoted. My stupidity had distorted the entire tournament and seemed to negate all my – perhaps all our – efforts over the previous nine days. I hated chess at that moment. Much of my fortnight at Wijk had been enjoyable and instructive, but now I just wanted to flee.

FILE E
From Russia with Angst

'For me, chess is life and every game is like a new life. Every chess player gets to live many lives in one lifetime'

— Eduard Gufeld, Soviet grandmaster
and chess writer

E1: HALF-TIME TALK

This is the square on which the white king sits. It felt significant. I was at the halfway point in my quest. I had not taken my wife's advice to stop here, admit that I would never be a chess expert. I had to keep the faith, even though that final-round disaster at Wijk was both depressing and alarming. How could I not have seen that the position was drawn? Why did I not even look when I still had a healthy six minutes left on the clock? How could my will have crumbled to such an extent? It was the antithesis of what a chess player should be – cold, calm, rational, implacable. I was a fool and felt I had compromised the integrity of the competition. I had given my opponent a soft victory and deprived two others of the rewards of their labours – some 50 hours of chess spread over ten days. I didn't sleep that night or for several nights afterwards.

Gradually, of course, a kind of normality asserts itself. The January English Chess Federation grades were published, and there I was still stuck in the low 130s. Stable – in chess terms at least. The grade was based on what seemed to me a poor six months between July and December, and just the two absurd losses on time at Asda and Hastings had cost me around seven grading points, so I was convinced I could do better in the next six-month accounting period. A grade of 150 was my initial target and then, who knows? The positive side of Wijk, once I started to set that final catastrophe aside, was that I had held my own with a likeable but competitive group of players rated around 1800 – men who had played all their lives. I had not been humiliated, except in that ludicrous final game. Indeed, when the monthly

FIDE ratings were recalibrated, I had actually gained a few points overall. I had competed, but knew I could do better. I was starting to get a feel for how to evaluate a chess position, but didn't yet have the ability to calculate with sufficient precision to nail my opponents. I tended to calculate on the basis of a player making an incorrect move. I shied away from looking at every alternative, and subconsciously suppressed my opponents' best responses – often unlikely or ugly moves that somehow kept them in the game. I had to factor those in; I had to anticipate a tough struggle. 'These old Dutch guys really wriggle and fight,' I had complained to my Italian friend at Wijk. 'Well, what do you expect them to do?' he said. 'Roll over and die?' I had to come prepared to fight, for as long and through as many phases as was necessary. Why should winning a chess game be easy?

I also had to work harder. It was mad that I had come this far – literally and metaphorically – without becoming more conversant with the openings. The man who beat me in round five mentioned that the player I was due to meet next favoured the Sämisch variation of the King's Indian Defence. I had barely heard of the variation and certainly had no idea how to play it. I bought a book on it from the chess store at Wijk and realised it would be dangerous to try the KID against someone who knew this line well – it is very aggressive and quite different from the systems I was (half) familiar with, so decided to avoid it and revert to my old standby, Tartakower's Defence. I didn't really believe in it, but it had to do, and on that occasion it paid dividends, producing the round-six victory that for a moment had taken me close to the top of the leaderboard. The opening was not everything, but it counted for a lot. I should at least know what the Sämisch was, even if I hadn't mastered its every detail. Unless I could plug these gaping holes in my theoretical knowledge, I was doomed forever to be a

1700-rated woodpusher, just about holding my own with the fiftysomething Jaaps and Joops, Toons and Tons, Pims and Wims at Wijk. But if I wanted to get better, move into the higher groups and get closer to the grandmasters at the top of the room, I had to study the openings. Play it again, Sämisch.

I had enjoyed, at least until that final loss, being locked into chess at Wijk: the daily walk on the misty beach, past the steamy steelworks which seemed so out of place in a quiet seaside location; a burst of classical music on the radio – I had stumbled on the Dutch version of Classic FM and found a bit of Mozart the perfect way to prepare; a liedown before the game to clear the head (I could see why Jonathan Rowson advocated meditation); and then the struggle itself, trying to concentrate and play only good moves for hour after hour. It felt very simple, very pure. Yes, it was only a game, and a woman serving in a café next to the playing hall looked at me as if I was mad when I told her I'd come to Wijk from the UK for a fortnight to play in this event. But I felt cleansed by the experience, divorced from everyday concerns, living in and through chess moves. I thought again of Duchamp: we should travel light, live in the moment, not take things too seriously. That, surely, was the appeal of chess: a glorious triviality, Julian Barnes' fragile profundity.

I felt differently about chess after Wijk. Now I knew what real chess and a real chess tournament felt like. I had enjoyed trying to play the tournament as well as the game, to work out who the stronger players were; who favoured what openings; when to play for a win or a draw. OK, it didn't work out in the end, but it was instructive, and I felt it would stand me in good stead for future tournaments. I liked the way the event evolved and drew you in, so that nothing else seemed to matter. Your whole being had to be invested in those daily battles, and you needed to have a strategy for both the game and the tournament.

Meeting Genna Sosonko and reading his books had also been crucial in forming a new attitude to chess, a new sensibility. He wrote about the game so beautifully and so seriously; memorialised these men who had devoted their life to chess and adored the game. A strange, vanished chess world, perfectly, sympathetically rendered. Chess mattered to me more after meeting Sosonko, and the game seemed worthy of even greater respect. I realised I could never be like the Soviet players – they were steeped in the game, had devoted their lives to it. But I could at least aspire to emulate their desire, their work ethic, their ability to analyse. I vowed – I seemed to be making a lot of vows – to stop flicking through grandmaster games, but instead to analyse each position that arose in a game I was looking at and try to work out what was happening. To learn the art of evaluation; to learn to think coherently about chess. I couldn't be Botvinnik, but I could try to think like Botvinnik.

To make a vow is one thing. To put it into practice is something else entirely. My first batch of league games after Wijk were disappointing. No fewer than five straight draws against so-so opposition – a few games where I was up, a couple where I had lucky escapes – and then two bad defeats against experienced opponents who just knew too much theory and had too much nous for me; players who were graded only 137 but packed a lot of chess years into that 137 and were more than able to deal with a fly-by-night latecomer like me. I had managed a draw against one of these opponents at Hastings and we were on email terms. After my league loss he sent me a long computer analysis of the moves, thanked me for an 'exciting' game and praised me as 'an imaginative player with good ideas'. This was kind of him, but I also felt it was a sort of code; he was, in a roundabout way, telling me I was a player who lacked a sound theoretical base and therefore had to engage in wild flights of fancy in a desperate bid to stay alive. Sometimes it worked, especially in blitz, but often it ended in disaster, as it had in these two league losses. Stuart Conquest had told me to toss the odd bomb into games, but he had also cautioned that you could not forever be tossing bombs. Sometimes you had to be laying foundations, building positions. The best chess had an implacable logic that defied the terrorists, the cavemen, the wild romantics.

I showed all my recent games to the Doc. It was our first meeting since Christmas – I had been in Wijk, while he had been at the annual tournament in Gibraltar. He liked the fact that I was playing the King's Indian – an opening with a bit of brio – and enjoyed my wild victory with the opening at Hastings. He ordered me to abandon the useless Scandinavian as black against e4 and take up a proper opening – the French Defence or the Sicilian, tricky and doubled-edged though they were. Saunders insisted that I was an aggressive player or I was nothing. I would never be a careful defender; I had to have the initiative, play games that were teeming with ideas. If I went down in flames, so be it. He also said that league games didn't suit me – short time controls, games that often ended in an adjudication rather than being played to their natural conclusion, wily old blokes who'd been around the block a few times. Stick to tournaments, he suggested. Overall, Saunders was not too dismissive of my recent games, despite what seemed to me a dismal record of two wins, five defeats and nine draws since the turn of the year. He thought there had been a few decent performances among the dross, and that there was some incremental progress. At this crossroads in the journey, he was not yet ready to despair of my prospects.

E2: THE JOY OF SETS

The other thing I did a couple of weeks after my return from Wijk was buy myself a proper chess set to replace my nasty, fading plastic one. I'd been planning to do this for months, and now it was time to shell out – as a statement of intent, a symbol of my renewed commitment. I visited the antiques dealer Luke Honey, a specialist London-based chess dealer, to see whether I could afford a late-Victorian Jaques set, but they were £1,000-plus and I couldn't. Honey did, though, give me a useful history lesson on the evolution of the chess set. National styles predominated in the 18th and first half of the 19th century – Biedermeier in central Europe, Régence in France and the elaborate Barleycorn design in the UK (so named because some of the carvings on the pieces resembled barley). But as players began to compete internationally, they disliked having to play with unfamiliar sets, and the middle of the 19th century saw the new set of chessmen designed by Nathaniel Cook – manufactured by the British boardgames company Jaques and bearing the imprimatur of Howard Staunton, then acknowledged as the strongest player in the world – begin to establish itself as the international standard.

Getting Staunton's seal of approval was a masterstroke – it is significant that the design is called the 'Staunton pattern' and poor old Cook has been largely forgotten. The early (and now very expensive) sets come with a warranty bearing Staunton's signature attached to the box containing the pieces, and he was paid a fee for every set sold – a nice little earner for the astute Staunton, who, as well as being a strong player, a chess entrepreneur and a prolific writer on the game, was also a highly regarded Shakespearean scholar who produced a complete edition of the Bard's works. Victorians, it seemed, were capable of anything, and chess for the English gentleman was still more pastime than profession.

One day I would have my Victorian Staunton set with the great man's signature – another vow! – but not yet. I had to husband my dwindling financial resources for lessons, tournaments, journeys to the heartlands of chess. So for the moment I would have to make do with a modern, though still very attractive, wooden set which I bought for just under £100. I hoped the big, wooden, weighted pieces would make me think more carefully before I traded them with such abandon. I used to dismiss the aesthetics of chess, thinking that a true player didn't care what he played on as long as the pieces were recognisable – rather than those awful themed sets featuring soldiers from the Napoleonic war. But I had changed my mind: now I wanted a generous-sized board and beautiful Staunton-pattern pieces. I wanted the quality of what I was playing on to direct the way I played. I would henceforth respect the game and try to live up to its traditions, not make a nonsense of them as I had in that final game at Wijk.

I christened the board by playing some training games against John Foley, chairman of Kingston Chess Club, a player graded 170-plus and a key figure in training the growing number of qualified coaches offering chess tuition in schools in the UK. A few days before our encounter he emailed me a simple three-point plan: '(1) Identify weaknesses (static analysis); (2) Improve position of pieces (dynamic analysis); (3) Work out your opponent's plan. Generally think about (1) when it is your opponent to move and (2) when it is you to move. [He had clearly been reading his Botvinnik.] Allocate more thinking on "critical moves", i.e., no-turning-back situations.' Foley told me he was unable to calculate variations when it was his opponent's move. 'It may have something to do with adrenaline,' he explained. 'It's the difference between watching from the stands and running on to the pitch. The brain seems to take matters much more urgently when the clock is ticking.'

Foley and I played four games on my lovely new set in the course of a single evening, not using a clock but trying to play at reasonable speed so we could get all the games in. I built up a very good position with white in the first game but blew it with a miscalculated and premature strike; won the second and third games (the former with an endgame grind, the latter with a good attack in the middle game), and lost the final game in a technical 'good' knight v 'bad' bishop endgame (where the knight has more freedom to manoeuvre and so is more potent). It was an encouraging performance and Foley thought the more relaxed atmosphere had benefited my chess. Certainly I noticed that I wasn't rushing off to the loo every five minutes as the tension affected my bladder. There was no tension; this was just a game of chess with nothing at stake – that seemed to liberate me. How, though, could I replicate that freedom in a match or tournament? 'Your playing ability is better than your grade,' Foley told me, 'but try to control your emotions – play as if the game is not that important. Perhaps aim to play more in the generous time control of a weekend event than the frenetic atmosphere of evening suburban chess.' It really did seem that to play the game properly I needed that bubble. Work and play just didn't mix.

E3: HEARTACHE IN HEREFORD

 A week after my training games with Foley I played in an under-160 congress in Hereford, with an exhausting six rounds over three days. The first round was on Friday evening, there were three rounds on Saturday and another two on Sunday. The congress was being played in a hotel in the centre of Hereford, cheap and a bit cheerless, a typical venue for myopic chess players who just want a large fried breakfast and a quiet room in which to play. It proved to be an odd event and my attitude was never quite right. In the first round I played solidly against a good player graded 150-plus, so a draw with black was OK, but I settled for the draw too early while he was determined to play on until a draw was inevitable. He was the one with the fighting spirit; I was just happy to hang on. More or less the same thing happened in round two, where I again managed a draw against a good player. Satisfactory in some respects, except that I had an advantage in the endgame but was reluctant to play it out because time was short. My nerve was failing me.

In round three I was winning easily against a German player who blundered his queen for two knights, but he played quickly, caused complications, used his knights cleverly, lured me into time trouble and eventually swindled a draw. He was apologetic, indeed embarrassed about it, but didn't need to be. He played well after the initial blunder, while as usual when I got my nose ahead I played slowly and feebly. I didn't seem to have the skill and technique to boss the game and put my opponent away. As I had discovered so often, when a player is material down he has little to lose and lashes out. Then you have to play accurately and implacably, but I just couldn't seem to do it.

My reaction to drawing a game I should have won perplexed me. A few months previously I would have been mortified, but now I just treated it as one of those things. Why wasn't I beating myself up? Was this the new calm, rational me (good), or was I being lackadaisical (bad)? A bit of both, perhaps, but mainly the latter: I had not come to this event, filled as it was with 150-plus players, to fight; I had come merely to survive. I was not, I realised, enjoying these games; not getting lost in the moment and in the sheer joy of thought as I had occasionally in the past; I was playing mechanically and trying not to lose. It made for dull chess. There was a hollowness in everything I did.

Most of the 50 players competing at Hereford were from the Midlands and the West Country, but one of my compatriots from the Surrey League, Adrian Waldock, had also made the journey up. He told me he had started playing at the age of seven and had now clocked up an unbroken 50 years as a player – unusual for amateurs, many of whom take a break in their twenties and thirties when job and family pressures intensify. What had captivated him over half a century? 'It's a flight of imagination,' he explained. 'Whenever I'm playing chess I'm not thinking about other problems in my life at all. I'm just focusing on the board, trying to play as well as I can.' Waldock told me he played about 80 graded games a year. I had watched the way he notated games: whereas my scores were scribbled, almost illegible and abandoned completely when I was in time trouble, his were beautifully clear, with the score in black and the clock time after each move written in red. They suggested the clearest and calmest of minds. My inability to score properly was a hallmark of my lack of lucidity when I was playing. 'I'm best when I'm that little bit more relaxed,' he said. 'It's relaxed concentration. A lot of players play better when they're just playing naturally and not agonising too much. Treat it as a game, as an art form.'

Waldock had a bye in the Saturday evening session, and I quickly wished I had one too. I was up against one of those bearded, grizzled old campaigners who populate chess congresses – not very highly graded but perfectly competent and certainly good enough to pounce on my inaccuracies. I miscalculated when trying to build an overly speculative attack in the middle game and my position quickly collapsed, leading to an ugly loss in which I resigned just before the inevitable checkmate. Once I would have been mortified, but by now I was almost immune to disappointment: I just shook his hand and went to the bar to have a beer. This is the way you are supposed to react as a chess pro – tomorrow is another game and another day – but I worried that the ease with which I accepted defeat was a sign of a lack of commitment.

At least on Sunday morning, following my Saturday evening defeat and a restless night filled with strange, hallucinatory dreams, I felt I wanted to get back on the horse in an effort to redeem myself. I had been getting into time trouble in every game, so was determined to play more quickly, but combining speed with accuracy was not going to be easy. In the endgame that I should have won in round two I'd told my much younger opponent – one of the few youthful players at the congress – that with only ten minutes left on the clock I didn't feel I had time to calculate a winning sequence. 'That's masses of time,' he'd said. 'I worked it out in 30 seconds.' This was not encouraging.

Sunday didn't prove much better. In the morning I had an advantage against a 145-rated player but again overpressed and lost. The result meant I had just 1.5 points from a possible 5 and was playing on the bottom board in the final round. Where you are sitting in the room reflects exactly how you have performed in the tournament, and it's an unpleasant feeling to be marooned in the boondocks with the other failures. My opponent must have felt the same way, because he played boringly, swapped off most of the pieces, produced a position of unutterable tedium and offered a draw on move 29. Stuart Conquest would not have been amused. Caïssa, the goddess of chess, was being mocked. But hell, who cares? The sun was shining, we had both had a poor tournament, I shook his hand. Hereford had not proved a happy hunting ground.

There was, though, a heartening coda. The evening I got back, I had to play in a crucial league match for Kingston's second team – in effect a relegation decider against Wallington. It was a six-board match, and after a couple of hours' play all the games had been decided except mine. The match score was level, so everything depended on me: I had the fate of Kingston second team in my hands! My opponent was elderly, wheezing and not very highly rated, but his play was sound. I had gambled an early sacrifice to try to set up a mating attack; he defended stoutly, exchanged queens and looked as if he might escape. The old me might have panicked, but I managed to conjure up a plan B, launching my pawns down the middle of the board. We were both in time trouble, but for once it was my opponent who blinked first, failing to make his 35th move to reach the one-and-a-quarter-hour time control. I had won the game; we had won the match; and I had contrived to play well despite being short of time. 'That was nicely played,' the veteran on our team (and president of the club) said to me. I swelled with pride and the travails of Hereford were forgotten.

E4: MAD, BAD VLAD

In the spring I went to Moscow to see if an encounter with chess in Russia – the heart and soul of the game for much of the past hundred years – would galvanise me. It was a peculiar time to go because the stand-off over the Crimea had frozen relations between Russia and the UK. I had visited the city before and loved its energy and openness – so different from the rest of Russia, the locals assured me. This time, with Russia and Ukraine close to war, I feared it would be different. But the flights were booked, the expensive visa had been arranged, there was no turning back. I was also, in truth, interested to spend a couple of weeks there at a time of tension and uncertainty. How much chess I would manage was anyone's guess.

My mentor in Moscow was Vladislav Tkachiev, a 40-year-old grandmaster from Kazakhstan who had reached the world top 30 in his twenties and was European champion in 2007. Tkachiev had had some well-publicised drink problems – in 2009, playing in a tournament in Calcutta, he was drunk at the board and passed out – but I found him delightful, expansive, boundlessly energetic (trying to keep up with him as he walked around Moscow was hard work) and stone-cold sober. Our first meeting was in a coffee shop in the centre of Moscow, and in his rapid, heavily accented English he recounted the highs and lows of his career. He was born in Moscow, but because his father was in the army he grew up in Kazakhstan, which is where he learned chess. 'I started pretty late,' he told me. 'I was almost ten years old – many strong players now start at four or five.' But his progress was rapid: 'I was sent to a special sports school, won everything that it was possible to win in Kazakhstan, and was soon playing in tournaments abroad.'

By the time we met, Tkachiev was playing less, but said he still had ambitions in chess. Having lived for a time in Cannes, he had been granted French citizenship and was playing for France – he was in the team which in November 2013 had narrowly lost out to Azerbaijan in the European team championship. He did, though, accept that his age meant he had to start looking at other options – writing and coaching. The writing he enjoyed; the coaching less so. 'I didn't feel my students loved chess as much as I did,' he said. 'I didn't feel they had the same passion, the same determination. They weren't like I used to be. For them it was a hobby; for me it was never a hobby and never will be. It was a religion. I don't know of any player of my level who doesn't have a chess position in his mind at any point in his existence. I'm talking to you; I have a position in my mind. No matter what I am doing – if I'm talking to you or playing football or making love with my girlfriend – I am thinking all the time about chess.'

Tkachiev outgrew chess in Kazakhstan, moving first to Moscow and then to Cannes. He chose France because there were many big tournaments and good opportunities to make a living, and Cannes because he was almost as passionate about the cinema as he was about chess. He achieved his best rating in his late twenties, but said that at the same time as he was reaching his peak as a player he realised he would never reach the very top: 'I understood that, if I worked very, very, very hard, I might become one of the best ten players, but no way was I going to become world champion.' That realisation was traumatic and it took him at least five years to adjust to his new expectations. 'I started drinking; I started to be, as they call me on Wikipedia, a hedonist. Most of it is true,

I don't deny it, but this is the main reason – I stopped considering myself as a professional to the last breath.' It was at that point that he started coaching – mainly the children of the wealthy – because that was an easier way to earn a living, but it had a detrimental effect on his chess. 'It was horrible,' he said. 'I started to think like them.' He carried on playing because he still felt the need to compete, but he was drinking and staying out until the early hours of the morning and his results suffered. 'The internet rumours are not just rumours,' he said. 'They are true.' Reports of his drunkenness in Calcutta in 2009 went around the world and quickly came to define him. 'Suddenly I became somewhat like a rock star – a chess version of Pete Doherty.' His range of western cultural references is impressive.

Setting up the World Chess Beauty Contest, complete with a website devoted to attractive female chess players, in 2005 with his brother Evgeny (they styled themselves the 'Blitz Brothers') added to the notoriety. The contest, for which he had high hopes, was well received in Russia and the countries of the old Soviet Union, but he was castigated in the west, especially in the US. No finance was forthcoming to back his website, and eventually the idea was dropped. He is unapologetic about it: 'My idea was to show another side of chess. We got coverage from all the biggest newspapers in the world because we broke the cliché. It failed, but I'm not ashamed to have tried it. If I did it again now, I would do two contests – one for men and one for women. That was one of the mistakes – not to do both.' Though finding enough attractive male chess players for a contest could be tricky.

Tkachiev said he believed he understood chess better than in his playing prime, but that standards had risen because information was now so readily available via the internet and computer analysis: 'Everyone is better prepared than when I started, and the way of playing is different now. The younger generation calculate much more; they are much more computer-like as chess players.' Whereas pre-computer players would avoid lines that were deemed dubious optically or intuitively, now everything must be concrete. Players who have grown up with computers have no fear of ugly positions. Tkachiev was having to adjust to this brave new world of youthful, automaton-like chess players. He was nevertheless still enjoying good results – within a year of our meeting in Moscow he had forced himself back into the world top 100 – and was sometimes optimistic he could win a major competition with the French team, perhaps even enjoy another big individual tournament victory. 'I want to leave on a high,' he insisted, 'and for sure I don't want to leave in the second hundred of top players, because this is humiliating for me. I want to leave while I'm in the top 100 because I believe I belong there.'

On his less bullish days, however, he felt chess had changed too much and that, whereas once he would have eaten 2300-rated players for breakfast, he was now struggling to beat them. At one point he had been as low as number 175 in the world. 'Somehow, invisibly, I became a little player, whereas once I was a big player,' he said. 'It happened just like that. I had the impression that I would be there [at the top] always. But somehow you stay the same and everything else changes.' The invitations to elite competitions had dried up, and he was having to compete in open tournaments – a certain way to drag your rating down even further unless you scored phenomenally well, since every draw conceded to a 2300 player or an underrated junior will cost you a hatful of rating points. He said it was important to work with young players to understand how the computer generation approached chess. 'Players of my age have to become like Dracula, drinking some young blood on a daily basis,' he said with a deep, guttural, smoker's laugh.

Tkachiev was realistic enough to know he didn't have long left as a chess pro. For him 40 really was a watershed, not least as he had so many other interests – journalism, literature, cinema, politics. He was already anticipating the moment when writing about chess would replace playing the game, and hoped to write books that would counteract what he saw as myths propagated by writers who, at best, were on the margins of chess. 'Look at Nabokov,' he said. 'He established an image of a chess player which is now very deeply rooted in the mass media, but Nabokov was a composer of chess puzzles, not a chess player.' Like Emil Sutovsky, Tkachiev said the unhinged central character in *The Luzhin Defense* was now accepted as the archetypal chess player, whereas in reality it described an extreme. 'I want to write about our happy moments, our desperate moments, from the perspective of a professional chess player,' he said. The *normal* chess player? I suggested. 'Never normal,' he said, 'far from being normal, but definitely not the kind of "beautiful mind" Nabokov writes about, because it is simply not true. Take a look at Karpov, take a look at Kasparov, take a look at Carlsen – they are very far from this image. They are very pragmatic guys.'

Tkachiev was worried about the declining popularity of chess, both in Russia and across the world, and said the sport needed to be transformed to meet the challenge of an age when there were so many competing leisure activities: 'The way the game is presented to the public definitely needs to be changed. If it doesn't change, chess is on the path to disappearing. Almost nobody believes any more that chess has a huge potential as a show, a spectacle, but I believe it does. I don't know how to do it exactly. I'm not a theatre director. But I believe it can be done.' He said he supported shortening time controls and playing more exhibition matches, putting him in opposition to Sutovsky and the classicists. I was doubtful. The problem with changing the way chess is played to attract the computer-games generation is that it would risk negating 500 years of chess history. The beauty of chess is that one can compare games and styles of play across half a millennium. That key attraction of chess – its glorious continuity – would be lost. Yet I couldn't help but admire Tkachiev's energy and entrepreneurial spirit, his willingness to think the unthinkable. A contest devoted to identifying the most beautiful female chess players may have been a terrible idea, but his ambition to transform the image of chess and attempt to secure its future in a world in which it felt increasingly marginalised was an admirable one.

E5: PLAYING AT 'THE CLUB'

 I was staying at the Vakhtangov Theatre in a vibrant street called Old Arbat, a 20-minute walk from the Kremlin and, more important, a 15-minute walk from the famous Central Chess Club, the heart of the known chess universe. I knew the artistic staff of the Vakhtangov because in 2012 I had written about a production of *Uncle Vanya* they had staged in Russian in the UK, and they were kindly letting me stay in a small block of flats next to the theatre which they used to house visiting artists. Metro trains rumbled deep below, and there was a tiny studio theatre attached where they sometimes staged performances, but it was more evocative than the average Moscow hotel and a lot cheaper too. I might not be playing like a professional chess player, but I was certainly learning to cadge like one.

The Central Chess Club holds rapidplay and blitz tournaments at weekends, and I planned to enter one. Whether this was wise, given the level of playing strength in Moscow, was questionable. Hans Ree, the Dutch GM I had talked to in Amsterdam, once said that when he visited the Soviet Union he had the impression that every tram conductor played chess better than he did. Chess in Russia was not the state religion it had been in the Soviet era, but the players who came to the imposing, yellow-coloured building on Gogol Boulevard were almost certainly going to be far too good for me.

Tkachiev was out of town on my first weekend in Moscow, so I pitched up at the club unchaperoned on the Sunday to enter the rapidplay. He had told me I needed to be there by 2.45pm to register, and that I would need to pay a small entry fee. It was a sunny afternoon and I arrived early. Only a few other players were there, and I was immediately buttonholed by an elderly man with a vast grey beard who sensed I was a foreigner. 'I am Russian poet,' he announced, before asking me where I came from. 'England,' I told him. 'Manchester United,' he announced. 'Chelsea.' The names of football teams seemed to be the extent of his English. He wrote his name, Konstantin Gumirov, on a piece of paper and challenged me to some practice blitz before the tournament started. We drew the first game – I was winning but ran short of time so agreed a draw – and he won the other two. I played an embarrassingly poor move in the middle game that allowed mate, and even before he could play – perhaps even before he saw it – one of the men watching said 'mate' loudly. This did not bode well.

After my games with Gumirov I managed to find a couple of people who spoke English – a well-dressed young man of about my strength called Dmitrii Loev and a FIDE master called Arman Erzhanov, who wasn't playing. Erzhanov said the event was too weak for him, despite it attracting a grandmaster, six international masters and two other FIDE masters, but had come to watch some of his students. Erzhanov told me he had a degree in business studies but for the moment was concentrating on chess. He had played at Hastings the previous January after a year-long lay-off, scoring 5/9 and drawing with a couple of GMs. He reckoned he could get to IM, but didn't seem sure whether he would make GM. 'I know how to do it, but it would be a lot of work,' he said. There was also the usual playing/teaching trade-off. He could make a living teaching, whereas he certainly wouldn't playing – the prize in the tournament in which I was playing was less than £100 – but the time he spent teaching was lost to serious study and competitive play. A vicious circle. I told him I was hoping to get to a FIDE rating of 2000. 'Read tactics books,' he told me.

'You have to be good at tactics. Forget opening books. And always remember – your best friend is yourself.' By which he meant don't rely on a trainer; learn to study chess on your own. Despite that advice we swapped numbers and agreed we would try to meet for a practice game during my stay.

The club was a lovely place to play – high ceilings, chandeliers, photographs in one of the rooms of all the Russian/Soviet world champions (male and female, on opposite walls) – but in all other respects I could have been back in Hereford or Torquay. The vast majority of the players were men, mostly over 60 or under 16; there were some very odd people playing, including one man whose head was covered in tattoos and who had a ring through his nose (I didn't see him speak to anyone all day); and there was a strong smell of body odour, even before the tournament began (perhaps it was a historic smell left over from the Botvinnik–Smyslov world championship match of 1958).

In my first game of the nine-round tournament I was drawn against an elderly IM. He played some odd moves and I was on top early on, but like all his compatriots he played very quickly – we each had 15 minutes to make all our moves – and time and his superior endgame technique eventually told. Still, given how nervous I was, it could have been worse. I lost my second game too, to a player rated 2250, who beat me easily, but won my third against a rather strange young man who refused to make eye contact and rocked back and forth nervously. I played the King's Indian Defence and got it all wrong as usual, but it was enough to flummox him. He played some feeble moves in reply and lost very quickly. I was on the scoreboard and mightily relieved – anything but a whitewash seemed somehow acceptable. I hadn't realised how long the tournament was going to be. We started at 3pm and would be playing beyond eight. I was already starving and had to raid the confectionery machine at the club for a KitKat *and* a Twix. This kept me going in the short term, but meant I had terrible stomach pains by round eight. The machine broke down later, which was probably a good thing.

I was annihilated in round four by a player rated around 2000, but in the next round recovered to win a game that could have gone either way. My not-very-highly-rated opponent played incredibly quickly and built up a huge time plus, pointedly staring at other games while waiting for the British slowcoach to move. But he became a little too confident, I managed to win a piece, and eventually he resigned with less than a minute left on my clock. This win was crucial: if I'd gone 1/5 I might have crumbled, but at 2/5 I was still clinging to respectability. I had the added pleasure that he was manifestly disgusted with himself for losing. 'Serves him right for watching other games rather than focusing on his own,' I thought, with quiet satisfaction.

By now I was tired and hot – the room was getting stuffier, though thankfully not much smellier. I was trundling along on or near the bottom boards, wishing I could have another Twix and a cup of tea, but the rounds were coming thick and fast, with the pairings read out in a loud voice by one of the two organisers. I, of course, had no idea what number board I was on, and had to pursue the man with the pairings at the beginning of each round to check who and where I was playing. After each round I would compare scores with Dmitrii Loev – we were performing at about the same level – and my poet friend would also sidle up occasionally to offer encouragement in rapid Russian.

Round six was not my finest hour – a feeble loss in which I miscalculated a great deal. A half-hour game is pressured, but there ought to be enough time to play without conspicuous blunders. Here, though, I made at least two serious errors and lost rather ignominiously. My genial opponent said just one word to me after the game: 'Trompowsky', the name of the opening he played and which he clearly felt I was clueless against. No doubt he meant well.

When you lose it plunges you down the table and, in theory, you get someone weaker to play in the next round. That's certainly what happened here, as I beat my next opponent – a charming middle-aged man with a ready smile – comfortably. That gave me 3/7 and I was reasonably content. Even if I lost my last two games, Britain's sole representative in the tournament would not have been disgraced.

In the penultimate round I encountered my first Russian junior – a 12-year-old already rated 1905. He had that distracted air juniors sometimes have and I thought maybe he wasn't concentrating, but he was still too solid for me. I fell behind on time, found it impossible to conjure up any sort of coherent plan and eventually got mated. It was back to a middle-aged opponent in the final round – smartly suited and not smiling. I was white and for once played a good tactical game that left him hopelessly behind on material. He resigned and gave me a look of cold fury, which again pleased me enormously. That left me on 4/9. The poet had 4.5, Loev 3. I had performed creditably, coming joint 44th – there were 14 players on that score, including the junior who had beaten me in round eight. My rating performance across the tournament was 1779, which was 40 points better than my FIDE rating in classical chess. Despite my Twix-induced stomach ache, I was satisfied. 'How many points did you get?' one of the more seasoned competitors asked me. I put up four fingers. 'It's enough,' he said. 'To begin with.'

E6: HANDSHAKE WITH HISTORY

 A couple of days later I was back at the club, this time
with Tkachiev in tow. We had come to see one of the
legends of Soviet chess – Yuri Averbakh, then aged 92,
the oldest living grandmaster and one of the few players
to have no less than three opening variations named
after him. He had won the Soviet championship in 1954 against
a hugely strong field that included Tigran Petrosian, who became
world champion a decade later, Viktor Korchnoi, Mark Taimanov,
Efim Geller and Salo Flohr. Averbakh also played in the great
Zurich tournament of 1953, to determine who would face
Mikhail Botvinnik for the world championship, coming tenth
out of 15 behind such legendary names as Smyslov, Bronstein
and Keres (who occupied the first three places) but ahead of
former world champion Max Euwe. Averbakh's other moment of
chess history came in 1972. He was president of the Soviet Chess
Federation when Bobby Fischer wrested the world title from the
grip of the Soviet Union after almost four decades. Better still,
Averbakh survived the Soviet regime's fury at the upstart
westerner winning the crown, and was still here more than four
decades later, the slightly hard-of-hearing conscience of the
Central Chess Club.

A Japanese film crew making a documentary about Fischer
were at the club to film the tall, stately Averbakh on the day I was
there, but Tkachiev and I spirited him away in the early afternoon
and asked him to reflect on a lifetime devoted to chess. There
were, he told us, six types of chess players. First, the knockout
players who didn't just want to win but to kill. In this category

Averbakh placed Botvinnik, Fischer and Korchnoi. The second group comprised the fighters, most notably Lasker, and the third the sportsmen – he cited Capablanca and Paul Keres as examples and said that, for players such as these, once the game was over they reverted to normality, not something that could be said for everyone. The fourth group of players included those who loved to play every type of game – cards, backgammon and board games other than chess. The best example of the games obsessive was Karpov. Only players from one of these groups could become chess world champion, he said. The fifth group was made up of the artists for whom the way of winning was as important as the victory itself. He cited Nicolas Rossolimo, one of my favourite players because of his cosmopolitan life as well as his approach to chess, as an example of a true artist. Analysts, for whom chess was a kind of scientific enquiry, formed the final group. He placed himself, along with Siegbert Tarrasch and Reuben Fine, in this final category. It was a brilliant and useful method of categorisation, though he admitted there were overlaps. Surely Tal was an artist, I protested, and the fact he became world champion contradicted his theory? 'No,' he said firmly, 'Tal was a fighter because he believed in himself completely.'

Averbakh bemoaned the fact that chess had become so narrow. Players, he said, started too early and had little experience of life. This was a common complaint among the older generation of players – that chess had become a mere game and lost its cultural significance. In the golden age between the First and Second World Wars, players believed chess was allied to poetry and philosophy and it was widely seen as a marriage of art and science. 'I consider chess an art,' Alekhine had said, 'and accept all those responsibilities which art places upon its devotees.' Another Soviet world champion, Vasily Smyslov, expressed similar sentiments:

'My study of chess was accompanied by a strong attraction to music, and it was probably thanks to this that from childhood I became accustomed to thinking of chess as an art, and have never regarded it as anything else, for all the science and sport involved in it.' Now, according to the sceptics anyway, chess was no longer an art form but merely an extension of computing.

Rafael Vaganian, an Armenian grandmaster who came to prominence in the 1970s and won the Soviet championship in 1989 as the regime tottered on the edge of the precipice, expressed the fears of the old-timers well in an interview he gave to the website Chess 24. Asked to compare Magnus Carlsen with the champions of his own generation, he said, 'It's hard to compare, because the chess is totally different. Those [old] champions worked in another setting, playing another kind of chess. With no computers, they worked and created on their own, and their creativity was immense. If they found something it was with their own minds, while now there are these amazing programs. Theory has "grown" to 30–35 moves, and you simply can't compare the two types of chess. Frankly speaking, I don't like modern chess, and I'm not sure what's going to happen next.'

Averbakh loved the rich history of the game, and worried that chess was losing its cultural significance. Everyone who had lived through the Soviet period, when crowds came to watch the great matches and games were relayed live over the radio, felt a sense of loss. 'It is ridiculous that the Candidates' Tournament [which had just been played in Siberia to decide who would face Carlsen for the world title, and which had included four Russian players] received only a small paragraph in Russia's most important sports paper,' he complained. 'Chess is in a spiral of decline.' He nevertheless refused to despair: 'Chess is a game with incredible resources. It has had many other ups and downs.

Card games almost killed chess after the invention of printing made cards very cheap in the late 15th century.' Chess responded with a new set of rules that made the game more dynamic. Perhaps it could evolve again, though he was far from clear about the nature of that evolution. Chess variants such as Fischer Random, in which the position of the pieces at the start of the game is determined by lottery (to negate existing opening theory), held some attraction and would counteract the malign effect of computers which made grandmaster chess in many ways a memory test, but he was reluctant to throw the classical baby out with the bathwater. Chess was in a bind but somehow it would come through was his hopeful message.

Averbakh was amusing about his role in the Fischer–Spassky match. He said the bigwigs in the Soviet Chess Federation realised Fischer would probably win and didn't want to be overseeing the game in the Soviet Union when that evil day dawned, so they elected him as president in his absence. 'I got married without being there,' he said with a laugh. Fischer's victory was a shock to the Soviet political system, and after 1972 the administrators reformed the structure of chess in the country and redoubled their efforts to win the title back. The result was another 30 years of Soviet and then Russian dominance, with Karpov, Kasparov and Kramnik holding the title until 2005. Averbakh said he regretted the fact that Fischer refused to defend his crown in 1975: 'Fischer needed a psychologist, because many of his decisions were completely illogical. He wasn't following his own interests. A Fischer–Karpov match would have had a colossal impact. Fischer is a mysterious figure in the history of chess. Even his decision not to be operated on [for kidney disease] in Iceland at the end is mysterious. He could have lived.'

The Fischer mystery is, in a way, one from which chess is still suffering. He made the game front-page news, but it has never been quite the same since he stopped playing. No one, not even Kasparov, could compete with the mercurial, at times maniacal Fischer, which is why the Japanese were here at the club, filming this dignified old man who had to organise the ill-fated Soviet fight against him in 1972. After we finished talking I watched the filming. Averbakh sat at a chessboard shuffling pieces around, as he had for more than 80 years. I so wanted to play some moves against him, but the Japanese film crew were becoming proprietorial and the moment passed. I had to be satisfied with my handshake with history.

E7: BLITZED IN GORKY PARK

One cool, drizzly afternoon, Tkachiev and I visited what may be Moscow's strangest chess venue – the White Rook Chess Club in Gorky Park, a wooden pavilion with chessboards inlaid on tables where every day a hard core of players, mainly elderly and retired, gathered to play blitz chess, cards and backgammon, drink some vodka when it was cold and have a barbecue when it was warm. It was a social club for the old, the dispossessed, the forgotten – a place to meet, escape and play games, something beloved of Russian men of a certain age who had grown up in a world where letting games take over your life was the only way of staying sane.

A middle-aged man called Marshan Karaketov, the de facto secretary of the club, recognised Tkachiev and insisted on playing blitz against him. Tkachiev won five, but Karaketov managed a win – quite an achievement for an amateur (his strength was hard to gauge, perhaps around FIDE 2000) against a GM. I was impressed that he didn't crow about it, just quickly reset the pieces for the next game. I would have been dining out on it for years. After the games Karaketov talked about the club, and it was clear how proud he was: of the fact it was free, open 24 hours a day, and in summer attracted up to 150 players. Even on the nippy afternoon we dropped by, there were more than 20. According to Karaketov, some chess-playing insomniacs showed up in the middle of the night. It was pleasing to see chess still had its fanatics. Nevertheless he admitted chess was nothing like as strong as it had been in the Soviet era, when almost half the population were occasional players and there were a million experts. He blamed capitalism for chess's decline: everyone was too busy to play now, except his little knot of retirees. He had no time for capitalism generally, pointing out a neighbouring café where a bottle of water cost 100 roubles (£2). Who could afford that? Not the impoverished old men at the chess club, that's for sure. Karaketov preferred the certainties and solidarities of socialism, when the state provided everything and the only entertainment – give or take ballet and the music of Shostakovich – was chess.

After offering his Marxist theory of the decline of chess, Karaketov and I played a couple of blitz games. With the pressure of Tkachiev and a dozen old guys watching and only five minutes for all moves, I played embarrassingly badly and lost both games without offering much resistance. Karaketov was fast and accurate; I was slow and incoherent. 'I could see that you're not used to playing blitz,' Tkachiev said afterwards. 'You didn't seem very comfortable. In fact, you were panicking.' I told him I felt he would be disappointed by my play. 'No, no,' he insisted. 'How could I be disappointed with your play when I'm not happy with my own play?' But he wasn't ready to overlook my limitations entirely, and said bluntly, 'You've got some problems with your general chess knowledge. This was quite evident. In the first game you were the victim of a typical tactical combination, allowing a double pin – a pin on a diagonal and a pin on an open file. And in the second game you allowed him a nice positional advantage, but basically he didn't do anything for that. You did it. Both of the positional themes were your fault, and both are very stereotypical.' He said my opponent was a classic product of the Soviet chess school, playing a sound positional game and fighting for good squares and open files. I clearly had a lot of work to do to become a true Soviet player.

Tkachiev had another chance to experience my chess in the evening when we went to the October Chess Club (so named because it used to be near the Oktyabrskaya Metro station). The club met twice a week in a long, narrow underground room at a social club – the Russian equivalent of all those draughty church halls and sticky-floored pubs in which UK chess clubs held their gatherings. It was the antithesis of the grandeur of the Central Chess Club: cramped, poorly lit and with smelly toilets. That 20-odd players should regularly pitch up to play a blitz tournament in such conditions certainly attested to their love of the game. I recognised several of the competitors from the rapidplay at the Central Chess Club. The poet, Konstantin Gumirov, was here, babbling endlessly, as was a man in a brown blazer festooned with coloured strips on the breast pocket which I took to be battle honours.

The time limit was a little more generous than in Gorky Park – ten minutes for all moves rather than five – and at least I felt I had time to think and construct a plan. But I never quite recovered from my first game, against a grim-faced young man, in which I would have won had it not been for the fact that for long periods his clock wasn't ticking. He must have had at least 20 minutes to my ten, and I had to keep checking his clock and telling him to bash it to get it going again. I was a piece up but inevitably going to lose on time, and suggested we agree a draw. This seemed the logical and just result, but he insisted on playing on to win on time. This instance of 'flagging' was particularly unsporting. There was nothing at stake and it didn't bother me especially, but it suggested a ridiculous desire to win at any cost and was a poor way to greet someone who had travelled 1,500 miles to play in this peculiar chess bunker.

I was winning the second game but then stumbled into stalemate with time running out – this was not going well – before managing a smooth victory in the third game. Cue high fives with Tkachiev, who had been having a lengthy and voluble conversation with the poet – a legend, according to Tkachiev, in Moscow chess circles. I lost game four, but had a fortunate victory in game five which helped to make up for my earlier disappointments. That, though, was the high-water mark of my evening. After that I started to feel tired and hungry (as usual), and suffered three straight losses. Chess, at this level anyway, is to a large extent a matter of will, and mine was non-existent by the end. This was functional, dog-eat-dog chess – there was no room for niceties at this underground club – and my opponents could sense my weakness. I finished on 2.5/8 and close to the bottom of the tournament, but if nothing else it had been another powerful lesson in the need to give no quarter. Moscow was not the place for gentlemanly chess players.

Tkachiev had left after round four – I hoped not in disgust at my play – and I had to make my own way back on the Metro. I would almost certainly have taken the wrong line but, as I stood deliberating on the platform, who should come into view but the poet, staggering down the steps in his stripy suit and battered felt boots. I pointed to the station I wanted to get to, and he indicated he was going in the same direction. He took me by the arm, announced he was my friend, and we took the next train north, with him singing some song in English I didn't recognise, and occasionally hymning the glories of Manchester United. With the help of my voluble guardian angel, I eventually found my way back to Red Square, and from there I could navigate the walk to Arbat alone.

The following morning I went to Sokolniki Park in the north of the city to meet Arman Erzhanov, the FIDE master and trainer I had met at the Central Chess Club a few days earlier. Erzhanov had emailed to say he would be playing a game at the club in the park, and that afterwards he would play some practice games with me. I was tired after my exertions at the underground chess club and, to be frank, a bit hungover because of some post-tournament beers I'd indulged in when I got back to the centre of town. It was not great preparation to face a player whose peak rating had been 2325. In each of the four games we played, I was already totally lost by move 15.

He told me the only way to improve was by working hard. Familiar advice. 'In order to be strong in chess, you need to know how to train correctly,' he said. 'You must have three things: time, desire and the right exercises.' He recommended two to three hours' study a day, split between problem-solving, studying grandmaster games without the aid of a computer and trying to guess their moves, and work on endgame technique. He was less interested in the opening, and recommended playing whatever I was comfortable with, ideally slightly offbeat lines that my opponents would be less familiar with. He suggested Alekhine and Fischer as grandmasters to study, because they were often beating up weaker players by executing very clear plans. Modern grandmaster games, he said, were harder to follow because most of the strategic thinking was below the surface. Today's GMs were so good and their strengths so comparable that only the most complex strategies would work, and to the amateur they often seemed opaque.

Erzhanov was interesting. Even though he had recently completed a postgraduate degree in business studies in Brussels, he had chosen to devote himself to chess. It was the opposite of Tkachiev, who I sensed had some regrets about having devoted himself to the game. Erzhanov was 30 and had worked as an actuary in his mid-twenties, but he told me the job bored him and that he found chess far more fulfilling: 'Working in an accountancy firm was like being a slave. I hated it. You earn money, but you have no freedom and just have to follow instructions. Chess is more about creativity.' He said there were many parents in Moscow who wanted their children to study chess, and that he could earn around £2,000 a month as a coach – not great for Moscow, which is expensive, but liveable on, especially when you remember that Russians are taxed at just 13 per cent. 'I have a free life,' he said. 'I can sleep as much as I want, and I can train those pupils who I like and who are talented. You need to follow your passion; you need to do what you like doing; and if you follow your passion the success will come automatically. Let yourself fly on the wings of your strengths, and then success is inevitable for you.' My fear was that my passion was inadequate, and so far I had not been able to locate the wings of my strengths, let alone spread them as I soared skywards. When, if ever, would I take flight?

Not on my second weekend of rapidplay at the club, that was for sure. I got there early and played a few training games against Eugenia Chasovnikova, a 32-year-old woman grandmaster who for the moment was doing more coaching than playing. I found working with her very instructive, and wished I'd met her earlier in my stay. She was serious without being humourless, and explained where I was going wrong in a way that I found easy to grasp. Chasovnikova told me my style of play was too risky. Everyone in Russia played solid, positional, Botvinnikian chess, not this hit-and-hope coffee-house nonsense. But she also encouraged me by saying I seemed a little stronger than my rating of 1739.

Sadly my performance in the subsequent rapidplay did not bear that out. Perhaps I was disturbed by the fact that Konstantin, the poet, was nowhere to be seen. I had assumed he was a fixture at every chess event in Moscow. But Dmitrii Loev, the nice young man I'd met the previous week, was back, and took it upon himself to tell me on which board I was playing. The man with the medals was also there. In fact he was a player of IM strength, was seeded one and went on to win the tournament – a 70-year-old who had retained his chess strength.

I again lost my first two games to 2200-level players, won the third easily against a weak player, had an excellent win against a good player in the fourth and lost the fifth. Then came the game that determined my day. I had a completely won (i.e., not completely won) game against a scary-looking man of about 40. I just had to play correctly and the game was mine. But once again I blew it in time trouble. I never quite recovered from that, managing only a draw in my final three games to finish on 2.5 and a rating in the tournament of 1689. I should have won the final game as well – I had an overwhelming position but again ran short of time. If I had won both those games I would have had a very respectable 4.5/9 and a rating in the tournament close to 1900. Such is the small margin between success – relative success, anyway – and mediocrity. I had nevertheless left my mark on Moscow's Central Chess Club. Not so much by my performance – I finished in the bottom six in the second tournament, and had only been mid-table in the first one. But halfway through this second event I spilt a cup of coffee on the red carpet in the playing hall and noticed later that it had left quite a sizeable stain. I may not have written my name in the annals quite as boldly as Tal, Smyslov or Botvinnik, but they wouldn't forget me in a hurry. At least the cleaner wouldn't.

E8: PRESENT V PAST

What state was Russian chess really in? That was the question that increasingly preoccupied me during my time in Moscow. It had a glorious past, but what about the future? This was a question not just for Russian chess but for the game all over the world in the computer age. One afternoon I went to the chess faculty of the Russian State Social University – chess is treated as a subject for rigorous academic training in Russia – to meet its founding director, Alexander Kostyev. It was one of five chess schools in Moscow and had produced more than a dozen grandmasters in its ten-year life. Kostyev introduced me to two of the current crop of students – Vladimir Belous, who was rated 2572 and had recently become Moscow champion, and Andrey Stukopin, whose rating was 2553. They were sitting side by side in a classroom studying complicated positions that their coach, Igor Yanvarjov, a veteran international master who had been a close friend of world champion Tigran Petrosian, had asked them to assess.

Belous and Stukopin were studying chess as part of a general degree, but with these two budding stars there was no question that chess was their focus and other subjects such as IT, management and psychology were add-ons. Whereas in the UK talented players faced the dilemma of whether to go to university or begin a career as a professional player, the Russian player – if he or she was sufficiently talented and motivated – could do both. In that sense the Soviet system lived on. Belous and Stukopin both came from southern Russia, had been identified as juniors with potential, left their homes and families, and from the age of 13 studied at what was in effect a chess boarding school, with everything paid for by the state. Now they had progressed to the chess faculty of the university, again fully funded, and soon they would have to start testing themselves in ever more demanding competitions to see how far they could get in professional chess.

I liked their optimism, especially after meeting so many old-timers who thought professional chess was becoming played out because of computers. I mentioned the Hungarian star Richard Rapport, who at the age of 18 was already rated 2700 and playing in elite tournaments. How could they bridge that gap, I asked them? 'He plays very unconventionally,' said Belous, picking up a pawn to indicate a wacky opening move. 'I would stick to solid Soviet chess principles.'

Young Russian chess players do not want for confidence. It amused me how little the grandmaster title meant to them. They had seen getting the title as inevitable – just another rung up the ladder – and what really mattered was getting to a FIDE rating of 2700. Then you would be in the world top 50 and have serious earning potential, attracting invitations to prestigious closed tournaments and deals with league teams across Europe – and, indeed, the US, where I noticed a year or so later that Stukopin was playing for New Jersey in the United States Chess League. The grandmaster title, for all its traditional mystique, had virtually become an irrelevance, devalued by the sheer numbers that now gained it and with the bar set too low. I had asked Tkachiev whether he had a business card that proclaimed his status as a grandmaster. He laughed. 'For me to put grandmaster would be like putting "Tkachiev, man".' With Magnus Carlsen at one point soaring to a rating of 2882, the real barrier was now 2700, perhaps even 2750. Only super-GMs really counted in the modern chess world.

I asked the two young stars how far they thought they could get in chess. Stukopin said he hoped to get into the world top 20; Belous went even further – why not aim to be world champion? He had the ambition that Tkachiev had had when he was 20. You couldn't help but wonder whether he would face a similar disappointment at some point when he realised that, while a hugely strong player, he was not destined for the very top. For the moment, though, he had to be allowed to dream, because that would drive his chess forward. Today Moscow, tomorrow the world! And if it didn't work out, he would no doubt become a coach at the school. They had ten masters teaching there, including one young, 2600-rated player I briefly met who had evidently opted for guaranteed income over the exigent life of the full-time professional. But I found the sight of him sitting in a small room teaching a seven-year-old boy sad. This was surely beneath him. It was too early for this twentysomething grandmaster to have given up on his dream.

Trying to take a considered view of the state of chess in Russia was as tricky as assessing a complex position on the board. There were as many differing views as there were rival candidate moves. While admiring the continuing strength of the Russian pedagogic tradition, Tkachiev was pessimistic about the future of professional chess. He argued that the curse of computers and a lack of strategic direction on the part of FIDE were marginalising the game. 'Your book is nicely timed,' he had told me mordantly in one of his more sombre, end-of-career moments. 'In a way you are writing about a human activity which is doomed to disappear. We are becoming marginal. Even the most respected newspapers don't cover the biggest chess events any more.'

Elmira Mirzoeva, a woman grandmaster who worked as a reporter on chess and other sports in Moscow, agreed with

Tkachiev's pessimistic outlook. She felt chess was no longer part of family life as it had been in the Soviet Union. It was one thing to teach it in schools, but its real strength in the Soviet years was that one generation passed it on to the next. Like Tkachiev, she believed chess needed a revolution, with shorter time limits and greater audience engagement, ideally through a popular programme on television. 'Chess is going down,' she said. 'The salaries are going down. We have to make a business out of it.' Chess, she said, was a sport, and needed to be presented as such, with a competitive tennis-style structure rather than a series of prestigious closed tournaments involving the same band of a dozen or so elite players who get almost all the attention and, more importantly, all the money. 'At the moment we are neither sport nor culture. We don't really know who we are.' Again this echoed a point made by Tkachiev. 'My favourite newspaper in France, *Libération*, used to put chess in the sports section,' he had told me. 'Now we are between crosswords and the weather forecast. It's really hard to define what we are.'

I asked Mark Gluhovsky, who at the time we met was editor of the renowned Russian chess magazine *64*, how he saw the future of the game in the country. 'In the Soviet Union chess was hugely popular, but now it is less popular than it should be,' he said. 'Our chess life is based on the Soviet tradition. The people who love chess were the ones who studied chess when they were young, and now they are businessmen and have the money to help it. But in 20 years, when these people will not be doing it, there is a danger that chess in Russia will fade away. We have a lot of tournaments, a lot of sponsors, a lot of people who want to organise something, and we have a good federation which has the money to organise tournaments, but the base has got a lot smaller.' Gluhovsky thought that, despite the efforts of chess schools such as the one attached to the university, the emerging group of players in Russia was weaker than preceding generations, especially that glittering galaxy of players who emerged from the 1930s on and dominated world chess for the next 70 years (apart of course from that tumultuous period when Bobby Fischer halted the Soviet juggernaut). 'There were no other career paths in the Soviet Union,' he explained. 'Chess was a way to get famous and to acquire money. It was a very fair and meritocratic game. Usually the best player won. It was hard for Jewish people to succeed in other fields, but in chess they could do it. Now they can succeed in other fields.' People who would once have been outstanding chess players, he said, were becoming computer programmers. He suggested that the former Soviet republics of Armenia and Azerbaijan were closer to the old Soviet Union. There, chess was still seen as a route to social enhancement and a good living.

Gluhovsky, who was in his early forties when we met, said he missed the cultural environment of chess in the Soviet days. While the system had been designed to win at all costs, the players themselves were highly cultivated, as my encounter with Averbakh had demonstrated. 'They read and enjoyed music,' said Gluhovsky. 'They were interesting people and formed an interesting world. Botvinnik was a serious scientist; Bronstein was a genius and had an interesting opinion about everything. The new chess generation is not in the least bit interesting. The players are chess machines and have no culture, education or even life beyond chess. They don't read books. When I started out in chess, it was a magical world. There were giants like Tal and free spirits like Bronstein playing in wonderful settings – the House of Writers, the House of Scientists and so on. When they gave simuls (where a master plays a number of amateurs simultaneously) and lectures, many people would go to watch and listen.' Now, though aficionados followed games online, events were ill attended. What is a sport without a public? A mere pursuit. 'The names of the players are still vaguely known to the public, but they are not gods in the way they were in the Soviet Union,' Gluhovsky said, pointing to the tyranny of computers as a key factor in the marginalisation of chess. 'In the old days, journalists would ask grandmasters what was happening. Now, after the game, the grandmaster will ask the journalist what the computer said. That's boring for the journalist.'

What was clear from talking to Gluhovsky, Tkachiev and Averbakh was that the period from 1930 to 1990 was a unique era in which a certain set of conditions came together to make chess a culturally central activity. Soviet society was monochrome, leisure activities were few, chess was a cheap but intellectually demanding way of passing the time. It was a macho society in which men loved nothing better than spending hour after hour playing chess, cards, dominoes, backgammon, and drinking and smoking together – the relics of those days were still doing precisely that in their cold wooden pavilion in Gorky Park. The Soviet state wanted to dominate world chess to prove the efficacy of their system, and poured money and expertise into the game. Chess was a low-level version of the space race.

But there was now a paradox at the heart of Russian chess. While there were rich backers – chess was benefiting from the cult of the oligarchs – and plenty of glitzy tournaments, the number of social players was falling, the level of public interest was declining, and fewer ultra-strong young players were coming through. The game wasn't in the country's bloodstream any more. Russia's wealthy elite – or at least that part of it that liked chess and were willing to support it – could produce a semblance of health by staging glamorous tournaments such as the Tal and Alekhine Memorials. The chess schools churned out grandmasters, most of whom then joined the schools as trainers – a closed circle that in some ways made it less likely Russia would produce another world champion. And old men still played in Moscow parks and amid the chandeliered elegance of the Central Chess Club. But what I had witnessed was residual affection, not true, urgent love. I feared that the passion that had sustained chess in this part of the world for so long was spent. It was now all icing and no cake. The substance, the obsessiveness, the centrality of chess to life had gone. Genna Sosonko's evocative books about Soviet chess were, indeed, memorials to a vanished age, and I left Russia more fearful for the future of the game than when I arrived.

FILE F
Meet Me in St Louis

'You can only get good at chess if you love the game'
– Bobby Fischer, world champion 1972–75

FI: IN FISCHER'S SHADOW

 I had felt emotional as I flew out of Moscow. Tkachiev was out of town on the day I left – he was giving a simultaneous display in the autonomous republic of Ingushetia in the Caucasus. We had had a farewell dinner the night before in a smoky, self-consciously hip Chinese restaurant – how Russians love to flash the cash – and I had met his girlfriend, Irina. I even got to play chess against her, and was winning easily until Tkachiev stepped in, took over her horrible position and turned it round. Bloody grandmasters.

It had been hugely enjoyable spending time with the cosmopolitan, free-spirited Tkachiev. I loved his energy, drive and questioning nature. He was at times neurotic, and I could sense his love-hate relationship with chess. But what it had given him was freedom. He had travelled widely, spoke French and English well, and, like his hero David Bronstein, had views about everything. He was a chess player of the old school: intelligent, cultured, sceptical, seeking all sorts of truths. He told me I had to develop my own ideas about chess, and showed me an opening variation he had developed independently early in his career. It was, he said, a seminal moment because he felt he was adding to chess knowledge and developing his own theories on playing the game. He was echoing Lasker's argument that you had to think for yourself and not rely on received wisdom or rote learning. Above all I could see that, as a chess player and as an individual, he valued freedom, honesty, integrity. For all the racketiness of parts of his life he was a thoroughly decent person who cared about the state of chess and about the society in which he lived. The independence of mind he brought to chess he also applied to life. There was no wall between them. He showed me that to play well and to live well you had to have freedom from fear. Tkachiev, living every moment to the maximum and searching for the truth as intensely in life as he did in chess, had shown me how life should be lived.

A couple of weeks after getting back from Moscow, I was packing my bags again – this time for a three-week chess tour of the US, taking in New York (the spiritual home of American chess and the place where Bobby Fischer honed his talent), the US championships in St Louis and a big open tournament in Chicago in which I intended to play. Chess in the US, with its hustler culture and peculiarly structured tournaments, seemed on the surface very foreign to the European sensibility, and I was keen to get inside it. But most of all I wanted to hang out in Greenwich Village, play with the hobos in Washington Square, go to the Marshall Club in downtown New York, and commune with the ghost of the Brooklyn-born Fischer. It would be a world away from Russia, that much was certain.

When I was coming through John F. Kennedy airport, the immigration officer asked me the purpose of my visit. 'Chess,' I said. He asked me if I was playing and whether I expected to win. I would be playing a bit, I told him, but didn't expect to do well enough to win any money. 'Well, you certainly won't win anything if you have that attitude,' he told me. There, in a nutshell, was the American approach to chess: it was a war, not a beautiful diversion, and winning was everything. Fischer sought to dominate his opponents psychologically, to smash them off the board. It was the American way, and the New York way. If nothing else, I hoped my US tour would toughen me up.

My first port of call was Frank Brady, the *éminence grise* of American chess. He had just turned 80 when we met and was about to retire as professor of journalism at St John's University in New York. In a wonderfully varied career, of which chess has always been a part, he had run the US Chess Federation, been president of the legendary Marshall Club, worked for *Playboy*, written biographies of Orson Welles and Barbra Streisand, and been chairman of the communications department at St John's. My main reason for visiting Brady in his restful apartment on the Upper West Side, though, was that he had known Fischer when the strange, immensely talented boy from Brooklyn was growing up, written two highly regarded books about him – *Profile of a Prodigy*, published in 1965, when all things seemed possible, and *Endgame*, which appeared in 2011, three years after Fischer's death – and tried to make sense of his heart-breaking 36-year exile from chess.

'I first saw Fischer when I played in a tournament four blocks from here,' Brady told me. 'He was about 12. Somebody was kibitzing and Fischer said, "Please, let's have some quiet, this is a chess game." The man was silenced, this 60- or 70-year-old man. I realised he [Fischer] was really powerful.' They became friends and, in Brady's words, 'bounced around' together, often a little unpredictably. 'I can see myself walking down Fifth Avenue with Bobby heading towards the Marshall,' recalled Brady. 'We wanted to get something to eat, and so we're walking down Fifth Avenue and we're at about 13th Street. There was a Howard Johnson's on Sixth Avenue and I said we could eat there, but he said, "I don't want to go to Howard Johnson's tonight," although he liked it. "I want to go to so and so [Brady forgets where exactly]," and he just turned around and walked away.' Everything you hear and read about Fischer underlines his complete singlemindedness and implacability. It is what made him a champion chess player and an impossible human being.

In *Endgame* Brady relates a telling story of Fischer visiting the California home of the US grandmaster Walter Browne in the mid-1970s, at a time when there was still some hope that Fischer would play chess again. He had arranged to stay with Browne overnight and, after dinner, embarked on a four-hour long-distance phone conversation. Browne became perturbed by the bill Fischer was running up and suggested he terminate the call. Fischer was so offended that not only did he leave on the spot, he never spoke to Browne again. 'Fischer saw himself as a godlike character,' Brady told me, 'and everybody had to do what he wanted.' He was the chess player from heaven and the house guest from hell.

Brady had been advising Tobey Maguire, who was making a film of the Fischer–Spassky match – the movie, *Pawn Sacrifice*, surfaced a few months after Brady and I met. Maguire wanted to know how Fischer walked – 'rangy, like an athlete,' said Brady – and talked and moved the pieces. The fact that a movie was being made of Fischer's life underlined chess's problem. He remains box office. No one has come along to replace him, whatever the inflated claims made for the appeal of Magnus Carlsen. Fischer was difficult, unpredictable, brilliant, mesmerising; a genius and a madman. He had everything and many observers in the US say that, if he hadn't walked away from the sport after 1972, chess would have implanted itself on the American psyche far more forcibly. Fischer is both the blessing and the curse of US chess: even now, more than 40 years after he won the world title, he casts a long shadow. His is still the name the public know; his death in 2008 made front pages around the world; it is Fischer who is endlessly debated and memorialised on film. Fischer's rise and fall, and to a lesser extent Garry Kasparov's defeat by the Deep Blue supercomputer in 1997 (also being turned into a movie as I toured the US), were the only stories in town for the mainstream media. It was as if chess time had stood still.

I had met Fischer very briefly in Iceland in 2005, just after he had been deported from Japan. On the day after he arrived I attended a press conference, which turned out to be an extraordinary occasion, with Fischer switching between jokes (always followed by his trademark nervous, staccato laugh) and venomous attacks on his usual targets. The presence of an American sports journalist called Jeremy Schaap added a frisson. He was the son of Dick Schaap, a New Yorker who had been a close friend of the young Bobby but later declared Fischer to be mad. Fischer quickly made the connection (the TV channel Schaap was working for, sports broadcaster ESPN, may have hoped he would). 'I knew your father,' he drawled to the youthful, dark-haired Schaap. 'He rapped me very hard. He said I didn't have a sane bone in my body. I don't forget that. I hate to rap people personally, but his father many years ago befriended me, took me to see a Knicks games, acted kind of like a father figure, and then later, like a typical Jewish snake, he had the most vicious things to say about me.' Schaap snapped at that, saying, 'I don't know that you've done much here today really to disprove anything he said,' and walked out. All on camera. Maybe it was a made-for-TV set-up, maybe not, but it certainly chilled the air. Fischer groaned and there was a half-minute silence before a woman from Icelandic radio got things back on track with a question about whether Fischer liked herring. The human being started to emerge from under the baseball cap, then, bang, he was off again with another lengthy exposition of his intricately wrought, completely bonkers theories, usually rounded off with, 'It's all on the internet! Why don't you go look it up?'

Fischer displayed an obsession with detail that, to my non-medical eye, appeared autistic. When he delineated his suffering at the hands of the US and then the Japanese, every letter he had received was cited, dated, described exactly. His was a world of tiny details; it was the bigger picture that eluded him, so he fell back on one stupid overarching theory, the world Jewish conspiracy. Mastery of detail, obsessionalism, relentless concentration, the ability to shut out the world are advantages in chess; in life they can be a disaster, especially when there is no screen between what you say and what you think. The black-and-white world of chess he could handle; the Technicolor world of life was more problematic.

In *Profile of a Prodigy* Brady has a beautiful phrase to sum up his endlessly frustrating hero: 'If he is the rainbow, he is also the storm.' That captures Fischer perfectly: the games he has left us are things of clarity, beauty, deep logic; his role in popularising chess in the 1960s and 1970s was immense; and yet his endless arguments with officialdom and his withdrawal from the sport without defending his world championship also did great damage. He was lonely, fatherless, had an intense but double-edged relationship with his brilliant and especially eccentric mother Regina, and once he had achieved his goal of winning the world championship went off the rails, spending more than a decade as a recluse in California and then another 20 years wandering the world looking for God knows what before dying from a kidney complaint which he refused to have treated. It was a sort of suicide – first as a player, then as a man. The once implacable Fischer had no resistance left. That he should die at 64 – the number of squares on the chessboard – was the ultimate irony, as fitting as it was tragic. What a waste, yet what a life. No wonder it is Fischer's story that film-makers still want to tell.

F2: LIFE AT THE MARSHALL

Fischer was a regular at the Marshall Club, which is housed in the lower two storeys of a classic brownstone building in downtown New York. It is a fantastic location: close to fashionable Greenwich Village and just off ritzy Fifth Avenue. The property is worth millions – the club owns the whole building but lets out the upper floors – but was left to the club by the descendants of Frank Marshall, who dominated American chess in the first third of the 20th century and played a match against Emanuel Lasker for the world title in 1907 (Lasker annihilated him). Without the bedrock of this building the club would most likely have suffered the same fate as its illustrious midtown rival, the Manhattan Club, which closed in 2002 after a 125-year history. The Manhattan was the second oldest chess club in the US, after the Mechanics' Institute in San Francisco, but that wasn't enough to save it from New York real estate prices. Having its own property gives the Marshall security and a place in the local, chess-savvy community. It has a full-time manager, several support staff, 500 members, is open every day, and has tournaments most evenings and at weekends. GMs and IMs hang out there and give lessons; lots of amateurs seem more or less to live there – I went about five times and kept seeing the same faces; if you played at the Marshall and in Washington Square Park, just around the corner, where the chess hustlers are looking for victims from dawn to dusk, you could not help but get strong. I immediately sensed my week in New York was going to be too short. I needed to spend a summer here, to imbibe all the Village wisdom – and whisky.

Chess in New York does not, I quickly realised, subscribe to Pietro Carrera's 'live well, play well' dictum. I played a tournament one Sunday at the Marshall, and my first opponent was a Russian called Sam who told me later he had drunk a bottle of vodka just before the game. This may have explained why he kept falling asleep at the board. On paper he was much stronger than me – his US rating was well above 2000 – and he launched an attack which threatened to blow me away. But the vodka kicked in, he failed to calculate with sufficient precision, I picked up a few pawns and had what should have been a won endgame. But he was sober enough to keep fighting, had a lot more time left on the clock – despite his somnambulism, he had still played a lot quicker than me – and we eventually agreed a draw. Afterwards we analysed the game with another very strong player. 'You're wasting time,' the latter, who was rated more than 2300, told Sam at certain points in the game when he thought a move had been weak. 'But life is a waste of time,' said Sam, simply and sadly.

Despite the fact that the weather on this Sunday was glorious – the winter had been cold and wet and this was one of the first warm, sparkling days of spring – 21 players had shown up to play four rapidplay games at a cost of $20 to members and $40 to interlopers like me. First prize was $120. Not much, but money is money, and from the way the players talked I could tell the cash was important, both practically and symbolically. For one thing it legitimised spending eight hours playing chess in the basement of the Marshall Club on a gorgeous spring day.

This was an open event and I was one of the lowest-rated players. There were two international masters playing, two FIDE masters, and two-thirds of the field could be called experts – with a US rating of 2100 or above. I realised I might get hammered, especially as I had got hammered the night before drinking absinthe in a Russian bar in the East Village and was feeling distinctly under the weather. But my good fortune in meeting someone who was in even worse condition than me in the first round encouraged me. I was on the scoresheet; I would not make zero; I had already avoided abject humiliation.

In the second round – this was what in the US is called a 'Game 45' tournament, with each player getting 45 minutes – I came up against a very good player: a veteran called James West who was rated 2200, had written books on opening theory and who was, I discovered later, a fixture on the New York chess circuit. He had a greying beard, which he stroked from time to time; his jacket was a little threadbare; he sighed a good deal (even though I didn't give him much to sigh about), and made a point of always staying a few minutes ahead on the clock just in case. He played the King's Indian Defence, and of course knew it back to front. After 15 moves my position was horrible; after 20 I was a pawn down and as good as lost. I wished he had been out on a bender with Sam the night before, but I could see he wasn't that kind of a guy: he was very businesslike, clearly lived for chess and loved to win. I had heard him earlier telling the story of defeating a grandmaster in a tournament being played in a hotel, and coming out of the lobby afterwards and finding the GM beating his head against the wall. He wasn't boasting; just telling it matter of factly. Chess does strange things to people – and especially to players who try to make a living from the game – was his point.

My game against West improved after move 20. More and more I was finding that I needed adversity to free me up. Also I realised that my real strength – if this solitary beacon in a sea of weakness could be called that – was the middle game, where I could randomise the play. Doc Saunders had been right all along. I didn't know the openings in any depth and my technique was unlikely ever to be great, but I did occasionally have ideas. I could turn my lack of theory to my advantage and play a kind of anti-theory. I needed to keep the pieces on the board, create complications, and not let more experienced players simply out-technique me. That's what I tried to do against West and, though he was never in great difficulty, the game carried on for another 30 moves, he did a lot more sighing and beard stroking, and once or twice it almost looked as if I might equalise. OK, in the end I lost, but it was a decent game, and afterwards I could walk down West 10th Street with him and two other players from the tournament to get a slice of lunchtime pizza on Sixth Avenue and hold my head up. I had not been crushed. I was a New York chess player.

But boy was I tired. There were two more games between 3 and 7.30pm, and I have no idea how I got through them. The first – against a pleasant, balding young man – became very wild and complex. We both made illegal moves in time trouble – the time control was 40 minutes with a five-second increment, so in theory you should be able to avoid a loss on time – which meant calling the arbiter and incurring a two-minute penalty. There were moments in this game when I felt I was going mad. One of the juniors in a parallel tournament for lower-rated players was sniffing constantly and I was desperate for someone to tell him to blow his nose; Russian Sam was playing on the table next to me, chattering to himself, commenting on other people's games, and behaving more and more erratically; a man with dreadlocks was sitting close by, playing while listening to music through large headphones; and then, when it scarcely seemed possible that things could get more distracting, a cockroach appeared, causing several juniors to squeal while others tried to stamp on it as it scurried round the room.

Somehow, amid the mayhem, I played on in an increasingly desperate and double-edged position. Thanks to the resetting of our clocks caused by the illegal moves, ours was the last game to finish, and – the cockroach dealt with – a gaggle of other players gathered to watch. I appeared to have the edge, but had underestimated my opponent's counter-attack and now I was under pressure. Activity, the much-vaunted initiative, is everything in these time scrambles. I almost went wrong and was within a whisker of playing a move which would have lost my queen, but saw the danger just in time – the seconds the arbiter spent resetting the clock gave me an undeserved breathing space – and I found a way to draw with a perpetual check. Once again my honour had been saved, and now I had one point from three, which in this company I felt was satisfactory, though no doubt the man at immigration (and Conquest and Tkachiev, too) would criticise my lack of ambition.

In the final game, against another man with a threadbare shirt who shook a lot as he played his moves, I had nothing left to give. Playing black I resorted to my tedious Scandinavian defence, played boringly and eventually made a draw. My opponent seemed pleased with the game, but I thought it was dull and devoid of ideas. The draw meant I had 1.5/4 and came joint 12th out of 21, with a US Chess Federation rating (thought to be 50 or 100 points higher than the FIDE rating) across the tournament of 1918. Considering my tiredness and the sniffing and the cockroach and the strangeness of playing in New York against hardened Marshallites, I didn't feel that was too bad.

On one of my visits to the Marshall I played a couple of blitz games (at $5 a throw) against New York chess legend Asa Hoffmann. Hoffmann, who was in his early seventies when we met and had recently married, had been on the New York chess scene for more than half a century. He told me he had learned to play chess at the age of three and had never stopped playing. Hoffmann also played numerous other board and card games; he said he liked any game where there was no risk of personal injury. A 2300-level player and FIDE master, he had hustled all his life, and combined chess with book-dealing and bric-a-brac selling. When we met, he had been to some New York flea market and come back with an obscure 19th-century travel book which he tried to sell to me. Playing a few games against him was a necessary New York rite of passage. I lost them both, but had a good position in the second game and with more time might have managed a win.

Afterwards Hoffmann showed me round the club – including the famous table at which Capablanca and Fischer both played – and talked in his rapid, rasping New York accent about his life in chess. I asked him if it was harder to earn a living now than it had been 20 years before. 'As a player it was always impossible,' he said. 'You have to teach. I won a lot of money playing in streets and parks and clubs. I won all the money that I made in chess – $5,000 at a time – playing blitz. I was a very good blitz player. I'm not playing so much now. I'm much older than I look – two weeks older than Fischer.' Hoffmann likened himself to a small-time professional gambler, and said the odds were poor these days as the competition – fuelled by all the eastern European players who had come to the US – was very strong and the prizes very small. He said he had a dictum: 'You can play against strong players for big stakes, or weak players for small stakes, but never play against strong players for small stakes.' He saw the latter as a waste of time: exhausting, attritional tournaments that, even if you managed to win, would net you very little. The fall of the Berlin Wall was tough for chess pros in the west, producing a flood of eastern European rivals who suddenly made earning a living much more difficult.

One of the many attractions of the Marshall is that it has a pleasant walled garden at the back – a rarity in New York – and there, one evening, I spent a couple of hours talking to grandmaster Andrew Soltis, a multiple champion of the club and author of *What It Takes to Become a Chess Master*, among many acclaimed books. Soltis never attempted to survive on the pittance most GMs earn. He spent his career working as a journalist on the *New York Post*, and fitted in his chess around it. 'I was never tempted to try to be a professional player,' he told me. 'The money is ridiculously low, and when the Russians started coming to the United States the competition was strong. Also I had a position [at the *Post*] that I liked, so I had the best of all possible worlds.' Soltis, who is disarmingly sane, is one of those rare grandmasters who enjoyed holding down a regular job. He doesn't think his play suffered by not playing as a pro: 'I got as far as my talent would get me. If I'd worked harder [at chess] I might have increased my playing strength by 50 points. If I'd gotten to be a 2550 player [his best FIDE rating] when I was starting out [in the 1960s] that would have been terrific, but by the late 70s and early 80s it was nothing.' He gave up playing in tournaments in 2002, but said he missed it and was now thinking about resuming, having retired from the *Post* shortly before we met.

Soltis played Bobby Fischer once, in a rapidplay game at the Manhattan Club, and said that at one point he was winning, though eventually the legend prevailed. The last time he saw him was shortly after the Fischer–Spassky match, when the new world champion was being feted at City Hall. I asked Soltis for his take on Fischer's disappearance from chess. 'He was terrified of losing,' he said emphatically. 'He was certifiable. A lot of players are marginal, but Fischer was ...' He never quite found the word, but crazy will probably do. 'My theory about Fischer is that in a lot of ways he was the reverse of his mother. His mother was into publicity whereas he was impossible to communicate with; his mother was anti-religion whereas he was always shopping around for a religion.'

Soltis was hopeful about the future of chess in the US, but a little worried about what life held for the pros, especially as they got older: 'One of the problems with chess is that no one's figured out what to do with players over the age of 40. Nobody goes into chess with the idea that they're going to reach the age of 40. They assume they'll become world champion and then their problems will disappear.' He paints a sad picture of ageing players slogging round open tournaments trying to earn a few thousand dollars: 'Chess is a great calling, but it's a terrible job. The idea that if you don't win this endgame you're not going to eat is just horrible.'

F3: BROOKLYN'S CHESS FACTORY

 One bright morning during my stay in New York, I took the subway out to Brooklyn to visit the Eugenio Maria de Hostos Intermediate School, where they take chess very seriously and mass-produce 14-year-olds with very handy ratings. The coach at the school, which usually goes under the more functional name of IS318, is Elizabeth Spiegel, a strong player who is reckoned to be the most inspirational chess teacher in New York. I watched her in action in a succession of classes, and was amazed by her energy and ability to galvanise children of vastly different levels of interest and ability.

The school teaches children between the ages of 11 and 14. Quite a few of them have already been playing at elementary school – scholastic chess is very well organised and deep rooted in New York – and many have opted to come to IS318, which is situated in a challenging part of Brooklyn, because of its reputation. It has won a host of national chess titles, its corridors are stuffed with trophies, and in 2012 it was the subject of an award-winning documentary called *Brooklyn Castle*, which traced a year in the life of five members of the team who won the national high school championship. When I met Spiegel, she told me the documentary was being remade as a feature film by chessophile producer Scott Rudin, though she would not be drawn on who she would like to portray her. The school's strongest players are rated around 1900 – not world-beaters but pretty strong for 12- and 13-year-olds. I played a couple of games against two groups of children and lost both.

Taking chess at the school is voluntary, and it tends to be the boys who opt for it. 'That's something I struggle with,' said Spiegel. 'The funny thing is that of our top four players two are girls, so when the girls do it they do it well. But they don't tend to do it very often.' Some of the best players are far from academic in other ways, demonstrating that there is little correlation between orthodox educational achievement and chess talent. Good chess players are often original thinkers and natural rebels. Conformists make very bad players. Everyone can spot a conformist's moves. Spiegel explained why schools liked to build chess into their curriculum: 'It's seen as developing pure analytical thinking. It makes thinking relevant in a certain way. There's a way in which school is totally irrelevant to everything you do, and for kids it's nice to have a game where if you think, you win, and if you don't think, you lose, because it makes thinking seem important. It also teaches children consequences; they see a chain of cause and effect.'

While I was at the school I met John Galvin, assistant principal, head of the chess programme and a keen 1600-level player who, like me, can never work out why he doesn't improve – 'I study a fair amount and I play a fair amount and I don't get any better,' he said. 'I'm just perplexed by that.' Galvin was in his room working while half a dozen youngsters were sitting nearby on their lunch break playing a wild chess variant called Bughouse, which involves two teams playing on adjacent boards. Chess variants are hugely popular with players at all levels – GMs are, of course, brilliant Bughouse players – but I tended to give them a wide berth. I was having enough trouble mastering mainstream chess, without getting diverted down the game's many tributaries.

Galvin gave me a quick rundown of chess at IS318: 'We have probably the largest scholastic programme in the United States in terms of the number of serious players we produce. My role is to manage the programme. I do a little bit of teaching and take the team to tournaments at weekends. Elizabeth is the heart and soul of the teaching programme and does some of the management. I do most of the management and a little bit of teaching.' I asked him why chess was so strong in New York schools, and he had a novel theory: 'In New York athletic opportunities are a little more limited due to the physical nature of the city. You don't have as many open spaces and soccer pitches. They just don't exist. Chess is a game you can play at a very high level at a very low cost. New York City has a long tradition as a centre for chess. It's an immigrant community, so a lot of European immigrants who came over brought the game with them, especially the big Russian community here.' He said many top players had gravitated to New York because there were opportunities for private coaching, and the city was now a hub for scholastic chess. He estimated that a third of the children who played in the national championship were from New York.

I asked the Bughouse players what they liked about chess. 'It's fun,' said one. 'I like to crush my opponent,' said another. The spirit of Bobby Fischer, who enjoyed seeing his opponents squirm, is alive and well in Brooklyn. I made the mistake of playing blitz against these boys, and while I wasn't crushed I did lose on time. I could at no point cope with the New York love of blitz, losing games at the Marshall, in the parks and here at the school. My brain just didn't work fast enough.

It matters to Spiegel that she works for a public (i.e. non-private) school, and by winning national titles can demonstrate that children from under-privileged backgrounds can succeed. 'I believe in public education,' she said. She could make a good deal more money and work in a less demanding environment by taking private pupils, but prefers to stay at this challenging, high-energy school in Brooklyn. Sometimes chess seems far removed from the real world – that, indeed, is part of its appeal – but in New York it is at the heart of the city, in the parks, at the open-all-hours Marshall and here in the schools. Chess is wonderfully classless and democratic, and nowhere is that better exemplified than in New York, where even the poorest and most marginalised can be kings if they have what it takes.

F4: THE VIEW FROM WASHINGTON SQUARE

 I enjoyed playing at the Marshall, but what I really loved about New York was playing in the parks. There is a chess and checkers area in Central Park, but I was told it was moribund, so gave it a miss. There is a new chess venue in Bryant Park in Midtown, where neat chess tables are laid out for office workers and you can borrow a clock from an attendant. I had a handful of games here and won them all – the King of Bryant Park! But the real action is Downtown – in the parks in Union Square and, most famously of all, Washington Square.

I played first in Union Square, where the chess players – almost all black or Hispanic – hang out in one corner of the square. On a sunny Saturday morning, with a bustling market nearby, it's a friendly, busy spot, and there are a dozen or so players anxious to relieve you of some money. Most of the hustlers in Union Square are not really hustlers at all. They won't play you for money. Instead they ask for a three-dollar 'donation' for a game, as if they were giving you a chess lesson. Most, though, are not strong enough to give lessons, and I won my first game with ease. Many of the park players are jobless or homeless and pick up chess as a way of making a few dollars. My first opponent, Fred, told me he was a retired counsellor, and had taken up chess as his new occupation. The park players learn from each other and gradually get stronger, but the general level is not especially high. I won about a third of my games, even though we were playing five-minute blitz at which the hustlers, many of whom play fast rather than well, were more adept than me.

'I need a chess player, I need a chess player.' The hustlers sit on crates, hunched over their boards, calling out for passers-by to take them on. 'Why go walking by the way? Stay to play some chess today,' one called out. I won a game and lost another against a middle-aged Hispanic man called Mr Moustache, one of the stronger players in Union Square. I hit on the idea of paying my donation only if I lost, which mostly they accepted. 'How much do you earn from playing?' I asked him. 'I try to make enough to eat,' he replied. Later I overheard one hustler complaining he'd made virtually nothing despite sitting in the park all day – I thought his rather sullen countenance might be a factor. The player to whom he was speaking said he had managed $42. They sit there from around midday until nightfall. This may be a business, but it is not a lucrative one.

I played a couple of games against a large, loud black man called Twitty – or 'Twitty from the City', to give him his full title. He gave himself white in the first game. 'How come you're taking white?' I asked him. 'Cos I'm tired of being black,' he countered without missing a beat. He was full of practised one-liners. 'How strong are you?' I asked him. 'I can lift 350lb,' he said. And he probably could, judging by the size of his neck. He told me he worked in airport security at night and played park chess in the day. It was not clear when he slept, but then no one sleeps in New York. Twitty was a pretty good – and very fast – player, beating me in both games and telling me off for what he said was misuse of the clock when I was in time trouble. 'You gotta use the same hand to move and to hit the clock,' he admonished me. Park chess, like blitz in Moscow, is not for fainthearts.

After half a dozen games in Union Square I was desperate for a coffee, but finding one at the organic market that occupied one side of the square was far from easy. There were handmade, hearth-baked European breads, naturally colourful eggs and wild mushrooms; there was 'bee wild' honey, heritage pork and chicken raised seasonally on pasture ('never frozen!'); but there was absolutely no coffee. In the end I had to go to Starbucks. When I got back to the chess, the players' corner had been colonised by a group of Hare Krishna devotees (including a small child) chanting, an all-women dance troupe clad in orange, and a man holding up a placard emblazoned with 'FREE HUGS'. It was a tourist-thronged New York Saturday morning and all a bit overwhelming. I decided it was time to move on to Washington Square where, according to one of the Union Square hustlers, the players were 'slimier'.

The scene there was equally bizarre. A young man was busking on an upright piano – playing Beethoven's Hammerklavier sonata and Chopin mazurkas and shouting 'AWESOME' at the end of every piece. He was good, and entertaining a crowd of 30 or so, but I did wonder what happened to the piano when it rained, which it did later in the afternoon. The chess players were out in force, and I played some games against a middle-aged man called David, who told me he had come to New York from Venezuela in 1985 and learned to play chess in a homeless shelter. He was pretty good – FIDE 1800, something of that order, I would guess – and clearly loved the game. When he wasn't playing, he would look at positions from a well-thumbed paperback he was reading – Alexander Khalifman's *Life and Games*. I played David for $2 a game and asked for a ten-minute control. He won three, I won two, so he made $2 for about an hour and a half's play, but they were nice games and we enjoyed each other's company. I asked him where he lived and he pointed to a nearby shopping trolley. All he had to show for 30 years living in New York was in the trolley. In the summer he slept in or near the park; in the winter he went back to the homeless shelters. His life was chess. He was the ultimate chess pro. To eat he needed to win chess games. Lots and lots of them.

A week began to feel like a month and, coming in and out of the park every day, Washington Square became my home from home when I was in New York. I loved hanging out there and trying my luck against the hustlers, who were more serious than in Union Square. There was always something fascinating to observe, including one man who was playing while carrying a 12-foot python. My biggest victory was against a tall, highly articulate black man who had beaten me earlier in the week in a couple of blitz games. I challenged him to a game at a longer time control, and he agreed if we could play for $10. I messed up the opening and he was the exchange (rook for knight) up within 20 moves, but then he got bored and careless and I got back into the game. By move 40, he was losing and becoming very agitated, telling me to speed up and saying long games were dull. Eventually, with a grimace, he turned over his king to signify defeat, but there was no sign of my $10. The hustlers are reluctant payers, but it's hard to make an issue of it as this is their livelihood and they are earning a pittance. I let it ride and agreed to play a return match under blitz conditions, which he won easily. I didn't try too hard: I felt I had made my point in the first game and this was just to square the money side of things.

In Fred Waitzkin's book *Searching for Bobby Fischer*, the author's son Josh – who went on to become a teenage prodigy and an international master at 16 – learns to play in Washington Square. Waitzkin paints an affecting picture of the hustlers in the park, and in particular one of its denizens, the Latvian IM Israel Zilber, who by the time the Waitzkins ran into him was suffering from severe mental problems. 'Thirty years ago, Zilber had beaten the brilliant Mikhail Tal, who would soon become world champion, for the championship of Latvia, and some of his games appear in evergreen collections of great chess games,' writes Waitzkin. 'But these days in the park, he offered chess players and tourists a choice: for a dollar he would pose for a photograph or play you a game of chess. Each game he played, no matter how powerful or pitiful the opposition, he scribbled in Russian notation on a napkin or an old envelope. At night he slept on a bench, his most valued possessions stuffed under his shirt and a few dollars rolled into a sock or an empty cigarette box.' *Innocent Moves*, the 1993 film based on the book, also portrayed life in the park, though the Hollywood version was a good deal more crowded and threatening than I encountered. Maybe that reflects the changing face of New York over the past couple of decades.

When it rained some of the Washington Square players sought refuge in the narrow back room of Chess Forum on Thompson Street in the West Village. There used to be two competing chess shops on either side of the road, and they fought a lengthy war for precedence. Eventually the Village Chess Shop closed, leaving Chess Forum to rule the roost. A young man in Washington Square told me chess was also played at the Zinc Bar in the West Village, but when I went along there was no chess, just a poetry reading. There was plenty of chess in Chess Forum: a dozen men doing noisy battle. Seniors paid a dollar an hour to sit there; everyone else paid $5. It irritated me that the young man at the counter charged me the senior rate. I realised New York was taking its toll, but this was ridiculous. Did I really look 65?

Two of the men playing in Chess Forum virtually came to blows, arguing over every move. 'Chess is a wargame,' declared one, to justify his bellicose attitude. What was remarkable was that, though every game descended into anarchy and shouting, once it was over and the dust had settled the two of them started all over again, much to the consternation of the other players in the shop who were hoping for slightly quieter conditions. I played against an Italian, who was visiting New York with his family and had left them shopping at Macy's while he sloped off to enjoy some chess. I won three games and drew the other, playing the best chess I managed in my stay in New York. He was immensely civilised and didn't really fit the New York chess scene, with its raucous running commentary on how the game was going. The hustlers are happy to use every trick in the book – and a few more besides – to undermine their opponents psychologically. I played one man in Washington Square who stopped the clock a couple of times to point out what I should have played. Maybe he thought he was being helpful, but the tactic also had the effect of unsettling me. I lost all my games against him on an evening that cost me $22.

I was in the park so often that the players in Washington Square got to know me and were very friendly – in part no doubt because I was a ready source of cash. When it was time to leave New York, I took one final walk in the park at dusk, when just a few players were left making moves under the lamps. David was still there and I waved. His life off the board was a never-ending struggle, yet part of me envied his freedom. Life reduced to a chessboard and a few possessions in a shopping trolley.

F5: THE CHESS PHILANTHROPIST

 I had timed my visit to the US to coincide with the American chess championships, which were being played in St Louis in the middle two weeks of May. I had planned to be there for most of the second week, but rain and thunderstorms in the Midwest meant I was delayed for two days in New York because all flights were cancelled. Not a bad place to be held up, of course: drinking all night in the Village and playing chess all day in Washington Square. Eventually I got a flight, albeit with a three-hour detour via Houston, and reached St Louis – the new hotbed of chess in the US and declared the country's chess capital in the Senate just before I arrived – late on Saturday, with three rounds of the championship left.

The rapid rise of St Louis's chess status is all down to the work – and more importantly the money – of one man: chess-loving billionaire Rex Sinquefield, who has ploughed millions into building a plush chess club in an upscale part of St Louis, paid for the transfer of the World Chess Hall of Fame from Miami – it is located just across the street from the club – and puts up serious prize money for the US championships. After years in the doldrums, the event is worth winning again: the winner of the championship gets $45,000; the women's champion wins $20,000. Twelve male GMs were battling it out in the Championship; ten top female American players were going head to head for the women's crown.

The championships were being played on the second floor of the club in front of a handful of spectators. Downstairs and on tables outside, lots of members of the St Louis club – it has more than 1,000 – were playing casual games. I must have played about 30 blitz games in the course of my three days in St Louis and won about two-thirds. But my blitz play remained uninspired, and anyone with a US Chess Federation rating of more than 1850 I found tough. It was a relaxing, fun place to sit and play chess, soaking up the sun, and I liked these club players a lot. They were sharp, funny, played hardball but were happy to laugh at their failings. The club, which was open from 10am till 10pm every day, was rapidly becoming a chess hub, a kind of Marshall Club with serious money. Resident grandmasters were employed to teach and give lessons; top players – including the US number one Hikaru Nakamura – had relocated to the city; and Sinquefield's largesse was underwriting a large educational programme. In the US everywhere you go chess is presented as an educational tool first, a diversion for perennial time-wasters second.

Mike Wilmering, the club's young, super-enthusiastic communications executive (one of an overall staff of a dozen or more), explained Sinquefield's purpose: 'His vision is to revitalise the US chess scene. This all started when he retired back to St Louis. He was born and raised here, was very successful in the financial world, and when he came back he wanted to play some chess.' Dissatisfied with the dingy rooms in shopping malls in which he found St Louis's chess players meeting, Sinquefield decided to create the fanciest chess club in the world. It made me wonder if one day a billionaire might walk into Asda on the A3 when Kingston Chess Club was playing a match against Wallington and make a similar commitment.

'What we've established here is unlike what anyone else in the country is doing,' said Wilmering. 'There are other chess clubs; there are other chess-in-the-schools programmes; and there are other people organising tournaments. But no one is doing all three together in the same package.' He admitted the challenge was huge: 'Chess needs new blood and a more widespread following, which is why we do a live show on the US championships' – an impressive, state-of-the-art broadcast that treats chess like baseball or basketball, playing up the drama, pressure and excitement.

St Louis is a baseball-obsessed city – everyone wears the bright red Cardinals gear and they were playing the Atlanta Braves in the stadium next to my downtown hotel on the day I arrived. I couldn't help contrasting the baseball mania – the metro was flooded with fans after the game – with the 60 or so aficionados who had turned up for the chess, in part lured by a free buffet in the commentary room, a big incentive for some of the more down-at-heel chess club members. Wilmering, a big baseball fan, accepted the vast difference in scale between the two venerable sports, but refused to be downhearted: 'We're never going to sell out a stadium to the tune of 40,000 a day, but it's growing in popularity and a lot of that is because of the scholastic, grassroots movement you see.'

The following day I got to meet Sinquefield himself, an unassuming man who was then approaching 70, dressed in the obligatory billionaire gear of shorts and baseball cap. Sinquefield was a hedge-fund pioneer, though he dislikes the term 'hedge fund' and prefers to talk about 'efficient markets' and 'financial optimisation'. In 1981 he co-founded the California-based wealth management company Dimensional Fund Advisors, which has built up an asset base of $400bn, and retired in 2005 saying he was bored. Sinquefield is a fiscal conservative and a major Republican donor. His father died when Sinquefield was five, leaving the family destitute, and he and his brother spent their early years in a Catholic orphanage in St Louis. He made it; why can't everyone else? The American Dream lives – in the mind of Rex Sinquefield at least.

Sinquefield was a little tight-lipped when we met over lunch – maybe my liberal *Guardian* background disturbed him – but his love for chess was manifest. Though not a very strong player (his USCF grade is around 1600), he told me he played every day online and, as we ate, he avidly followed the broadcast commentary rigged up in the neighbouring bar. 'I wanted to learn as a child, but didn't find anyone to teach me until I was 13,' he explained, in his flat monotone. 'My uncle Fred taught me and I beat him the second game that we played. I always felt a little bad about that.' He started studying the game and then discovered Bobby Fischer, a collection of whose books and papers he had recently bought at auction. Sinquefield told me his real interest in founding the club was to teach local children how to play and to provide a welcoming space for chessophiles. He recalled once driving to a local venue looking for a game and finding a small knot of people playing who just ignored him: 'I felt thoroughly rejected and turned around and left.' He vowed that his club would be open, friendly and hospitable, which indeed it is. Subscription rates are low, so anyone can join; even registered Democrats can join. Rich and poor trade blows (metaphorically speaking, of course) across the board, half the members are students, and there is a moving plaque to a member who died a couple of years ago of pancreatic cancer. It is everything most hole-in-the-corner chess clubs aren't: the sort of club that existed a century ago but no longer seems to be able to sustain itself.

The club opened its doors in the summer of 2008 and has hosted the last six US championships. The Hall of Fame came a couple of years later, and Sinquefield has added a big art-and-chess dimension to it. When I visited there was a fascinating re-creation of the musical chess set created by composer John Cage and artist Marcel Duchamp, in which the moves made interact with music on a continuous loop to create new sounds, the uniqueness of each game producing infinitely varied musical tracks. 'We intend to make it a destination spot for art,' said Sinquefield. His chess coach, the former US women's champion Jennifer Shahade, is interested in the performance art possibilities and in the way Duchamp was able seamlessly to combine chess as game and art. She thinks this could be a means of both expanding chess's appeal and shaking off its nerdy image.

Sinquefield said that, in terms of its membership, the club had grown organically. 'We never advertised for members. They just came out of the woodwork, truly like roaches. The first two or three years we were over 700. Now we're over a thousand. We're the largest chess membership club in the country and we've never advertised.' This is the folksy Sinquefield, but I suspect he can be a little sharp when the urge takes him. You can't make a fortune in business without having an edge. When I asked whether he now saw himself as 'giving something back', he bridled: 'That phrase "giving back" has always bothered me,' he said tartly, 'because it implies that you took something inappropriately and now you're returning it. That certainly isn't the case.'

I got a sneak preview of an exhibition on Fischer that was being prepared at the Hall of Fame. Most of the material came from the auction lot bought by Sinquefield – books and papers that had been held in store by Fischer in Pasadena and forfeited when he failed to pay rent on the storage unit. The museum's assistant curator, Emily Allred, walked me round the exhibits and it was thrilling (even wearing the obligatory white gloves) to touch the early manuscripts that, after much labour in the mid-1960s, eventually became Fischer's *My 60 Memorable Games*. The early manuscripts are variously titled *My Life in Chess*, *52 Tournament Games* and *My Memorable Games* – all staging posts on the way to the iconic title. It was fascinating to look at Fischer's annotations on the scripts: his writing is child-like, his spelling erratic, sometimes so much so – 'engame' for endgame, 'quicly' for quickly – that I wondered whether he was dyslexic. He was, of course, a great fiddler with proofs – the chess equivalent of James Joyce, for whom each set of page proofs was an opportunity for a new set of thoughts. Fischer was so implacable – in publishing as in chess – that at least one publisher withdrew.

The collection includes the books of openings that Fischer prepared for his match with Spassky in 1972 and a book of all Spassky's games in which Fischer had ticked off the games he had analysed. There are also letters back and forth about Fischer's possible participation in the Piatigorsky Cup in 1966. Chess philanthropist Jacqueline Piatigorsky is friendly, encouraging, admiring; Fischer respectful but demanding about money and other conditions. The Fischer that withdrew from competitive chess in the mid-1970s is there ten years earlier, fully formed. The saddest part of the show is the collection of books from friends and admirers that kept on arriving through the 1970s, inscribed to Fischer. It seems his interest in chess had not diminished: there is evidence he read the books and even put some games on to floppy discs to run on early computers. He still loved the game, but for some reason – fear, cussedness, madness perhaps – he wouldn't play any more. What a loss. Even out here in St Louis, with its fabulous new chess facility, the ghost of Fischer lingers, casting its sombre shadow.

F6: CLOCKED BY BIG BEN

While I was in St Louis, I met Ben Finegold, a funny, fast-talking, larger-than-life figure who was resident grandmaster at Sinquefield's club for a while and is still a fixture there. He agreed to play a game with me and give me a few tips about my play, but first he gave me a résumé of his career. Finegold said that he had played hundreds of tournament games a year as a youngster, and didn't care how many he lost: 'I loved chess and if I lost it didn't matter to me. That's the main thing you have to do to get better at chess – if you lose hundreds of games in a row, that's OK.' Eventually something sticks. 'Between nine and 19 I got much better every year, and by the time I graduated high school I was 2400 and decided I was going to play chess.'

Finegold didn't go to university, started playing professionally, followed his girlfriend – a woman's international master who worked for the Grandmasters' Association – to Belgium and played chess all over Europe. In 1992 he moved back to the US, playing mainly in opens and not worrying that he had yet to gain the necessary norms – performance ratings in high-ranking tournaments that have to be achieved before a player is awarded the master title – to become a grandmaster. 'I didn't care,' he said. 'I knew I was GM strength. Everyone else knew I was GM strength. Most players are like, "I've got to get this norm and that norm and the other norm," but I didn't want to pay $1,000 to play in a chess tournament where I might get a norm. I just wanted to play chess. My US rating was over 2600, my FIDE was over 2500, and I was an IM. I was a strong IM rather than a weak GM.' He did eventually become a GM at the age of 40, but said he was no stronger when he got the title than he had been in his early twenties. Finegold is the sort of man who takes life as it comes and, while happy to have got the title, is not one of those players for whom it is the pinnacle of existence. The child who didn't mind losing hundreds of games has become the expert who still likes to play for fun – and to earn enough to get through the day.

The more chess players I met, the more I realised that freedom was the key – to their lives and their chess. Finegold was another of nature's rebels and in chess had found a passion to sustain his fast, counter-intuitive mind. He had no intention of stepping back from the game, and when I raised the rival examples of Hans Ree and Genna Sosonko – one of whom played on in the face of decline while the other quit – he said he would definitely fall into the Hans Ree camp: 'I'm not going to stop. I know I'm getting weaker [he was 44 when we met and said he could feel his powers starting to diminish], and that's the way life goes. But I like playing chess. I'll still be able to beat strong players sometimes.'

Finegold described his style of play as boring. 'I like to get my opponent out of their preparation and play chess. I like to not trade, to play really boring, outplay my opponents slowly and take advantage of mistakes they make. I'm a big believer in mistakes. I don't make mistakes and you do. That's what I hope. I'm not trying to overpower or make threats. I'm just being solid.' In the game we were about to play I told him he had nothing to fear – there would be mistakes aplenty on my side of the board. He let me take white and I played Queen's Gambit, which I was still employing with white despite Doc Saunders' doubts. All was fine for about 12 moves, then my central pawns got into a tangle and after that I was suffering. As I made errors – an incorrect pawn push here, a misplaced piece there – he told me where I was going wrong. It must have been tedious for him, but he did it with good grace.

'I figure out what I want to do and what you want to do,' he said. 'Most lower-rated players don't figure out what their opponent wants to do. That's their big weakness.' He explained what sort of pawn structure he hoped to achieve, where he wanted to place his knights, and what he thought my best two plans were. He was trying to build a complete picture of the position and of where the game was going, whereas I was just trying to hang on. He told me to try to be flexible; not to get hooked on a particular plan but to try to respond to what was happening across the board. It was like trying to keep 32 plates spinning at once; eventually one was sure to come crashing to the ground. Early in the game, he pointed out that my king lacked defenders and that one day that might come back to haunt me. Sure enough, 15 or so moves later his queen and rooks ganged up to bear down on the king. He had had a long-range plan in the back of his mind but was willing to change course if the game dictated it or if I suddenly found a counter-attacking idea – 'You never know what you're going to get. That's why I love chess.' He admitted there had been times when his enthusiasm dwindled and he wondered whether he should have got a proper job. But the moods didn't last long, and he reckoned the people he grew up with who were now successful in business were envious of him. 'Nine to five and life in the boardroom is not for me,' he said. He preferred to be the true chairman of the board.

'The best way to get stronger is to play stronger players,' Finegold said when I informed him I hoped to reach expert level. He told me to play a lot of tournaments and put up with the pain of losing to higher-rated players: 'No pain, no gain. You should always play in the higher section if you can. That's how to improve your game.' I asked for some other tips before he left for dinner. 'Never trade,' he said. 'Always take your time. Never underestimate anyone. Never offer a draw; never accept a draw. Draws are stupid. You don't get better at chess by drawing. You want to go to king versus king. If you sat there and didn't play chess for a year, you wouldn't be a better chess player. You play 15 moves and you agree to a draw instead of playing 15 more moves, you just took away chess you could have played. Never even think about a draw; think about what chess move you should make. Live like a man; fight like a dog.'

F7: THE MILLION-DOLLAR MAN

Maurice Ashley, the first African-American to become a grandmaster, is a dynamic, super-sharp operator. It is not just in chess that his moves are good. I saw him on the dancefloor at the party after the conclusion of the US championships – Gata Kamsky and Irina Krush had retained their titles – and boy could he move. A New Yorker with a taste for expensive suits and expansive rhetoric, Ashley is the face of 21st-century chess. Or would like to be. He was the main presenter of the broadcasts from St Louis, backed up by the whizzy Jennifer Shahade and the reassuring bass tones of former world top-ten player Yasser Seirawan (himself no mean mover on the dancefloor), and proved a television natural.

Ashley was born in Jamaica and told me over coffee that he learned the rules of chess there when he was nine, but started playing seriously only when he came to the US at the age of 12. He went to school in Brooklyn, met a group of boys who played chess, started reading books on the game and fell in love with it. He became a grandmaster in 1999 at the age of 33. 'That was a pretty big moment,' he said. 'I'd been working towards it for quite some time.' Becoming a GM made him a role model for African-Americans. 'I was in a lot of newspapers and on a lot of talk shows. It made the front page of *USA Today*. It was a good time for me, and people were proud of it.'

After he got the title he had to find a new motivation: 'Becoming world champion was not on the cards, so it became a question of why was I doing it? Was I really going to reach the heights when I was so old? Sometimes I thought I could try to make a push because I'd started so late, but the reality of family life really affected me – I have two children – and after the age of about 35 I turned to entrepreneurship.' He started running chess tournaments so US players could get IM and GM norms, and then hit on his big idea: a million-dollar tournament. In 2005 he managed half that – a half-million-dollar tournament – but when we met he was close to realising his dream, with a million-dollar tournament in Las Vegas.

From the beginning of my stay in the US it had been clear that money was the main driver in American chess: the man at immigration control, the hustlers in the park, the players at the Marshall who really cared about their $63 joint second prize … and now this goal of a million-dollar tournament. 'Money in the United States means a lot,' said Ashley. 'It means a lot everywhere but especially here. The American mindset is very much rooted in the profit motive. There has to be money on the table. If you play for small-time stakes in the US, nobody pays attention. They really don't care. If chess is going to move to a big sport, getting any kind of attention, it needs more money.'

He was planning a tournament at Planet Hollywood in Las Vegas the following October, with a whopping entry fee of $1,000, a prize pool of $1m and a top prize of $100,000 – the most money ever given away at an open chess tournament. It would, he hoped, be the ultimate US chess event and would make an indifferent American sporting public sit up and take notice. But could he really win over the public? '"Public" is a big word,' he said. 'There are lots of people who will hear the word "chess" and never be interested. They just say, "It's not for me." But there is a group of people bigger than where the chess population is right now who would be interested but have never heard about chess tournaments or realised that they can be lucrative endeavours, and you need to get that story out.'

Ashley would clearly have been a success in whatever line of work he had gone into, and I asked him if he regretted having stuck with chess, given how limited were the rewards for a 2500-level grandmaster. 'Not really,' he said. 'I've always been locked into chess. There have been times when I was frustrated that there wasn't more money in the game. If Bobby Fischer had stayed in the game, there would have been real money and I would be Tiger Woods. He would have raised the profile of chess and you'd have had two million more people playing chess now.' It was an interesting take and one I had heard from others: that the Fischer 'boom' was more a Fischer blip and quickly turned to bust. 'The boom was so short,' said Ashley. 'It was like fireworks going off. That was part of the motivation for why I wanted to organise chess tournaments. The events I was playing in were crap.'

Ashley said it was hard for anyone with a rating below 2700 to be a fully fledged chess pro. Below that, he said, almost inevitably you would have to become a chess coach. We decided a rating of around 2730 was the real threshold these days. Above that and you could make a living as a player; below it you would make a sparse living unless you were willing to teach too. He admitted that having been the first African-American GM had given him certain advantages that offset his unspectacular grade. 'I see myself as a grandmaster rather than a black grandmaster,' he said, 'but it has helped me to promote chess among youth, which is a big part of what I do, and in particular to tell African-American youth that they can succeed.'

I asked Ashley whether chess in America was seen as an art or, as I suspected after my experiences in New York, a war. 'Any competition in America has to be win-lose,' he said. 'Once the word "competition" comes out of your mouth, that's it. Somebody's got to win, somebody's got to lose. The idea of drawing will not penetrate the American mindset. They will not take to draws very well if chess starts to get big, so I'm trying to take measures against them. Play to a draw and people will be very upset if they have to watch. To the average American, it's like kissing your sister. To capture the public imagination in the United States you need a winner and you need money on the line. And you also frankly need to speed up the game a little bit, because sitting around for five hours is not going to work.' The classicist would be horrified. Surely this is changing the essence of chess? 'There are different essences to chess,' he insisted.

The alternative, according to Ashley, was chess becoming ever more marginalised. 'Chess is in a horrible place at the moment. You could talk to 90 per cent of the people right here and ask them if there is a chess club nearby, and they might say "Maybe" – they might notice the big king outside the Hall of Fame – but you say, "Do you know there is a big chess tournament in town?" and a lot of them won't know. If you're in the capital of chess in America and most people don't know that, it's a sign. Take it outside of here and what do people know? For me chess is in a great place when there's visibility, when there are big tournaments and when there is broadcast interest. We are trying very hard here in St Louis to make that happen, but it hasn't broken through into the American psyche yet.'

F8: CHASING THE BIG BUCKS

After watching the play-offs for the US championships, I took an Amtrak train north to Chicago to play in the Chicago Open. Amtrak journeys are wonderful – if only the whole of life could be lived in one of their dining cars, watching the endless prairies roll past. But don't trust the schedule. Away from the east coast, because they don't own the lines they have to give way to freight trains and often run hours late. Still, it is a disembodied pleasure and a beautiful way to travel.

The tournament was being held at an anonymous conference-centre hotel in a prosperous, car-dominated, road-bisected suburb to the north of Chicago. After the energy of New York and the quirkiness of St Louis, it felt a bit like being buried alive, or incarcerated in a very posh, air-conditioned prison, though I enjoyed having a morning swim in the pool. I hadn't worked out how to book online so signed up for the tournament at the hotel – an outrageous $250 for a seven-round event. I entered the section for players with a US Chess Federation rating of less than 1900. The high entry fees are justified by the equally high prizes: $5,000 for the winner of my section; $10,000 for the winner of the nine-round Open, which attracted 20 grandmasters and plenty of other titled players. This was an event on a scale and with a prize fund – $100,000 in total – that made every British event look ridiculously small.

One of the peculiarities of US tournaments is that you have to bring your own set and clock. I hadn't bothered, assuming my opponents would have one, but the organiser, Bill Goichberg, a veteran of the US chess scene who has been running tournaments for more than 50 years, pointed out that if my opponent didn't show I couldn't claim a win by default unless I had the equipment. So I had to shell out another $91 on a board, a set of pieces and an electronic clock that I didn't have the faintest idea how to program. This was turning into an expensive venture. I really needed to win that $5,000.

Unfortunately my hopes of scooping the pot were almost immediately dashed. My opponent in the first round was a nice old chap with the delightful name of Valdis M. Tums, who played slow, solid chess. I built up a useful edge and could have won the exchange (rook for bishop), but thought I saw something better. What I thought I saw proved to be a mirage. I went a pawn down without realising it, tried some trickery in an endgame where I had two rooks against his queen, but failed to stop his two extra pawns from becoming decisive. 'I've won from a lost position,' he said afterwards. It was a miserable beginning. 'Do you come from the Chicago area?' he asked sweetly. 'From the UK,' I spat. I couldn't face talking. He must have thought me extremely rude.

I had trouble concentrating in this opening game. My head was still in New York, I was used to the rhythms of blitz. I wasn't enjoying this slow game – 40 moves in two hours; then half an hour for the rest, with a ten-second increment on every move. That's a near six-hour game. There were more than 700 people playing in eight sections – from the Open for the strong, brave or foolhardy, down to a section for players rated less than USCF 1000. It didn't seem noticeably different from a UK event, except in scale, with all the participants gathered together in the huge hotel ballroom. Everyone, even the grandmasters, arrived carrying their sets in little canvas bags. It felt like a Masonic gathering, which in a way I suppose it was. Earlier in the week the hotel had been filled with lawyers and doctors meeting in the convention rooms, but now the chess players had taken over and would be in occupation over the Memorial Day weekend. The money on offer didn't seem to induce any extra tension or aggro. There were no screams, no obvious abuse, no fistfights. Old guys, middle-aged men with baseball caps and inscrutable poker faces, and Asian kids just got on with it. I hoped my play and my application would improve as the tournament progressed. In that first game I was far too impulsive and lackadaisical, and forgot to look once I thought I had the game won. The same old elementary error. Still, at least it made an old man happy. And my new electronic clock worked.

There wasn't much recovery time. My first game finished at midnight. I didn't get to sleep until around 3am, the critical, game-losing move reverberating in my head and keeping me awake. The second game, played on a lovely Saturday morning when I would have much preferred to be heading for nearby Lake Michigan, began at 11.30am, with another game following at 6pm. It was, as one of my rivals said to me, a marathon – seven long, arduous games in quick succession. 'And you pay $250 for this?' I said to him incredulously. He didn't seem to find it so remarkable. The prizes were big; you saw old friends on the circuit; this was a pleasant venue. 'We play in so many crap places that it's nice to come to this hotel,' he said.

Before each round one of the tournament directors made an interminable speech about security. All chess is now plagued by the threat of cheating – using programs on handheld devices to supply the best moves – but with such large winnings on offer the danger is multiplied. I would just have a blanket ban on all mobiles, iPads and laptops, but here the organisers adopted what seemed to me an unsatisfactory halfway house – mobiles were allowed in the playing area but had to be switched off at all times. They were especially exercised by the possibility of players consulting them in the restrooms, and stationed a member of staff outside to make sure no one took a device in. They had sticks which could supposedly detect a mobile if they waved it over you. 'We may randomly wand you,' warned Goichberg before the start of the opening round, to much ill-mannered sniggering.

My second-round game was a dull, technical, passionless struggle – my wretched Scandinavian again – in which I was outplayed in a knight v knight endgame. My opponent, who had had an eight-hour drive from Omaha to get here, had an outside pawn and in the end made it count. I was very disappointed by my play and by my low energy and concentration levels. It was the end of a long trip; I was tired and playing in a strange environment – excuses, excuses. I feared the worst, but in round three Caïssa, the goddess of chess, sent me an opponent who was pretty clueless, and I won in less than 20 moves, using only about a quarter of an hour on my clock. As well as having a point – my first tournament game win in the US in seven attempts – I also had a free evening and could get some proper rest ahead of the two games I had to play on Sunday.

I used part of my unexpectedly free evening to buttonhole Goichberg, and ask him about his life as a tournament organiser and why the entry fees for US tournaments were so high compared with the UK. There were, he said, lots of tournaments you could enter for $40, but the chess public liked these big jamborees where players had the chance to win a lot of money. They got a good rate on the hotel and a chance to challenge themselves with the possibility of winning some cash. 'The stronger players can make money, but the majority of players play in tournaments like this because they are exciting. They don't really expect to win money. They see it as a vacation. You have a shot at some big money, but I have people in the World Open who have never won a cent yet come every year because they love it.'

A bonus of talking to Goichberg was that he had known Fischer, an almost exact contemporary who used to come to his tournaments in New York in the 1960s. He told me a funny story about Fischer coming along once and, without being recognised, joining a simul being given by an expert-level player from South Carolina. The expert was horrified that, after nine moves, he was completely lost. Only then did he realise who he was playing. Goichberg said that on one occasion Fischer came to a high-school tournament and was fine until the kids started badgering him for autographs. He ran off, pursued down the street by his fans. Fischer, said Goichberg, was living in a hotel in Manhattan at the time. The kids discovered where he was, went up to his room and renewed their requests for his autograph. Eventually he gave in – a rare example of Fischer giving way to pressure. The hotel eventually threw Fischer out for not obeying the house rule to let the maid clean the room at least once a month. Fischer refused, saying she was sure to sell his opening secrets to the Russians if she ever gained admittance.

I felt more relaxed on Sunday. Getting a point on the board is always crucial and makes you feel you're at least in the tournament. Unfortunately I ran into a truck in the morning game, in the form of a 48-year-old accountant from Ontario who hit me with an opening called the Nimzo–Larsen (it starts with pawn to b3, looks weird but has a nasty kick). I was completely out of my depth, he had a very comfortable game, won a host of pawns and closed out the game easily. When we analysed the game afterwards, it was obvious how much more he had seen than me – as well as being strategically lost from about move ten I made two significant miscalculations which hastened my demise. I tried to justify my feeble play to the accountant by telling him I had returned to the game and started playing seriously only seven or eight years ago, but he trumped that by saying he, too, had enjoyed chess as a child and come back to the game five years ago. His objective was also to become an expert, and he seemed to be advancing more rapidly to that goal than me. He clearly loved the game, played tournaments in Canada and across the US, and said he played for the joy of competition rather than the prospect of winning a big prize. He said this event was far bigger than anything in Canada, had more of a buzz and presented a greater challenge. He gave me a mini-tutorial on the Nimzo–Larsen, one of his pet openings, and also showed me some more active lines in the Scandinavian. I had been thinking of abandoning it, but he convinced me to persevere.

I was starting to realise what a tyro I was in this tournament, and how much less I worked at the game than my rivals. To pay $250 to enter you had to be obsessed, and they were. In the breaks the kids played on iPads; the adults sat in the restaurant playing; one man just sat in the tournament room staring at a position. They had the chess bug bad. These people were sick. Asian tiger mothers were drilling their knuckle-hard offspring; fat, bearded men were engaging in intense chess chat; 99-year-old Erik Karklins, a master-level player in his pomp who was still playing at a US Chess Federation rating of more than 2000, was being feted everywhere; amiable American GM John Fedorowicz was on hand to do the post-mortems of players' games and had a long queue of takers. There was much more of a convention feel than in the UK. It was a fun event, a gathering of a strange clan, a land where everyone spoke chess.

Sadly in round five I proved far from fluent in the lingo. I seemed to have an edge in the opening against a nervous, thoughtful young man with an embryonic moustache, but he outmanoeuvred me in the middle game, trapping a knight I had been convinced I could free. I got tired and depressed, and just started making random moves. 'Do you give up?' my opponent said to me with surprise when I muttered my resignation. 'Of course I give up, you thundering idiot,' I wanted to say. 'You're about to queen a pawn, and your position is overwhelming.' This was turning into a chastening experience.

There was just pride at stake now. It would be nice not to finish last of the 120 competitors in my section, but I wasn't the only one having a tough time. 'I'm either winning or I'm losing,' said one of the players in the lift on the way down to the Monday morning game. 'I'm learning a lot,' said someone else to general laughter. At last, though, in this sixth-round game I played well: I stuck with the Scandinavian (my opponent, another personable Canadian, clearly didn't know it), built up a decent attack, sacrificed rook for bishop, and mated him in 30 moves (see Game 5 on p384). I hoped it would be enough to get me off the bottom of the table. I offered to go through the game with my opponent – I wanted to show him the two or three passive pawn moves early in the game which I felt had given me the initiative – but he declined. 'By this stage I'm just demoralised,' he said. He looked as if he was going to cry. I gave his arm a friendly squeeze. What a gracious winner I was.

In the final round I tried to keep my focus; 3/7 would be almost respectable. I was up against an 11-year-old boy, one of the many children of Chinese parents at the tournament. Luckily for me he wasn't very strong – the advantage of having scored so abysmally in the early rounds – and made a few inaccurate moves that gave me an extra pawn and eventually a win. So in the end, without scaring anyone, I managed to claw my way towards the middle of the table, avoiding the ignominy that before my Super Monday had seemed likely. It's amazing how a couple of wins can boost the spirits.

I noticed Valdis M. Tums had won a small prize for finishing somewhere near the top in the section and thought that might have been me if I hadn't made that stupid oversight in our first-round game. But despite that early blow which affected everything that followed, I was content. I'd gradually come to enjoy the festival atmosphere and the camaraderie among the players, locked together in their airless hotel in the middle of nowhere, oblivious to the world outside. It was the ultimate chess bubble. All being in the same hotel and heading down in the lifts for each round engendered a communality of spirit. I hoped to come back at some point to play more events on the US tour. After playing here and at the Marshall I had an official US rating of 1779. I was now an Anglo-American chess player. I also felt changed by my journey through the US: it had given me a taste of freedom, space, adventure. Going back to the UK did not appeal. My heart was still in Washington Square.

FILE G
Awakening in Aberystwyth

'Chess is a sea in which a gnat may drink and an elephant may bathe'

– Anonymous

G1: HOME TRUTHS

 My odyssey seemed to be turning into the ultimate shaggy dog story, a journey leading nowhere. Was I becoming a better chess player? Maybe, a little. But true expertise, let alone grandmasterdom, remained a distant dream. Was I becoming a better, more focused person, as I'd originally hoped? Absolutely not. The reverse was true. I wasn't sure I even believed any more in the Carrera hypothesis – that to play well you had to live well. Indeed, I doubted whether he believed it. With his sideline forging historical and religious provenances, he was as rackety as the rest of us. My stay in the US had convinced me – if I hadn't known it already – that playing chess was above all a quest for freedom. I loved the tale in Arnold Denker's amusing memoir, *The Bobby Fischer I Knew, and Other Stories*, about the chess and poker hustler Jacob Bernstein, one of a rich cast of characters active on the New York chess scene from the 1920s to the 1950s. Bernstein was at a Woodrow Wilson-for-President rally. 'Mr Wilson, is it true that if you're elected, every man will have work?' asked Bernstein. 'Yes', replied Wilson. 'But Mr Wilson, I don't want to work!'

Spoken like a true chess pro/player/hustler. I no longer believed in the distinctions between those categories either. Once the bug gets you, what else matters? How tedious and workaday is the 'real' world beyond the board? How I longed to be back in Washington Square, where all that mattered, all that was real, was the game. The rest of the world could go hang. It was the most perfect example of living in the moment I had ever experienced, though I realised Washington Square in the spring sunshine was a different proposition from Washington Square in January, when the hustlers would freeze in the day and seek shelter where they could at night.

Denker, whose book I had read on my dreamily delayed Amtrak train from St Louis to Chicago, came to a conclusion which seemed to me quite profound: 'As I mentally rummage through the years and try to capture with memory's eye the great players of the last several decades, I find one characteristic common to almost all of them: a bitterness about and rebelliousness against the inequitable social and economic conditions of the real world . . . For them, playing the royal game was a purely personal statement against social injustice.' Devoting yourself to chess was an act of rebellion; a rejection of the conventional world; a statement of solidarity with the marginalised. I now realised that this was what had made me come back to chess. I was uncomfortable with, or perhaps just bored by, the pressing world; I wanted this small, beautiful, meaningless world; I wanted to possess it and to be possessed by it.

Chess – among many of the pros at least – is the game of those who don't fit with conventional norms; hence their pursuit of grandmaster norms. In his 1974 book, *Idle Passion*, a provocative psychological interpretation of chess, Alexander Cockburn seeks to give this observation a political thrust: 'Chess is *par excellence* the pastime of a disinherited ruling class that continues to crave political domination but has seen it usurped. Just as, in psychoanalytic terms, chess is a way of sublimating oedipal conflicts, so, in social terms, it is a device for sublimating political aspirations; the empty omnipotence exercised by the player over his pieces is consolation for lost power.' This brilliant generalisation, prompted by Cockburn's musings on the game in the Middle Ages when the declining nobility took it up, is hugely contentious, yet it seemed to me there was something in it. Many of the people I encountered in chess were intelligent misfits; they had in some way been dispossessed, losing their job or suffering a marriage breakdown or feeling some grudge against the system; chess empowered them, gave them a space in which they felt comfortable and in control; it was an antidote to their powerlessness in life, a simulacrum of success, a satisfying narrative they could cling to. A game of chess was a battle they felt able to fight – perhaps had to fight – because they had lost life's greater war.

Chess, if my earlier contention was correct, tended to be dominated by societies on the way up – Spain in the 16th century, Italy in the 17th, France in the 18th, Britain in the 19th, the US and the Soviet Union in the 20th, China and India today – yet within those societies it was often the powerless and the marginalised who became the experts: monks and misfits, rebels and occasionally charlatans, in retreat from the bourgeois values that dominated the materialist, go-getting world around them. After all, the rich and wealthy tended to have better things to do, leaving true expertise at mere games to others. I felt there was probably a PhD thesis in this.

Returning to the banalities of domestic chess after my perspective-shifting stay in the US was difficult, but I had to apply myself. My immediate target was the under-140 tournament in the British championship at Aberystwyth in late July – a competition I had convinced myself I had a chance of winning – but real expertise was proving as elusive as ever. While in St Louis I had talked to the American grandmaster Yasser Seirawan, four times US champion and a former world top-ten player. He described chess as a game of 'unlearning': 'The prejudices and biases you had as a beginner and a club player, you have to realise they were wrong, and you have to revamp your way of thinking.'

He was right, of course, and I needed to do some serious unlearning, because I was repeating many of my old errors.

Within a fortnight of returning to the UK I was playing in the Felce Cup, the Surrey individual championship for players graded under 140 (this was bathetic after Moscow and New York, but it had to be done). I really believed I could win this damn thing, though one of the players in my preliminary group was my old friend/foe Adrian Waldock, who had a grade of 137 but in reality was a good deal stronger than that. Overcoming him would not be easy, and I would need all the hustler's fearlessness I hoped I had absorbed in the US.

My first-round game was against a junior, who played quickly but inaccurately. She used only a third of her time, but what's the point of that if you lose the game? I rather pompously lectured her afterwards, but she was quite rightly having none of my patronising homilies. Anyway, I was off to a winning start in the Felce. The second round was even better: my opponent played a disastrous opening, was in trouble by move six and somehow missed the fact that he was about to be mated on move nine (see Game 6, my shortest encounter in any serious competition, on p385). I felt both euphoric and a little sorry for him. What should have been a three-hour struggle was over in 20 minutes. We played some lacklustre blitz to allow him to regain his composure and pride, but he still looked shellshocked at the end of it and went away muttering. I would have had great difficulty recovering from such a reverse and felt for him. But it meant I was 2/2 in the tournament and now facing Waldock, against whom I had a poor record. This would be make or break.

Except it wasn't. I was in a spot of trouble in the opening – I played d4 as usual and he played the Benko Gambit, which I knew only sketchily. I equalised and on move 15 he suddenly offered me a draw. I was playing white and he must have reasoned that a draw would give him the advantage as he would play white in the deciding game. By all the laws of the goddess Caïssa, and with the protestations of Stuart Conquest against quick draws revolving in my head, I knew I had to play on. 'No,' I said firmly, 'I want to carry on.' But then I looked at the position further, thought the fact he had a pair of bishops against my bishop and knight might eventually tell, and accepted the draw offer. 'If your opponent offers you a draw, try to work out why he thinks he's worse off,' Nigel Short says. I couldn't see anything especially concerning for him, but perhaps I wasn't looking hard enough. The peace offering was too seductive. It was a touch feeble, though I rationalised it by telling myself I could beat him with black in the return when he would have to play to win. I was also consoled when I looked at the game on the computer. In the final position it gave him a small edge, suggesting I had been correct in not seeing any immediate advantage for me. Our decisive meeting was deferred, and next time he would have the white pieces. I hoped my chance hadn't slipped away.

G2: HOWELL AND HAPPINESS

The draw with Waldock left me at 2.5/3 in the Felce Cup, and I consolidated that in the weeks that followed with another easy win against the junior in our division and a tedious draw against the man I'd beaten in nine moves in the previous game. The draw took me to 4/5, but I knew I'd played poorly in the most recent of those games – without imagination or any real will to win. I had settled for a draw by move 20. He was fairly solid playing white and I let him play on his own territory – a bog-standard Queen's Gambit Declined. A proper player would have thrown him off balance with an attacking response – the Budapest Opening or the Albin Counter-Gambit, openings I kept intending to learn but hadn't got round to yet.

That, in fact, had been the problem ever since I'd returned from the US. From more or less complete immersion in chess I had reverted to being a very occasional player. I had had a tough six weeks at work, trying to edit as well as write, and working long hours. My mind was frazzled: I still wanted to be in America, just travelling and playing chess. Back home I had little or no time to study games, or even play online, and I was getting rusty. I found I had to play every day, be obsessed by the games, have knight moves revolving in my head as I fell asleep, or the whole thing just went. It was all or nothing. In my tedious drawn game in the Felce, I was devoid of ideas, and, if you have no ideas, chess is a bore, a mechanical procession of hollow moves, the bland leading the bland.

My only hope now was the British championship in Aberystwyth. I had booked ten days off, and intended to play in one competition only – the under-140 championship. The games would be played in the morning, starting at 9.30, with a reasonably generous time control – 110 minutes plus a ten-second increment. The rest of the day I would devote to walking, swimming, reading chess books and watching some of the country's finest players do battle for the British title. I would be back in the chess bubble, give the under-140 championship – a notch down from the level in which I had played at Torquay – my best shot, and hope that would prepare me for the game against Waldock in the Felce that would determine which of us would progress to the final against the winner of the section being played at another club in Surrey.

As I packed for my less-than-dreamy six-hour train trip to Wales, I felt far from confident. I had just a weekend to switch myself properly back on to chess, and it didn't seem long enough. My convoluted train journey to Aberystwyth – via Birmingham, Shrewsbury, Welshpool and Machynlleth – confirmed my worst fears. I was restless, bored, unable to concentrate on chess or anything else. The focus I had felt at, say, Wijk was missing. At that crucial moment chess didn't feel like the core of my being.

I arrived on Saturday afternoon and went in search of my B&B – an idiosyncratic (and necessarily cheap) guesthouse a couple of miles outside Aberystwyth but reasonably close to the university, where the British championships were being staged. I could have stayed in the halls of residence, but didn't fancy sharing the facilities with hordes of chess players – you had to draw the line somewhere. Being a mile further up the hill in this secluded hamlet gave me a degree of privacy into which I could withdraw each night.

Sunday morning was warm and sunny, and I spent it sunbathing on the shingly beach, swimming and listening to the England Test match on my little transistor radio – a throwback to my teenagehood when cricket and idling in the sun were the essence of my summers. I perfected the art of doing nothing early in life, and have always resented having to depart from it. Spending the morning on the beach, trying not to look at my mobile phone too often, calmed me a little. In the afternoon I made my way to the hall in which the championships were being played. The main event had started the day before – 60 players, all but two of them men, with the usual smattering of GMs and IMs, though fewer than in previous years because Aberystwyth was less convenient than the south coast of England and, as usual, the prize money was far from enticing. But the previous year's champion, David Howell, was back to defend his crown, and after he had finished – chalking up a straightforward win against a promising junior – we talked in the early evening sunshine.

Howell was only 23, but he seemed to have been on the chess scene for ages. He became a grandmaster at 16, the youngest ever British holder of that esteemed title, and won his first British championship at 18. I had first met – and indeed played him – when he was eight. He had beaten grandmaster John Nunn (my great victim, too!) in a game, and been hailed as the next British star. I interviewed him and his parents for an article in *The Guardian*, and played a ten-minute game against him. It had always rankled that I was winning the game – or at least doing pretty well – but lost on time. It would have been nice to have beaten a future British champion. I met Howell again just before he left school, to write an article in *British Chess Magazine*, and we played again, but this time he slaughtered me. At that second meeting, I tried to get some sense of whether this prodigiously talented but not necessarily world-beating young man saw his future as a professional chess player, or whether he would go to university. At the time he wasn't sure. He deferred taking up a place at university, but in the end did go – to study English literature and philosophy at Cardiff – and at the time of this third meeting, in Aberystwyth, he had just finished his degree. Now he was once again facing the choice that confronted him when we had met five years earlier – whether to become a professional chess player.

'I do sometimes feel that I handicapped myself by going to university,' he said. 'I haven't done so much chess work or playing in the past few years. But I now feel my love for the game has come back, and that I have unfinished business. I have a lot to prove.' Howell's rating at the time of this meeting was 2650 – dangerous territory for a grandmaster; extremely strong and not far off the world top 100, but not strong enough to get invitations to elite tournaments. He was in the same boat as his great English rival, Gawain Jones – a strong player but one who would struggle to make a decent living just by playing. Howell had fewer qualms than Jones about teaching chess – he said he had done some coaching and believed that in some ways it helped him by making him more analytical. He was also thinking of writing a book aimed at the parents of talented young players – drawing on his own experience as a prodigy – and had visions of helping to boost chess's profile, perhaps by getting it on TV. Chess, he said, needed to be 'sexier'. There was no doubting that, and Howell – tall, athletic, strikingly handsome, far from the stereotype of the nerdy chess player – could be the man to do it. 'It's a long shot,' he said, 'but I do feel there is more that chess can give if the public could see that there are personalities behind the long games. I want the perception of chess to change.'

His immediate goal was to get to a rating of 2700 and, within a year of our meeting, he had indeed surpassed that magic number (whereas Gawain Jones seemed becalmed at around 2640). Howell was a warm favourite to win the British title for the third time at Aberystwyth – in the event he emerged as joint winner after suffering a surprise loss in the early stages – but said that was not the be-all and end-all of his participation. 'It's more about improving and feeling that I can hit another level, because when I do play these 2700 guys I feel on the same wavelength; it's just that I've been slightly disadvantaged over the past few years.' He hoped playing well in Aberystwyth would get rid of the rustiness in his game and engender a confidence and 'momentum' that would carry him through the sterner tests to come. It was good to hear that even 2650-rated grandmasters got rusty; perhaps there was hope for me yet.

It was Howell's misfortune to be born in the same year as Magnus Carlsen and Sergey Karjakin, two superstars of the world game. He was part of that prodigious generation, and said that 'inspired me for the first few years, but then, after a while – when Carlsen gained 300 points in a year and shot up to world number three – that was intimidating, and I did feel either I had to abandon everything just to stay in touch or I had to be more philosophical about it and be less intense.' Having had some run-ins with authority and, by his own admission, felt detached from the rest of the chess world in his teens, he had now learned to relax more and put the game into perspective: 'I try not to get too stressed out about things nowadays. I empathise more with my fellow chess players than I used to. I realise that they've been through struggles too, and have had to make the same decisions as me. I get along with everyone far better now.' Whereas once he kept his distance, he was now happy to be part of the curious chess world, without ever quite sharing its occasional myopia: 'I feel I've split my life in two – chess and non-chess. It's never been completely about the 64 squares for me and I don't think it ever will be, but as long as chess is part of my life I think I'll be pretty happy.'

G3: IF YOU CAN'T STAND THE HEAT ...

 Before the start of the first round in the tournament in which I was playing, I bumped into Will Taylor, the young man I'd met the previous year who was blogging his 'Road to Grandmaster'. Except he wasn't any more – he was about to start a full-time job and had abandoned the blog. I wasn't the only one who was finding this mountain a tough one to crack, though since his grade was now in the 170s he was making a better fist of it than me. He had managed to shimmy up a few cols; I was still barely out of base camp. Still, we were all, in our peculiar ways, struggling. This game had the capacity to make fools of everyone.

My first big decision about the under-140 tournament was what to wear. 'Dress for competitors should be smart casual' said the championship programme. This was ridiculous – no chess player below super-GM level (where jackets and ties tended to be de rigueur) even knew the meaning of 'smart casual'. But would it be disrespecting my opponent to turn up in discoloured, sun-bleached, strawberry yogurt-stained shorts? In the end I decided that it would, so I opted for combat trousers and a 'Chess is war' T-shirt I had bought in Chicago.

I was black in the first round against an opponent graded just over 100, a middle-aged northerner on crutches. Despite the crutches I was determined to show him no mercy. To have any chance of winning the championship I would need a score of at least 4.5/5. He had white and played the English opening. For 35 moves there was nothing in it and I had a horrible feeling that my lowly graded opponent would get a draw. But he went wrong in the endgame, my knight proved more potent than his bishop, I hoovered up his pawns, and he resigned on move 53. Hurrah! I was off to a winning start. Because we were playing on the specially wired-up boards used in the main event in the afternoon, the game was even transmitted in real time on the championship website – a kind of demonstration of how not to play chess. I hoped not too many chess wannabes in Lagos and Lapland were watching. Being exposed to my play could be seriously damaging. But a win is a win. Doc Saunders, who followed the game online, told me I'd played OK and that it was an ideal 'workout' ahead of the tougher struggles to come. Quietly satisfied, I retired to the beach for the afternoon with a book – a non-chess one – and sat on a rock roasting in the decidedly un-Welsh sunshine.

The first of the tougher tests came next morning, when I was up against one of the two highest-graded players in the tournament – a man called Herring, with a grade of 139. I feared that, despite his name, he wouldn't be a fish. But I was determined to enjoy it, and to try to play with a bit of vigour. I also told myself to be more assiduous about time – in the first game I had fallen hugely behind my opponent on the clock, by 45 minutes at one stage, and that had imposed additional pressure. I had somehow to play more quickly and with more panache, or Mr Herring would net me with ease.

As I had suspected, Herring proved to be no fish (indeed he won the under-140 championship the following year). It was, in fact, hard to judge just how good he was. He had returned to chess because he had a teenage son who played – he was here playing in a higher-level tournament – and Herring Snr must have learned the game a long way back because he still used the old descriptive notation (P-K4, P-KB4, etc.) which had been supplanted by the algebraic system decades ago. But he played reasonably well and grabbed the initiative in the middle game. I defended stoutly and soon we were both running low on time. With 15 minutes left on my clock, I started thinking about offering him a draw. Sacrilege, of course: I had come all this way and had hopes of winning the tournament, and now I was thinking of offering a draw in my second game. 'Are you a man or a mouse?' I started repeating to myself. Naturally, I was a mouse, because after playing my 29th move I offered him a draw. At first he turned it down but, after thinking for a few minutes, he renewed the offer and I accepted. I had been hamstrung by the thought that what had been a good, tense, tactical, technical struggle would be decided by a blunder in time trouble. That, in any case, was my excuse for suing for peace. The Doc told me later that my position when we agreed the draw had been slightly inferior, so I felt vindicated. Even mice can sometimes be right.

While I was playing this game, I had something close to an out-of-body experience. As Herring and I sat there hunched over the board – playing very slowly, two middle-aged men who had returned to this infuriating game after long breaks, trying to find the thread, any thread – it suddenly struck me as ludicrous. It was a gorgeous day outside, and here we were playing a four-hour game of chess in a room with a couple of hundred other deluded aficionados of this batty pursuit. With the beach beckoning, I could suddenly see that Wells, George Bernard Shaw – who said chess was 'just a way of wasting time' – and all the other chess-haters had a point. This was, as George Steiner said, an 'ultimately trivial human enterprise', though no doubt had I been smashing my opponent with a brilliant sacrificial attack I would have felt differently.

Unfortunately I wasn't. I was low on both confidence and energy, hanging on in there but not much more. I felt less focused than I had a year earlier at the British championships in Torquay, where I had acquitted myself fairly well against a higher class of opponent than I was meeting here. After my game had finished I watched two strong players analysing, and their speed and depth of thought were in another league from mine. It was desperately depressing, and yet I was not depressed enough. I was settling for the level I'd reached – an insipid competence. Maybe I was just too old and clapped out to do anything else.

I managed a win in round three, largely because my opponent donated a knight to me just as we were heading for an endgame that might well have been favourable to him. He was a man of around 60 from Yorkshire, and afterwards as we looked at the game he told me a nice story. He didn't play chess until he was 38, when a friend asked him to go along to Scarborough Chess Club to test the water. The friend, sensible fellow, never returned, but my opponent was hooked and now came to play in the British championship every year. I asked him why he wasn't playing in the under-120 section, which he would have had a good chance of winning. He said he wasn't interested in winning weak tournaments; he preferred to play stronger players, even if that meant suffering. 'I'd sooner lose a good game than win a poor one,' he told me. An admirable attitude, but one I doubted many chess players shared. I knew I didn't. For all my lofty ideals about beauty and artistry, nothing beats the almost sexual surge of winning. I loved the half hour of this game when I was a piece up and knew I was going to win. He played on hoping for a miracle, but it was never going to happen. That's a wonderfully (or perhaps pathetically) empowering feeling.

We had now reached what golfers like to call the 'business end' of the tournament. I was up against a confident-looking young man graded 136 who was also on 2.5. Doc Saunders sent me an encouraging email: 'Forget today's game for now and enjoy the score – 2.5/3 is very good and exactly where you want to be. A little bit more confidence and fight needed from here on in, but don't overdo it. None of these guys is any great shakes, and on your day you're as good as any of them [was that a backhanded compliment?]. Stay calm and inscrutable.' I wished he'd added 'don't spend too long on the beach', because I overdid it after my round-three win, turned pink and felt a bit dizzy. I hoped it wasn't sunstroke – previously unheard of in west Wales but Aberystwyth seemed to have turned into the Algarve. I had an early night to prepare myself for perhaps the most important game of my life. If I could win in round four and other results fell my way, I could start to dream about being British champion.

'It's not the despair; I can cope with the despair,' as John Cleese's deranged headmaster in the film *Clockwork* said. 'It's the hope I can't bear.' And so it proved for me. Joint second going into the fourth round, I was filled with expectation. I wasn't even put off by the fact that my bronzed and muscular twentysomething opponent, who was half-Dutch, came into the playing hall clutching a book called *Grandmaster Chess Strategy*. A feeble psychological ploy, I felt. Or that he cracked his knuckles menacingly every so often. I tried to do the same, but couldn't make it work. What did put me off was that he played a peculiar defence to my usual d4 opening, outplayed me strategically and had me beaten after 25 moves (see Game 7 on p385). I soldiered on playing for tricks and trying to manufacture an attack, but it all came to nothing and after four hours I was done for. I had lost the game and also felt exhausted – this had been a far more demanding intellectual exercise than my three previous games. I hadn't been able to make the steep step up in standard.

After the game I went along to the bookstall and couldn't resist buying a pleasingly short guide called *Why We Lose at Chess*. I really wanted to know. When we spoke on the phone a few minutes later, Saunders had his own ideas. He said I had been mugged in the opening and had played too passively. He also suggested, a little brutally, that I had to be realistic: 'There just aren't enough years left for you to become a really strong player, but there's still pleasure to be had in beating better players. You need to play more violently.' Only the first part of his remark really hit home; I ignored the more encouraging bit. Maybe I was destined to be eternally mediocre, an old bloke taking his annual holiday at the British championship and struggling along among the also-rans in some lowly rated satellite tournament, never progressing, never really getting it, continuing to make the same mistakes and play the same feeble moves in perpetuity. It was a vision of chess hell.

G4: TIME FOR AN MOT

 The new mid-year grades were announced when I was in Aberystwyth and I had managed to add five points – crawling to 136, an old codger's grade if ever there was one. I was about to 'celebrate' my 57th birthday – an age to consider retirement, not to set yourself improbable challenges. Saunders liked to see the battle for chess excellence as a mountain to be climbed. If Carlsen and the super-GMs were at the peak, and their lesser brethren were a couple of thousand feet below looking up enviously through the clouds, I felt I was still struggling to find a route up from base camp ('No, you are still on the tarmac at Heathrow!' said Saunders bleakly). How on earth could I begin the ascent? I would settle now for a grade between 150 and 170, and for a FIDE rating as close to 2000 as possible, but even those relatively modest objectives seemed distant dreams. This was one battle the clock appeared to be winning.

When I got back to London I had very little spare time and played much less online blitz than usual. I didn't miss it. OK, my synapses might be slowing down a bit and I was no longer dreaming of knight combinations, but I felt a better person for eschewing the lure of the instant (and almost invariably imperfect) contest. I would listen to music, read books, and *work* at my chess instead. I was preparing for my make-or-break game against Adrian Waldock in the Felce, and decided it was time for an MOT. The chess mechanic I chose to give me a full check was the English-born international master Andrew Martin, who had carved out a career for himself as a commentator and highly regarded trainer. I had seen him commentating at the British championships and been impressed by his wit and speed of thought. Martin, who was just a few months older than me, and as a teenager was also inspired by the Fischer–Spassky match, was born in east London. I hoped his blunt, no-nonsense style would put my faltering chess career back on course.

'Are you really keen to get as good as you can be?' he asked me at the beginning of the long training session we had together. 'Or do you think you're already there?' I wasn't sure how to answer this. I felt I had improved, but could offer very little evidence from my rating progress. He reckoned I'd made less progress than I should have done, and when he looked at my games thought they were inconsistent – not just between games but within games. I played some good moves – moves that a 170-graded player might have been happy with – but then blew it with a very poor move. Martin said I had to aim for greater consistency, which meant applying myself properly at every point in the game, not relaxing for a moment.

The tricky questions did not stop there. 'You've got all these books, a lot of very good books. Have you read them?' He laughed at my hesitation. 'Chess is not just about working,' he said, 'but working effectively.' He was echoing the Doc's point that chess geniuses do not necessarily have a genius for chess but for systematic study. But I'm old, I squealed, it may be too late. 'You can't see that as a barrier,' he said. 'You've got experience of life to guide you.' But what about my congealed brain? 'What about your intuition? You've got everything you need in this library to become really strong. You could get to 200.'

Martin had been a great natural talent in his youth, but told me he had never tried to make a career as a playing professional. He had realised early on he wouldn't be strong enough to make a good living and turned to teaching. More gregarious and outgoing than many chess players, he said teaching suited him. He also enjoyed writing, and not being on the playing circuit meant he had time – and money – for his four children. Though an international master who had reached a peak rating of 2433, he had never made it to grandmaster, but not having the title didn't bother him in the slightest.

As we played through my games, what struck me most was his intensity and the excitement with which he responded to certain positions. 'Don't go too quickly,' he'd say. 'This is interesting.' Here was what distinguished the true chess player from the patzer: the former was willing to spend a huge amount of time studying a single position, looking for that elusive truth. The patzer just wanted to play. As Bobby Fischer said, 'I give 98 per cent of my mental energy to chess. Others give only 2 per cent.' I was definitely one of the two-percenters.

Martin said there was no magic wand that could be waved. I had to work harder, learn to analyse properly, stop relying on the computer to do the post-mortems for me, seek to play more consistently. He also said I needed to learn some new openings. I was giving my opponents an easy life with the dull, unchallenging openings I was playing, and would never beat a strong player with that repertoire. 'You are playing games in which the strong player will always win,' he said. He advised me to drop the Tartakower Defence against d4 and play more actively, to play the Sicilian against e4, and to learn some surprise openings as secret weapons. He gave me a book about the Sokolsky, which begins with the unlikely move pawn to b4. Work, study, learn, innovate. 'You don't want to be 140 for ever, do you?' he said breezily.

G5: BANISHING THE DEMONS

I had attached great importance to winning the Felce Cup – the annual under-140 championship for Surrey players. The Waldock game in the end had not been make or break – we drew again and he preferred not to contest a play-off, so I was through to the final where I faced another old foe, French-born Wimbledon player David Cachet, with whom I'd had several close encounters. I had won the most recent game and felt I had at least an even chance, but on his day he was a good, thoughtful player and an able exponent of the King's Indian Defence. I told myself to play e4 as white – to avoid getting into his favourite lines – and to try to play dynamically. I also needed to stay relaxed: if I wanted this too much and put pressure on myself, the likelihood was I would lose. Relaxed concentration, remember – an intense focus on the game but sufficient mental flexibility to avoid freezing and to allow yourself to know when to strike. With such psychological mumbo-jumbo, I readied myself for my latest date with destiny.

Incredibly, for the first time in months, everything went according to plan. Playing e4 surprised him; he had a tiny edge in the opening but I neutralised it and got a little plus myself (see Game 8 on p387). I trapped his knight and forced an exchange of piece for pawn; he got some counterplay and we ended up in an endgame where I had rook and two pawns against bishop and four pawns – very tricky, though it helped my cause that he was under his usual time pressure. I swapped rook for bishop in a position where I thought I had a passed pawn and a certain win. To my horror, when I looked at it on the computer later, with correct play he could have got a draw. But he had only a couple of minutes to play six moves and didn't play the all-important pawn move that would have drawn. After a few more perfunctory moves, and with my pawn about to become a queen, he resigned. I was one up and had banished the demons that had been dogging me. I had played more dynamically, taken a few chances, and it had paid off. I had one hand on the Felce Cup.

In the week before the all-important second game, I tried to apply myself to some proper study, and began by watching two DVDs of a programme called *The Master Game*, a television series which had run for seven series in the chess boom years of the 1970s and 1980s. Top grandmasters – Karpov, Korchnoi, Tony Miles, Bent Larsen, a young, nasal-sounding Nigel Short, the ineffable Hein Donner – played against each other and gave a running commentary (recorded immediately after each game) of their thought processes. It was amazing to think that chess was on peak-time national TV only a generation or so ago. Would it ever return? Almost certainly not, sadly. But for me these DVDs were gold-dust – a way of getting into the heads of some of the strongest players of all time.

In some ways it's sad to watch these series from 30-plus years ago. Donner – tired-looking here and with hooded eyes, a great fire extinguished – had a stroke soon afterwards; Miles, the UK's first grandmaster, died at the age of 46; and several of the players – Svetozar Gligorić, Lothar Schmid, the American Robert Byrne and the elegant, delightfully deadpan Dane Larsen – had died recently in their seventies and eighties, legends of the game when somehow it seemed to have more resonance, more meaning. The cultured commentary of these old GMs was splendidly aphoristic: 'That seems a natural move, but I hate making natural moves,' said Larsen. 'It's a good position, but a little sleep will wreck any position,' cautioned Byrne. But what was most useful was to see the way they started anticipating the endgame while still deep in the middle game. They didn't try for knockouts or even material advantages. Instead they sought to create tiny advantages which might come to fruition 30 or 40 moves later. You of course had to be constantly aware of tactical opportunities, but if your opponent played sensibly they were likely to be limited. And where there was no chance of landing a tactical blow, it was important to play organically and fluidly – seeing the board as a whole and making every detail count.

Some of these old legends captivated me, especially the suave, worldly Larsen – amusing, highly cultivated, original in his style of play, and, according to *New in Chess*, 'one of the greatest fighters chess has ever seen'. 'I always have confidence and I always try to win,' he once said. 'I never make deals and I always compete to the end.' If only I could be so combative. He held that 'the stomach is an essential part of the chess master', and his attitude and humour were summed up in a Q&A with chess magazine *Kingpin* in 1999: 'Greatest weakness as a chess player – "No respect for authority". Greatest strength as a chess player – "No respect for authority".' I read through Larsen's best games collection, *Fighting Chess with the Great Dane*, and it was instructive to observe the way he would wait and wait until precisely the right moment to strike, not starting the final battle until every piece in his armoury had been called up to the frontline. By playing through Larsen's games I hoped I might absorb some of his attacking flair and sense of adventure. Or at least remember his point about the stomach being a key part of the player's make-up, and eat something healthy before the second leg of the Felce final.

I took the day of the big game off, stayed in bed late and rested ahead of the evening encounter at my rival's home club in Wimbledon. Larsen would have been proud of me. Well, up to a point anyway – see Game 9 on p387. Though black, I managed to get a small edge by move 15, forcing my opponent to double his pawns. This seemed to provoke him and he launched an unwise thrust with his h-pawn. This was not his natural game, but he needed to win to force a play-off, while for me a draw would be good enough to take the title. I won his h-pawn (or rather he sacrificed it for a speculative attack), he went for broke by launching an attack on my castled king down the now open h file, I parried and launched a counter-attack, he failed to see how potent it was and, on move 31, faced with a simple three-move sequence that would force checkmate, he resigned. I was champion of the great, historic county of Surrey (brackets and in very small letters, division three). Perhaps, after all, this whole stop-start odyssey, characterised by good intentions and a bad work ethic, had been worthwhile. I would now have a cup to fondle, polish, cherish.

Naturally I obeyed the old dictum 'win with grace, lose with dignity'. Just as you should not turn over the board or assault your opponent when you lose, so you should never crow about winning. And I didn't. I liked David, a cultivated chess aficionado with a filmic French accent. He worked for an oil and gas company, and was about to be posted to Japan. This was his last serious game in the UK before his departure, but I didn't feel any guilt about giving him such a send-off. At least, I told him, he wouldn't have to pay all that yen to send the cup back to the UK in time for the start of the following year's competition.

The Doc was ecstatic when I showed him the moves – I had stressed this was his triumph as much as mine. 'Excellent! Really pleased for you. You were note perfect. He had to try to make the running but you gave him nothing to bite on. Once he had weakened his kingside, you did all the right things, at the right time and in the right order. 100/100. I feel like that athletics coach in *Chariots of Fire* played by Ian Holm when he hears "God Save the King" being played in the stadium nearby after Harold Abrahams wins the Olympic 100 metres final. It's a good feeling!' He was right: I had played a near-faultless game, and it was a very good feeling. All the ups and downs of the past three years were forgotten. Sometimes the pleasure of winning really could outweigh the pain of defeat. I was a champion and no one could take that away from me. Henceforth I would answer only to the name of 'Champ'.

G6: IS CHESS GOOD FOR YOU?

After winning the Felce I felt wonderful, but there was still part of me that accepted the carpers had a point. Was chess really a pursuit worth wasting your life for? Was it a boon or a curse? The American writer, inventor and statesman Benjamin Franklin, a keen (though by all accounts not very good) player, insisted it was the former, producing a much-reprinted essay called 'The Morals of Chess' (published in 1786 but written half a century earlier) which argued that it was good for the soul. 'The Game of Chess,' he wrote, 'is not merely an idle amusement. Several very valuable qualities of the mind, useful in the course of human life, are to be acquired or strengthened by it, so as to become habits, ready on all occasions. For life is a kind of chess, in which we have often points to gain, and competitors or adversaries to contend with, and in which there is a vast variety of good and ill events that are, in some degree, the effects of prudence or the want of it.' Franklin said chess taught you foresight, circumspection, caution and optimism.

More than two centuries later Garry Kasparov made the belief that chess offers signposts for life the basis of a self-help book, *How Life Imitates Chess*. The game, he argued, was an 'ideal instrument' for developing effective decision-making. 'Psychology and intuition affect every aspect of our decisions and our results,' said Kasparov. 'We must develop our ability to see the big picture, and deal with and learn from crises. Such decisive moments are turning points – every time we select a fork in the road knowing we won't be able to backtrack. We live for these moments and in turn they define our lives. We learn who we are and what truly matters to us.'

Jonathan Rowson, the former British champion and an immensely thoughtful writer on chess (and much else besides), had gone further, describing chess in a column in the Glasgow *Herald* newspaper as the rock on which his early life was founded: 'Chess gave me a way to channel difficult emotions into something creative and constructive. From the age of about five to about 25, whatever sadness and confusion I held inside me became fuel in my quest to improve.' Rowson was expressing the reason many people play the game. It was an arena to find yourself, a source of validation, a place where the rules and rituals made sense.

So much for chess's true believers. The antis were just as vehement. 'Amberley excelled at chess – one mark, Watson, of a scheming mind,' Conan Doyle has Sherlock Holmes say in the short story 'The Adventure of the Retired Colourman'. Victorian writers saw chess players as devious. The villainous Count Fosco in Wilkie Collins' *The Woman in White*, for instance, is an expert chess player. Deviousness was not the only charge laid against the game; it was also dull, at least according to the novelist Herman Melville, who in *Billy Budd* describes it as 'an oblique, tedious, barren game hardly worth that poor candle burnt out in playing it'.

George Bernard Shaw, the hater of all pastimes, could safely be ignored; H. G. Wells, though, was more interesting. On re-reading his essay 'Concerning Chess', I thought that, beneath all the bombast about the debilitating effects of the game, it was in reality rather affectionate. Wells was writing as a spurned lover of a game he could never master, a sentiment I could appreciate. 'There is no happiness in chess,' wrote Wells. 'No chess player sleeps well. After the painful strategy of the day, one fights one's battles over again. You see with more than daylight clearness that it was the rook you should have moved, and not the knight!' He was warning, mock-heroically, of the dangers of chess mania, but it was clearly a mania to which he himself had succumbed at some point in his life. Like all of us he had suffered those sleepless knights.

At the outset of my odyssey, I had hoped chess would be good for me – that it would make me a better, more complete, more focused person, able in some way to engage with life in a less superficial manner than in my first five decades. I had largely been disappointed: I had become a marginally better chess player, but there was no great evidence I had become a better, more focused person. I was still overweight – my dietary and gym regime, designed to back up my assault on this chess Everest, had never quite clicked into place; my commitment to work, in both chess and my rather understated career, remained uneven; I still felt I was underachieving and too inclined to drift along. Chess was supposed to change all that – to make me a more driven, purposeful individual, to give me the sort of moral boost Franklin had talked about and teach me the life lessons espoused by Kasparov. Some hope! Tarrasch said 'chess has the power to make men happy', but I thought former British champion James Plaskett's observation that 'the pure and solitary nature of chess attracts some fragile minds and helps hold them together' was nearer the mark. Or Bill Hartston's quip that 'chess doesn't drive people mad, it keeps mad people sane'.

Chess might not bring joy, but it could at times bring contentment and provide equilibrium for people who previously had none. 'Chess reflects how people long for meaning and purpose in their lives,' says Robert Desjarlais in the conclusion of his book *Counterplay*, 'how we want to live intensely, craft something of beauty, test ourselves against others and achieve a sense of mastery in our endeavours. Chess speaks to the place of ritual and cultural forms in our lives, and how we seek rites, devices, or magical charms to keep anxiety at bay.' I liked the idea of chess as rite – a sacred rite, which was how Luzhin's father described the way his gifted son approached the game.

In an essay in the *New Republic* in 1983 called 'The Romance of Chess', the writer, political commentator and chess enthusiast Charles Krauthammer defended the game against critics such as George Steiner who derided its sterility. Why should it have to produce some tangible benefit? asked Krauthammer. 'To indict chess for not producing monuments is to indict all play and many of the arts ... It is in the nature of beauty to have no use and few products. Why turn somersaults on a four-inch (not three, not five) balance beam? Because it is difficult and demands perfection of certain human faculties, the exercise and apprehension of which are beautiful. There is no other answer.' Chess was pointless, but rather wonderful in its pointlessness, like so much human play.

According to his biographer, Calvin Tomkins, Marcel Duchamp knew why he loved chess, and why it sustained him all his life. 'Duchamp's working methods were marked by an almost mathematical precision,' wrote Tomkins, 'and one of the things he loved about chess was that its most brilliant innovations took place within a framework of strict and unbendable rules. "Chess is a marvellous piece of Cartesianism," he once told me, "and so imaginative that it doesn't even look Cartesian at first. The beautiful combinations that chess players invent – you don't see them coming, but afterward there is no mystery – it's a purely logical conclusion."'

Infinite variety and possibility within a strict framework was one of the joys of chess, and one reason I dismissed all the chess variants. It had become apparent to me why Duchamp likened chess players to artists. It was not so much that they created art, more that they strove to enjoy the mental freedom of the artist and give themselves scope to create. It was an attitude of mind. Chess, whatever Franklin and his followers might have thought, was not a moral good or a guide to living. Like much of art it was an assault on bourgeois convention. Why shouldn't you play for a living or, in the case of many professional chess players, a pseudo-living? Chess might not make you a better person, but it could make you a freer one.

G7: MY CUP RUNNETH OVER

 A new season was beginning, and at one of my first matches – against Dorking, the home club of the organiser of the Surrey individual championships – I picked up the Felce Cup, newly inscribed with my name. It was a huge silver trophy that the tournament director had wrapped in a plastic bag – the symbol of British chess. Kingston's second team were playing Dorking firsts, and I had hoped for a smattering of applause from my team-mates, but they were oblivious to this historic moment, which passed with merely a handshake between the organiser and me. Still, I felt the hand of chess history on my shoulder. The evening got even better when my opponent in the match handed me a knight for nothing early in the game. The game was over by move 24 and suddenly I felt anything was possible. I spent the train journey home studying the inscriptions on the cup, listing all the winners since 1922 (annoyingly the names from the 1920s were in larger letters than mine). Several of the former winners had become well-known players, though it had to be said they had tended to win this trophy very early in their careers. I was one of the more mature champions. Nonetheless, I felt I had chiselled my tiny niche in chess history and immediately made the cup the avatar on my Twitter feed.

Hubris, was, however, lurking. The following Saturday I headed down to Horsham to play for the Surrey under-160 team against Sussex (this was based on grade not age). These matches were anachronisms and the travelling was irritating, but I still got a bit of a kick out of 'representing your county', in the evocative lingo used by the team captains when they were trying to persuade you to play. It felt like something out of the 1930s. On this occasion, though, I rather wished that I hadn't been representing my county, as I was soundly beaten by one of those middle-aged men whose outward affability disguises an inner steel. We lost the match narrowly, and I felt my lacklustre performance had played its part. Thank God I could cradle my cup when I got home and remember the ups rather than the downs.

'Chess is a foolish thing; sometimes it works, and sometimes it doesn't work,' said Efim Bogoljubov, who twice challenged Alekhine for the world title. Increasingly I felt this to be true: there were good days and bad days; days when you saw everything (or at least enough) and days when you saw nothing. My excursion to Horsham was a bad day. I played poorly; ate a cold, unhealthy, unappealing pasty; and got stuck on a crowded, slow-running train on the way home. It was a day when chess, that foolish thing, really didn't work. But I no longer beat myself up too much about such failures. I was teaching myself to feel disappointment in defeat but not pain. Rather than berate myself, I tried to learn from the loss, putting the game into the computer as soon as I got home and looking at the four or five key positions where I could have chosen better moves. I was at last getting some sense of perspective. I'd lost a rating point or two; we'd lost the match; but I had my trophy, my shiny, silver talisman – symbol of a succession of days when chess did work – and the wheel would turn again. At least I hoped it would.

I had an early opportunity to put my new-found equanimity to the test at a weekender in Bury St Edmunds – five rounds played over a Saturday and Sunday at an arts venue bang in the centre of the medieval town, which was populated by a curious combination of affluent middle-aged English gents in thick brown corduroy trousers and new workers from eastern Europe. In round one, on a bright and unseasonally warm Saturday morning in October, I was black against a classic codger. He played the Stonewall Attack, a well-known d4 line that is much loved by tournament amateurs, and the game seemed to be heading for a draw. But he made a small imprecision at around move 40 that allowed me to win a pawn, and after three and a half hours I managed to grind him down. I had only seconds left on the clock when he resigned – there was no increment, so it was easily possible to lose on time. As the flag on my clock started to show danger signals and with the five-minute rule in operation, I stopped recording my moves to save time. He complained afterwards that he thought this was unfair, which I thought was a touch ungracious, but I didn't really care. I had the victory, and was up and running.

At several points in the game, when I felt he had a small plus, I considered offering a draw. Had I done so, that would have set the tone for a very different tournament. I would have been chugging along in midfield looking at my usual mediocre result. But the win seemed to change everything. In the second game I chanced my newly acquired King's Gambit against a bright young junior who played very quickly (indeed, too quickly – a common fault among juniors). I built a powerful attack in a complicated position, won some material, and resolved the position into a winning endgame. I was 2/2 and feeling great. It was, as ever, a struggle to maintain focus and stop the rest of the world intruding on the 64. But when you are doing well and starting to get a sense that you might be in the shake-up it becomes possible to hone your concentration and tell yourself that all that matters is winning the next game.

The Saturday evening encounter was tough. I took another gamble and played a King's Indian – another of my recently acquired (and still imperfectly understood) openings. The battle was tense; I started to get into time trouble; I won a pawn. But the position was far from clear, and as my time started to run out I offered a draw. My opponent rejected it – he told me later that he was sure that with just a few minutes left on my clock I would make a mistake. But I didn't. He lost two further pawns, I promoted one of my extra pawns to a queen, and managed to mate him with seconds left on my clock. Again a lucky break – I could have lost on time and would have been mentally shot. He could have accepted the draw and I would have been in a pack of players on 2.5/3. But he didn't. He chose to play on and the win meant I was now sole overnight leader on 3/3. The line between winning and losing, doing well and being one of the also-rans, is perilously thin.

I slept badly after too large a Chinese meal. But I wasn't panicking. I knew what I had to do and none of my opponents in this under-145 event (it was officially called the 'Intermediate', still de facto division three as there was an Open and a Major) seemed too terrifying. The morning game was complicated and I failed to anticipate several key moves by my opponent. By move 20 he was a pawn up, but I had a small positional advantage which gave me some compensation. To my surprise he offered a draw and I took it, realising I would then be at least joint leader going into the final round. In fact, it turned out better than that. All my closest rivals drew, so I was a half-point clear after round four and knew that a draw in the last round would mean I was certain to be joint winner of the tournament. And if I could win the final round, the prize would be mine alone. As I sat in a café eating a rather unappealing jacket potato and reading Andrew Soltis's book on Bobby Fischer for inspiration, I felt complete contentment: 3.5/4, top of the tree, in line for a prize. Oddly I harboured no fear that it might all go wrong in the final round. I had feared round four more, thinking back to my fourth-round disaster in Aberystwyth when I was starting to have visions of winning the British title. Now I realised that, whatever happened, I had had a good tournament. I also had no thoughts of trying to draw my final game, to get a share of first prize. I would play to win, even though I had black.

My opponent, half a point behind in a batch of players on three points, had the same idea. He went all out for a win and built a massive attack that looked as if it would secure him victory. But he kept giving up material to get the attack – first rook for bishop, then a bishop, leaving him a whole rook down. Even then, again in horrible time trouble, I could have gone wrong. But I kept finding good defensive moves (see Game 10 on p389), and in the end his attack ran out of steam. I felt relief rather than excitement at the end. It really had looked at one point as if I would be crushed. But above all I felt a surge of pride. I was champion of Bury St Edmunds (OK, champion of the third-tier competition), and stayed on into the early evening to pick up my £200 prize. Matthew Sadler, one of the strongest English grandmasters of all time (his ECF rating is a towering 280), won the Open tournament, and just for a moment I could share the limelight with a truly great player. It was a wonderful feeling. I had played well, fought hard, coped with time trouble, and enjoyed the necessary good fortune that turned an average score into a winning score. Something had clicked. And sometimes, it seemed, chess really could be good for you.

G8: 'WE ARE ODD,
BUT NOT BARKING'

 After winning the Felce and triumphing in Bury St Edmunds I felt I was close to the top of what I had come to regard as the third division of chess in the UK. My live rating, which I was now assiduously calculating, was about 143. Could I go higher? A couple of weeks after Bury, I played in the strongest tournament in which I'd ever participated. There were a dozen grandmasters, including reigning British champion David Howell, former world number four Jon Speelman, the immensely strong Matthew Sadler, who had recently returned to chess after a lengthy break, and Bill Hartston, who was playing his first over-the-board chess for 20 years. Add a clutch of other titled players, and 50 other experts, and this was an outrageously strong field.

I realised it would probably be an embarrassment for me, but went along because it was primarily a social occasion – an invitational blitz tournament at the Kings Head pub in Bayswater, a famous chess hangout in the 1970s and 1980s, played in memory of the English international master Andrew Whiteley, who had died a couple of months previously. Whiteley had run the Kings Head Chess Club and this was a fitting way of communing with the spirit of one of those dedicated old English amateurs who had devoted his life to the game he loved. The tournament was sponsored by David Norwood, a grandmaster who had made a fortune in investment banking and now lived in Andorra but who made periodic sorties to the UK to support chess. I wasn't quite sure why I had been invited to play in such exalted company, but was very pleased to have been asked.

At least I thought I was pleased. As defeat followed defeat I wondered whether it was really wise for me to be playing against such a field. We were divided into groups of ten, and I was 40 grading points weaker than any other player in my section. In fact the next weakest player was my coach, Doc Saunders, so from the off I knew I had my work cut out to make even half a point. I lost to grandmaster Simon Williams in the first game; got horribly beaten up by a 200-graded player in game two; was mated beautifully by an IM in game three – 'Thematic,' he said, admiringly, as he administered the *coup de grâce*; gave a bishop away in one game, a queen in acute time trouble in another. We were playing five-minute blitz, and to try to compete against players of this strength with so little time was impossible. I ended up with 0/9 and just hoped my ego – bolstered by those recent tournament wins – was robust enough to withstand the onslaught. I reckoned I'd played three reasonable games, including the one I lost on time against the Doc. The rest I consigned to oblivion, entering into the spirit of the occasion by drinking a couple of pints of London Pride in honour of Whiteley, who had sat on a stool propping up the bar hereabouts for decades.

A few weeks later I went to meet Speelman, who had been runner-up in the tournament, at his flat in Hampstead, north London. He was now nearing 60 and his full-time playing days had ended a decade earlier, but his rating was still comfortably above 2500 and, as I had seen at the Kings Head, his competitive spirit remained undimmed. He had been a shaggy, friendly, somewhat unworldly presence in British chess for 40 years, instantly recognisable with his shock of wiry hair and shapeless sweaters.

Julian Barnes, in his essay about the 1993 Kasparov–Short world title match, offered a wonderful description of Speelman, who was acting as one of the on-screen experts for Channel 4's rather optimistic blanket TV coverage of the event: 'Tall, gawky and shy, with downcast eyes, thick-lensed spectacles and a circular shrubbery of comb-free hair, Specimen is the ultimate boffin version of the chess player.' 'Specimen', as Barnes explained, is Speelman's nickname – the result of a gloriously apposite *Times* misprint from a tournament report in 1981, though over time 'Specimen' has tended to be abbreviated to 'Spess'. Barnes thought Speelman an untelevisual figure, but I would beg to differ; he is everyone's image of the dedicated chess player and should be given his own TV programme immediately. He would be perfect in a reconstituted Master Game alongside a cluster of other glorious eccentrics. What a boost that would be for chess, even if some players might feel it was pandering to the media and the public's idea that all chess players were potty.

Speelman, who was chess adviser on the 2000 film *The Luzhin Defense* – 'I tried to get John Turturro to look a bit like a chess player,' he recalled – is one of those who rejects the all-chess-players-are-certifiable argument: 'We are odd, but we are not necessarily completely barking. And for players who are eccentric, chess offers a way of living quite fulfilled lives in a safe environment. Chess players generally are not bad to each other when they're away from the board; they just try to kill each other at the board, which is a lot more healthy than many things.' I asked him whether he agreed with Hans Ree's suggestion that chess was a game beautiful enough to waste your life for. 'It doesn't have to be as deliberate as that,' he said. 'I went to university, got a reasonable degree, thought, "I'll play chess for a couple of years because I really don't want to get a boring job," and then I got a bit better, and the idea of the boring job became that much more something I didn't want to do, so I carried on. It wasn't a very deliberate idea to become a professional chess player and, when I did it, it was hugely easier than nowadays.' He said he had never regretted his decision.

Speelman once said chess was 'a medium through which concentration and a higher state of mind is achieved … it is like contemplating your navel, only better.' When I reminded him of this quote, he explained what he had meant: 'My concept of time changes completely when I play chess. Five or six hours hardly seems to take any time at all.' He said that when he played in a team match, so intense was his concentration on his own game that he would have no sense of the games being played on either side of him: 'The normal continuity of viewing the world outside goes. Once I'm playing I'm completely focused, until it's over and I'm unfocused. I like that very much. It's an endeavour where you can transcend yourself.'

Since retiring as a player he has earned a living by writing about chess and doing a little coaching where, rather than dogmatically laying down rules, he encourages his students to learn by osmosis: 'I don't like telling people what to do in any circumstances, especially in chess, where people have to take responsibility for themselves at the board.' He is not one of those players who was marooned by the coming of computers, and quickly adapted to the way they changed chess. Nor is he worried they will kill chess, either by solving it any time soon or by making human players seem irrelevant. In Speelman's view they are calculating machines and don't really understand chess. 'They don't outplay humans,' he said. 'They out-error-check them. They take things when we leave them *en prise*. It doesn't matter that human beings blunder, because it can't be helped; we do. Computers don't often do anything very original, and when they play each other they quite often have really awful games. You need some sort of guiding hand behind the fact that they can calculate to infinity and beyond.' Speelman was the first person who introduced me to the idea of 'truth' in chess when we met a decade or so previously, and his belief that only humans had access to that truth was reassuring.

Speelman was an optimist about the future of chess, and rejected my nostalgia for the golden age of the first half of the 20th century. He admitted chess had declined in Russia – its dominance in the Soviet era, he suggested, reflected an era in which people had nothing else to do – but pointed to its growth in China and India, and to the renewed enthusiasm in the US thanks to Rex Sinquefield's money and several top players becoming naturalised Americans in a determined bid to produce an Olympiad-winning team. 'Chess has always been a minority activity in the west,' he said, 'and I don't think it'll slip off the radar completely.' I told him there had been times during my journey when I felt I might be writing an elegy for the game. 'I hope not,' he said simply. Chess evolves and the past always has a golden glow. It may be that the pros have a less rose-tinted view of the game's former glories than us amateurs.

After talking together for a couple of hours, Speelman showed me his large, chaotic study, which was packed with trophies and plaques, scores of mementoes of a chess-playing life. It made my Felce Cup look rather lonely. To keep them for so long, down to every last dusty little shield, showed how much they meant to Speelman. But it wasn't his entire life: he has a son and said he had never sought to 'inflict' chess on him. 'Why should he suffer?' said Speelman. 'I see no reason why I should inflict the suffering of losing games of chess on someone I love. I don't think it's fair. It's a type of suffering you choose yourself. Having chosen it, it's tough; you have to get on with it and accept that it will be incredibly painful sometimes.'

It reminded me of a story grandmaster John Nunn told me when I bumped into him at the launch party for the Candidates Tournament played in London in 2013. He recalled being at a tournament with Speelman at Chester in 1979 when he overheard a father talking to his son. 'Those two are strong chess players,' said the father sagely, pointing at Speelman and Nunn. 'You don't want to grow up like that.'

FILE H
Fail Again, Fail Better

'I was playing chess with my friend and he said, "Let's
make this interesting." So we stopped playing chess'
                                    – *Comedian Matt Kirshen*

H1: VLAD COMES TO TOWN

In December my Russian grandmaster friend Vladislav Tkachiev came to the UK for the annual London Classic, where he was playing in the Open. It was wonderful to see him again, feed off his energy, and experience the Classic vicariously through Tkachiev's participation in a tough nine-rounder. He beat a young English junior in the first round, dispatched a good Polish player in the second, and dismissed an up-and-coming British IM in the third. I was getting enormous satisfaction from his wins, while constantly panicking that he was going to blow up. He was now past 40 and I wasn't sure how up for the fight he was in this field of youthful wannabes. But he didn't let me down. He pressed for a win in game four against Keith Arkell, the veteran English GM I'd met at Hastings. The wily Arkell escaped with a draw, as did the young Chinese IM Jinshi Bai – the eventual joint winner of the tournament – whom Tkachiev met in round five.

On the Saturday and Sunday the players in the Open had to play twice each day, and I was anxious Tkachiev would forget there was a morning game – the preceding games had all been in the afternoon. He had a tendency to show up late, which panicked me (though I wondered later if it was a psychological ploy), but he eventually arrived and won in great style against a young German IM. After another victory in the afternoon he was on 6/7 and going well, but on the Sunday he was suffering from a cold and accepted two short draws. That left him undefeated in the tournament on 7/9 – a good result which meant he gained a few rating points, but not quite good enough to win the event. He was joint third with five other players behind Bai and 19-year-old Polish GM Kamil Dragun. For his week's slog at Olympia, the west London home of the Classic, he won £750, not even enough to cover the costs of the flight and the cheap hotel he'd stayed in for the week.

While he was playing the tournament, Tkachiev entered a kind of purdah and didn't communicate much, but the day after it ended we met for coffee and a debrief. He was happy with his level of play. 'I hadn't played for five months, so it went surprisingly well,' he told me. He said he was undermined by the cold and by what sounded like nervous exhaustion. He said when he was young, nerves affected him in a positive way, but as he got older they became more problematic. It was that, above all, which tended to reduce the potency of older players: 'I was always stressed, but in my twenties it helped me to become stronger. I even cultivated the stress inside of me because I knew it was going to help. But now it doesn't. I have the same habit of being tense, but it has the contrary effect on me. I understand chess better now and have a much wider vision of the game, but I have less energy and am much more likely to be destabilised psychologically.'

The time controls were tight at the Classic – even classical chess is tending to speed up in our unreflective age – and Tkachiev, used to playing in more leisurely tournaments (and despite being a noted blitz player), found that added to the pressure. Nevertheless he seemed happy enough and was no longer talking of retirement: 'If I'm continuing to play chess, it's because I can still teach those youngsters some lessons. Once I am not capable any more I am going to leave chess. I am not playing just for the sake of playing chess. I'm playing to win. I'm a very competitive guy. I don't just want to participate; I want to win.'

I managed three trips to the Classic – the nearest thing the UK has to an international festival of chess, with GMs competing alongside amateurs and a big emphasis on encouraging children to play. On one of those visits, I played a blitz game against English grandmaster Stephen Gordon. Gordon, whom I'd met before at a couple of events, was a friendly 28-year-old who had recently taken a proper job in accountancy, in effect turning his back on professional chess. It was a sensible decision, given the earning potential of a 2500-rated GM. He was sitting out the Open in which he would normally have been playing and taking on all-comers for a few quid a game to raise money for Chess in Schools and Communities instead – I played pretty well in our game and he showed me a chance I'd missed towards the end.

I wondered what choice I would have made if I'd been that good at chess: to try to survive as a pro, despite the penury and the dangers of getting stale and going downhill after the age of 40, or to join the workaday world and either stop playing – as many strong players do when they cease to be pros – or play as an amateur. I was almost certain I would have tried to eke out a living as a professional. The beauty of the game and the simplicity of the lifestyle appealed to me. The board was a country I could imagine inhabiting always. The idea of never having a proper job, which I had come to believe was the main incentive for chess pros, was also infectious. Some may claim to be artists but most, I had concluded, were professional layabouts, hoping to suspend the normal rules of life and forever escape the world of work. 'I have the life of a restaurant waiter,' Marcel Duchamp told art critic Pierre Cabanne, describing his free and easy lifestyle. That was the freedom I craved. To be a Duchamp, living on my wits or my art, or a Tkachiev, living out of a suitcase and a chess database. If only I had a rating of 2730 rather than 1730, I could have put my theory about my career (or anti-career) inclinations to the test.

H2: THE FULL ENGLISH

 Despite my chilly memories of the previous year I had once again decided to try my luck at Hastings in the New Year weekender. The portents, though, were far from good. I had twisted my knee a month or so before and it was intermittently aching. Worse, the day before leaving for the south coast I had played some New Year's Day blitz with Doc Saunders and my Kingston team-mate John Foley and performed dismally. To say I had low expectations would be an understatement. I was looking to avoid ignominy, no more.

It was at least a beautiful winter's morning when I limped off, and even dowdy Hastings sparkled in the sun when the dawdling train from Waterloo finally deposited me there just before 2pm. True to the promise I had made to myself to avoid cheap hotels, I had booked to stay at a pricier 'holistic' B&B close to the playing venue. My old guru Carrera, who had been rather sidelined since my American adventure had taught me to value freedom ahead of discipline, would have approved: organic breakfasts with lots of fruit; emphasis on a stress-free environment; no television in the room; space for intense contemplation and the monkish devotion Alekhine said was necessary to do well in a tournament.

After checking in I had a couple of hours to kill before the evening game with which the five-round weekender began. I wanted to look at Hastings Chess Club – one of the few clubs in the country which, like the Marshall Club in New York, owns its own premises (a four-storey building bequeathed by old member Victor Pelton in 1953) and opens every day of the year (except Christmas Day). The tournament only exists because of the club, which was founded in 1882 and organised the magnificent event in 1895 which attracted world champion Emanuel Lasker and former title holder Wilhelm Steinitz, as well as a host of other legendary figures, including Siegbert Tarrasch, Mikhail Chigorin, Richard Teichmann, Joseph Blackburne and Carl Schlechter. That inaugural tournament had been won, surprisingly, by the 22-year-old American Harry Pillsbury, one of those troubled geniuses in which US chess seems to specialise. His career after his great victory at Hastings was undermined by persistent illness, almost certainly syphilis, and he died in 1906 aged 33, another of those lost champions.

Unfortunately my plan to see the Hastings club was thwarted. It transpired that 'open every day of the year except Christmas' actually meant closed – unless you were a member and had a key. I buzzed a few times, but the members were either asleep or elsewhere – probably up at the sports centre watching the Masters event, a pale shadow of the great tournament of 1895 but still able to bring together a score of titled players, including a few overseas grandmasters and English GMs such as Keith Arkell, Mark Hebden and joint British champion Jonathan Hawkins. I decided to join the spectators at the sports hall and headed up the hill, which made my knee ache even more. Once there I settled down to watch former British champion Chris Ward's incisive and amusing commentary of the day's games. His analysis, conducted in a room close to the playing hall, is a tradition at Hastings, though it was rather sad that he kept quoting the number of viewers watching him online, since it rarely rose above a hundred. Chess, for all its manifold virtues, is a backwater. It's been a long way down since the glories of 1895. I did at least have the pleasure of suggesting a move which he thought was very good, and was rewarded with a small Snickers bar – the award of sweets in his occasional 'guess-the-move' competitions was another much-loved Hastings tradition. This was probably the high point of my tournament.

My first game, against a player graded 114, was a tense four-hour struggle. At one point, so twisted were my facial contortions as I battled to get some sort of initiative that my opponent asked me whether I wanted to go to the toilet. A first, for sure. I managed to get a pawn up by about move 20, but then became over-defensive – once again falling victim to 'won game' syndrome – and my opponent missed an obvious move which would have secured a draw. Ours was the last game to finish, on the stroke of 11pm, and I did in the end manage to win, but I was extremely fortunate and could not claim to have played well. Still, I had eked out a victory and could return contentedly to my room (which was called 'Khayyam' and filled with improving books such as *The Self-Sufficient Life and How to Live It*) at the peaceful, holistic, organic, Persian-themed B&B.

I played a good, controlled game on Saturday morning, as white against a player graded 147, and won well. The Doc was impressed with this game when I showed it to him later. 'With most of the games that we've looked at where you've won I've been able to say, "Well, your opponent made a mistake – he left a piece hanging." But here I can't say that. He's made a very slight positional error, that's all. You've maintained a slight advantage right the way through to winning the game, and much stronger players are very happy to do that.' I had won without my opponent doing anything obviously wrong – the sign of a strong player. 'This game is quite significant,' said the Doc portentously – and extremely encouragingly.

As so often, however, morning joy turned into ashes in the afternoon, when I came a cropper against a player who used ear-plugs to increase his concentration and showed great intensity at the board. At one point he told me to stop making notes in the little black book I always carried with me – note-taking during games was illegal, he pointed out. He even chastised me for toying with my water bottle, which certainly wasn't illegal. None of this really put me off, but it did suggest a great will to win on his part. I played my tedious old opening standby, the Scandinavian, and it went horribly wrong, putting me at a big disadvantage after just a few moves. I squirmed through the rest of the game and came close to equalising a few times, but he nailed me in the end in a time scramble. He had wanted it more than me, but, more to the point, he had played better than me. I had, though, managed to play 12 arduous hours of chess in the past 24, and was on a respectable 2/3 going into Sunday.

My Sunday morning win, against the man to whom I had lost on time at Hastings the year before, was hugely satisfying – a crushing win in 20 moves. It owed more to some bizarre moves by my opponent than to any stroke of genius by me. Indeed, the line I had calculated following an exchange (rook for bishop) sac didn't work, and I was lucky there was another way in which I could win. But when we came to analyse it, I could massage this and claim to have seen everything. It was quick, beautiful, deadly and put me on 3/4, suddenly in with a chance of a prize.

Once again, though, the final afternoon and my weakness with the black pieces did for me. My opponent in the final round was one of those grizzled technicians who play the English opening. I had always struggled against the English and did so again. He got a small plus in the opening, went a pawn up, got it to the seventh rank, and then tied me in knots. It was horrible, pointless, embarrassing. I hated this game and told myself to learn to play against the English or give up. He wasn't very highly graded yet he had beaten me with ease. I didn't even have the pleasure of resigning with a flourish. I had noticed earlier in the tournament that the player next to me, when he resigned, did so by laying down his king theatrically and smiling – an admirable way to accept defeat, I had thought. But I just couldn't bring myself to do it: all I managed was a shrug and a mumbled 'Well played.'

The last thing I saw as I left the playing hall a few minutes later was my opponent giving his name and address to the organisers, so they could send him his £100 prize for coming joint second. That could have been me if I'd won. As it was, I'd finished joint ninth with 3/5. I had lost my 'death match' and I hadn't even made my opponent sweat. He had simply out-techniqued me. I vowed never to let it happen again, though as the Doc, who was there for the final game, said, I had vowed to do an awful lot of things. This was at least the third time I had vowed to learn the English, yet it still remained a foreign language to me.

H3: 'I'M LIKE A WEST BROM MIDFIELDER'

One of the veteran – or, at 38, near-veteran – English grandmasters playing at Hastings was Danny Gormally. I had been pursuing him for more than a year – he lived in the north-east of England and had kept eluding me – but I finally managed to grab him for a couple of hours before a Saturday evening blitz tournament at the White Rock Hotel on the seafront at Hastings, a gathering point for many of the GMs playing in the Masters. Gormally fascinated me because, on his blog, he was so honest about the demons that plagued him, his love-hate relationship with chess, and the anger and self-loathing he felt when he played badly. He was having a poor tournament, losing to two players rated well below him, and had tweeted a sad summing up of his form: 'Lost to 2100 players with white and also lost to a 1900 player – the worst year of my chess life. If 2015 is like this, I will quit chess.' Another tweet a week or two earlier had also attracted my attention: 'Without chess my life would be completely pointless. As it is, it's only 99 per cent so.' Could the life of a chess pro really be so grim?

Gormally had lost to a young female player with a FIDE rating around 2300 on the day before we met and told me how it felt: 'I got a great position out of the opening, she played a move – b4 – and I should have spent some time and thought about the position, but instead of that I played too quickly and missed her reply. I was really angry with myself afterwards. After that, though objectively I was about equal, I was demoralised because I had stood better earlier in the game. It's very difficult when you play not to be consumed by your emotions, and very hard to adjust psychologically to a change in circumstances. Chess takes you on an emotional journey, and what you play is informed by what happened earlier in the game. It's psychological warfare against yourself.' Gormally is disarmingly honest. Whereas many GMs present themselves as paragons of objectivity, striving for a quasi-scientific approach to chess, he admits he's as prone as us amateurs to moods that affect the way he plays.

Gormally is proud to be a GM, but with a rating around 2500 is realistic about where he is in the pecking order: 'The difference between me and the top players is very large. People think, "You're a GM, so there can't be that big a difference," but there is. One of the misconceptions that people of my strength seem to have is that they're only losing to these top guys because they're making one or two moves better. But the reality is that they are just on a different level and are outplaying you almost every move. It's like in football: when you watch Ronaldo and Messi play, you instantly see the difference between them and the average player. I'm like a Premier League player, but a bog-standard West Brom midfielder, whereas someone like Magnus Carlsen is like a Messi. There's a big difference.' That said, though Gormally realises he can never be a Lionel Messi and play for the chess equivalent of Barcelona, he wouldn't mind being touted for a transfer from lowly West Brom to middling West Ham: 'Why I get angry is because I don't feel I'm achieving my potential. I feel I'm a good player and feel quite sharp at the moment, but there are weaknesses holding me back. I play too quickly, lose my objectivity and don't look deeply enough into the position.' He is not one of those players who can laugh off defeats, and said he once walked into a forest next to the playing venue and screamed with anguish. But he reckons the plus side is that would-be champions should feel mortified by defeat – Garry Kasparov took defeat notably badly. 'Show me a good loser and I'll show you a loser,' said Gormally, quoting American football coach Vince Lombardi.

Gormally was a relatively late developer in chess (remember that most truly world-class players becomes GMs in their early teens). His father taught him to play when he was seven, and the young Danny showed ability. But he never got any formal coaching and became strong only in his mid-teens. He said he was an introverted, anti-social child, flunked school and thought chess might allow him to succeed at something, so worked hard at it. He became an international master at 21, but then lost his focus and didn't become a GM until he was 29. Becoming a grandmaster is, he told me, a double-edged sword, because once you have the title you're inclined to coast and let your rating drift downwards. His peak rating was 2573 in 2006, but he'd lost almost 80 points since.

He told me he was still inspired by the creativity of the game and motivated to try to reverse the decline in his rating – but at the same time earning a living was difficult. He had been given a hotel room to play in Hastings and a fee of £100 to appear, but that isn't much for ten days' slog. He failed to get a prize, so ended up making a loss on the tournament. It's no sort of career. The only player who could afford to smile after the event was Chinese grandmaster Zhao Jun – part of China's accelerating takeover of the game – who took the £2,000 first prize. Three foreign titled players came joint second and earned just over £800 each. Then came four GMs, including Keith Arkell and Jonathan Hawkins, in joint fifth, for which they each won the princely sum of £160. If they were eastern European fruit pickers, the Department of Work and Pensions would be taking a close look at their hourly rates.

Gormally does very little coaching – he doesn't enjoy it and, in any case, lives in a thinly populated part of the country where potential students are few. 'I struggle to get interested in my own chess, let alone someone else's,' he said, with a laugh. 'I'm quite a bad coach because I lose patience with these people.' The only way he can survive as a pro is to reduce his overheads almost to zero, which is why at 38 he was still living with his parents. He told me he had occasionally tried jobs outside chess, but that they had always ended in disaster, notably when he dropped a £100,000 painting on his first day working for a furniture removal company. 'Most of my jobs have only lasted half a day,' he said. Work was a hostile environment and chess offered a sanctuary, albeit an extremely ill-paid one. But what could he now hope to achieve? 'Let's be realistic, I'm not suddenly going to get to 2700. You don't improve that much at 38. But I do feel there's the potential to improve. The problem is that you need to play better players to get better. When you play in England, you're playing 2100 and 2200 players, and you won't learn anything from that.'

Gormally is funny and self-deprecating, but the bleakness of some of his tweets is real. 'I wish there was more to my life,' he said. 'I've got a lot of friends in chess, but I don't have much of a social life outside that.' In a notorious incident at the 2006 Olympiad, he punched Armenian grandmaster Levon Aronian on the dancefloor of the Turin nightclub Hiroshima Mon Amour because he was dancing with a female player he admired. The unfortunate blow was the result, he explained at the time, of a combination of love, alcohol and jealousy that Aronian was 'the world number three and I'm the world number two hundred and something'.

The incident made Gormally contemplate giving up the game. 'There are a lot of egos, a lot of competitiveness; it just doesn't interest me,' he said immediately afterwards. 'I've always been a very lazy person and the problem with chess is that you have to be completely obsessive about it. You have to have the passion, but gradually I think I've lost it.' Yet here he was a decade later still playing, still studying, still hoping he could get back to where he was at his peak, and still oscillating between love for the dreamy glories of the game and loathing for the nightmares it induces when things go badly. Would he ever quit? 'I'll talk a lot about how I'm going to do something different, but in ten years' time I'll probably still be here at Hastings. There's no pension in chess. You get to 50 and you have to carry on. I've often said I'll give up – it's an emotional reaction: "I'll never play chess again!" – but I never do. There's nothing else I'm good at. If I gave up chess, I'd just be another pleb, another nobody, going into some other activity, starting from scratch.'

H4: DEATH OF A STALWART

Early in 2015 I made my debut for Surbiton II in the Four Nations Chess League (4NCL) – the premier British club tournament. On five weekends a year dozens of teams gather at hotels in the Midlands to contest matches in three divisions. There are 16 teams, packed with grandmasters, in division one; another 16 very strong teams in division two; and everyone else – more than 50 teams in all – playing at another hotel near Northampton. I managed a draw against a player of about my strength and suffered an honourable defeat against a very strong player who, I discovered later, had drawn games with English grandmasters Michael Adams and Luke McShane.

Though I played solidly in the latter game, my attitude towards the end annoyed me: I was telling myself that I had played reasonably well and given him a decent game; I should have been telling myself not to be satisfied with dignified defeat, to keep fighting and to enjoy the laborious endgame. The Germans have a useful word for this (as for most things in chess) – *Sitzfleisch*, the ability to sit there indefinitely, playing 100-plus moves and enjoying the battle. As well as improving my endgame technique, I needed to toughen up, though when he saw this game the Doc reckoned I had played well. 'If you had managed to get a draw, it would have been a tremendous result, easily your best ever,' he said consolingly. So near and yet so far.

The 4NCL weekend was overshadowed by the death of my Kingston II captain, Chris Clegg. Clegg was in his mid-sixties and had played chess all his life. Indeed, by the end chess was his life.

He had had several nervous breakdowns and been forced to give up his job as a solicitor in his thirties. He lived alone, said little, dressed shabbily, clearly did not look after himself, but he still played good chess and took the game very seriously. For me he was the quintessential English club amateur and one reason I began my own journey through chess. I was fascinated by people such as Clegg, who had more or less given up on life (or perhaps been given up on by life) and now just lived on and for the board. Former world title contender Viktor Korchnoi called his autobiography *Chess Is My Life*, and that phrase is just as applicable to Clegg and many other club amateurs.

There were moving tributes to Clegg on the online English Chess Forum, and a couple of his former opponents posted the moves of games he had played against them. 'His dedication saw the club through some difficult times as membership levels declined,' wrote Kingston chairman John Foley. 'He never complained about anything.' Chess teacher and writer Richard James, co-author of *The Complete Chess Addict*, had known him all his life and caught him perfectly: 'Chris was one of those highly intelligent, rather introverted people who tend very often to be drawn to chess. Chess kept Chris going and Chris kept Kingston Chess Club going.' 'He was one of those fixtures on the circuit,' said another player. And that, indeed, is what he was: part of the furniture of English club chess, one of that generation of grammar-school boys who grew up with chess in the 1950s and never lost their love for the game. With Clegg's death I felt even more that I was writing an elegy for an era of chess – the anoraked, pens-in-the-top pocket, draughty-church-hall brand of the game played in the UK by men who, in some respects, had never ceased to be small boys.

The small band of ancients who make up Kingston Chess Club held a meeting-cum-wake in a noisy local pub for Clegg, and somehow in the course of it, weakened by a couple of glasses of red wine, I accepted the position of second-team captain left vacant by his death. The problem of finding six bodies a match from a club with such meagre human resources and playing in a benighted 24-hour supermarket on the A3 would henceforth be mine.

In late January the latest English Chess Federation grades were published. I had risen another five points to 141 – reasonable progress, I felt, though I knew I was still playing patchily. On the day the grades were published I played in my first match for Kingston as second-team captain. Everyone had said captaining weakened you as a player because of the distractions – fretting over players turning up late (or not turning up at all), explaining the rules, arbitrating over disputes, keeping track of scores – and so it proved. I was beaten by a player graded 128, though happily the team won the match, so I was able to accept my defeat with something approaching equanimity. I was starting to wonder whether my skills were better suited to organisation than playing. I was eyeing the possibility of inventing the position of 'head of enterprise' (which I thought had a nice whiff of modern management gobbledygook) for myself at Kingston and trying to reinvent the club, make it relevant for the 21st century, connect with local schools, the university (which supposedly had a chess club) and the community. It was perhaps the first flickering of a chess messiah complex. Perhaps I could save this wonderful game. First Kingston, tomorrow the world.

H5: THE TROUBLE WITH WOMEN

 Women were reckoned to make up just 6 per cent of the competition chess players in the UK, and the sport's governing bodies were desperate to get more involved in the game. Soon after the end of the London Classic I had gone to meet Jovanka Houska, one of the UK's leading female players and winner of the British women's championship five times in succession between 2008 and 2012, to ask her what the problem was: why were so few women attracted to chess? Many girls played at primary school – and, indeed, as I had found on my trip to the US when I visited the strong chess school in Brooklyn, showed a lot of promise – but few carried on. What was turning them off the game?

Houska had played in the Open at the Classic and finished in joint 20th place with 6/9. Joint 20th overall, that is, but joint top with Georgian IM Sopiko Guramishvili among the women players who, as ever, were a tiny percentage of the overall field. This was a familiar situation for Houska, who had spent her career flying the flag for women in chess. 'Growing up I didn't really realise chess was a man's world,' she told me. 'My sisters had always played chess, and I would always find other girls to hang around with and play against. It [the maleness of the chess world] hits you round about puberty. Quite often I'd be the only woman playing in a chess tournament, or maybe there'd be three of us at most. We're just seen as the special attraction. We get a lot of attention, some of it very nice, some of it very unpleasant. Often when you want to play chess you want to play in peace and do your own thing. You don't want to be watched by 20 people in every game you play. Everyone knows you, everyone knows your name, people will comment on your appearance, they write things about you on the internet. It feels awkward.' Houska, who coaches England's female juniors, is doing her best to 'drive the numbers up', and Malcolm Pein, organiser of the Classic, does his best to incentivise women's participation. It's an uphill battle, but there are signs of progress.

Houska was a prodigy as a junior and her rise was mainly due to her father. 'He was the one who was pushing me,' she said. 'My dad always loved chess and that was always the plan – one of his children was going to play chess.' Houska senior was not an especially strong player – his daughter calls him 'an ambitious 120' – but that is often the pattern: a parent who can play a bit invests all his hopes and desires in his offspring. 'My father was very controversial,' said Houska. 'I was ten years old and he would make me play in the under-21s. He wasn't very popular on the English chess scene, but he said, "I don't care. I want her to be good."'

Her upbringing, with two other chess-playing sisters (and a brother who was a good player), was similar to that of Hungarian grandmaster Judit Polgar – the strongest female player of all time. Polgar, too, had had a pushy, protective father who had educated her and her two sisters at home and consciously set out to turn them into world-class chess players. In Judit's case he succeeded beyond his wildest dreams. She became a world top-ten player – an astonishing achievement given that women have rarely managed to break into the world top 100. Polgar's father was gender-blind – he would not allow her to compete in women-only events. She took on all-comers from an early age, became the then youngest ever grandmaster (male or female) at the age of 15, and didn't bother competing for the women's world championship because she could have won it in her sleep. She simply aimed to be the best in the world, regardless of sex, and got remarkably close to the top of the tree. She gave the lie to the notion that men were better chess players because of some innate wiring in the brain, and, though now retired, is an inspiration for other women players. She showed that women could aspire to beat men at what the latter like to consider their own game.

I had met Polgar a few years earlier at the 2012 edition of the Classic, and asked her whether she felt she had struck a blow for women by showing they could compete with the best men. 'There are many guys who say, "OK, you are an exception, so you prove the rule. Show me the next,"' she told me. 'I say, "Yes, I am so far exceptional, but I don't think I will be the only one in the upcoming decades."'

The issue was an enormously touchy one for chess, as was demonstrated when Nigel Short got into hot water for writing an article in the magazine *New in Chess* in which he argued that men were 'hard-wired' to be better chess players than women. The media, loth to cover chess games but intrigued by any sign of freakishness or controversy, had a field day. Short, who insisted his article had been misinterpreted, was vilified, not least by Judit Polgar's elder sister Susan, herself a grandmaster, former women's world champion and now a well-known chess teacher and commentator based in the US. Susan Polgar insisted the disparity between the sexes had nothing to do with brain power. 'It's a numbers game,' she said. 'If you have a lot of girls playing chess, then there'll be a lot more girls who are good at it. Just imagine if Nigel Short had said blacks don't have the brains to play chess; how crazy that would sound. It has nothing to do with race or gender. It has to do with the opportunities.'

Houska hoped the Polgars would be proved right and that more women would break into the upper echelons of chess. There are certainly signs that is happening in emerging chess nations such as India and China. The latter has already produced the prodigious Hou Yifan, winner of the women's world championship at the age of 16 and now taking the Polgar route of eschewing women-only events. But Houska worried that the structure of chess teaching, in the west at least, was holding women back. 'It favours boys,' she said. 'There's a lot of competition and there's not a big enough social element. Girls need companionship, they need someone to talk to – at the moment everything is internalised and there's a lot of competitiveness. What you need is a group of girls, friends of course, to go around to tournaments and play. The way chess is taught needs to be more female-friendly.' She said boys were happy just to learn the moves, but girls needed to have chess explained more metaphorically. Why are we playing these moves? What is the meaning and purpose of this game? Women, as I always suspected, were more human than men; less willing to lose themselves in the board-as-world. As anthropologist Margaret Mead said, 'Women could be just as good at chess as men. But why would they want to be?'

Hein Donner, with characteristic dogmatism, took this view to its extreme. It wasn't, he contended, that there was a problem with women; the problem was entirely to do with chess itself. Chess, like all games, was a way of avoiding true interaction and intimacy – a way, according to Donner, of 'imitating human contact'. 'During their game chess players are "incommunicado"; they are imprisoned,' he said. 'What is going on in their heads is narcissistic self-gratification with a minimum of objective reality, a wordless sniffing and grabbing in a bottomless pit. Women do not like that, and who is to blame them? They easily hold their own in games in which human contact is incorporated, as in bridge for instance, because in such games a feeling for another's intentions, throwing a bridge to one's partner, is of paramount importance. But they cannot keep up in the total isolation of chess ... For unsolvable riddles they have little patience.'

A typically Donnerian provocation, but, at the risk of inviting the opprobrium that was showered on Nigel Short when he contrasted the male and female brain, there may be some truth behind the bluster – chess, like trainspotting, pigeon-fancying and building scale models of the Eiffel Tower with matchsticks, has traditionally attracted far more men than women. There will of course be cultural reasons for that, but might there also be neuroscientific factors at play? We should at least be able to suggest that without being immediately condemned as chauvinists. If Houska accepts boys and girls need to be taught differently, that surely suggests there is something in the notion that the genders approach chess differently, though no one is disputing women can make it to the very top as chess players. Judit Polgar showed that more than 20 years ago, and Hou Yifan is now demonstrating it again as she climbs towards a rating of 2700. In many ways chess's greatest hope of a revival is a woman vying for the world title, as Judit Polgar did when she played in the Candidates Tournament – a key stage on the path to determining the world champion – in 2007. That would be the sort of supra-chess story that tends to win mainstream coverage for the game, akin to man v machine or Fischer v anyone.

When I was in St Louis for the US championship, I met Jennifer Shahade, former US women's chess champion and author of *Chess Bitch: Women in the Ultimate Intellectual Sport.* Shahade comes from a chess family – her father and brother are strong players – and reached a FIDE rating close to 2400 before turning her attention, like many other chess players, to the more lucrative world of poker. She told me she had written *Chess Bitch* because she 'wanted to examine this interesting subculture that people knew so little about'. To my surprise she said she was much more interested in the place of chess in society than in the toxic question of whether women could play as well as men. She reckoned the latter was really an issue for biologists, but my sense was she believed that in many ways it was a non-question and that Susan Polgar was right in believing it was all about the numbers. 'The percentage of top female players is similar to the percentage of active female players,' Shahade argues in the book. 'For instance, there is one woman, Judit Polgar, in the top 20 players in the world [this was written in 2005 – Polgar didn't retire until 2014] and about four or five women in the top 100 players in America [mirroring the percentage of competitive players overall in the US]. So there is little evidence that women play worse than men.'

Little evidence or no evidence? I asked her. 'Obviously, I think women are just as talented and intelligent as men. I also believe the backlash against women can become a positive force for some women. The fact that people say women aren't as good as men can hold some women back, but for other women it can serve as a positive force. There are some issues that make it a little bit harder for women to become elite players – if they want to have kids or something, that may make it a little harder.' Or maybe they're just too sensible to want to play chess, to live on those 64 squares, I suggested. 'People say that sort of stuff about women all the time, but to be successful in anything these days you have to be somewhat specialised and obsessive. Sure, you could just be a normal person and not have a good job, especially in the United States now. You're not going to get very far if you never master any skill and you're too sensible to take anything too seriously.'

Shahade didn't buy my argument that men, being more prone to Asperger's, were therefore more drawn to chess: 'There are a lot of socially well-adjusted people in chess. Generally it's so difficult to be a good chess player that ultimately your gender becomes irrelevant. You might be slightly more apt at something in your first chess lesson, but to be a great chess player you generally have to override your personal instincts.' I asked if she thought a woman could be world champion. 'Yes, though there's definitely a smaller pool to deal with and it seems women are a little bit less encouraged. I think that if there was more money in chess, there'd be more women in it.' So, in that sense at least, women are too sensible to devote their lives to the game.

Houska insisted chauvinism was rife in chess and that it starts early: 'It's not done deliberately. It's just that the boys are very boisterous while the girls who are playing aren't.' The effect is that the girls get marginalised. 'I was watching a game in Brazil where I was teaching,' she recalled. 'There was a girl playing, partnered by a nine-year-old boy. The boy was very confident and the girl wasn't, so even though she was older than him she referred to him for advice.' The problems for older female players are even more marked – male players tend to come on to them sexually. 'It happens all the time,' said Houska. 'One player was very persistent and kept inviting me out to dinner, even when I told him I was married. It's hard, especially if they're famous. I want to be friends, I want to hear their chess stories, but I don't want that aspect. It's a male thing: they're very competitive, and if there's one female they will try to be the person who gets her.' Chess really is all about mating.

Men, as Houska has discovered, also get very upset when they are defeated by female players. '"That's the first time I've lost to a woman!" – I get that a lot,' she says. 'I just go, "Yeah, OK, fine." It doesn't bother me any more, but I used to find it annoying.' I suddenly felt guilty about feeling extra-irritated when I lost to an 11-year-old girl in the Felce Cup back in 2012. Why shouldn't 11-year-old girls be able to play good chess? I would show more grace next time I lost to a woman. At least I hoped I would.

Meeting Houska – a normal, friendly, baggage-free young woman – was a breath of fresh air. Perhaps chess didn't have to be nerdy and introverted after all. She was also, like many female chess players, extremely attractive, though she warned me not to make too much of this. 'It's not that women chess players are any more attractive than women anywhere else,' she said. 'It's just the situation they're in: there aren't that many of them and the male players are really quite horrendous, so they become extremely attractive.' I tried not to take this personally.

H6: ALMOST IMPERIOUS

The early months of 2015 were an unhappy time. I was playing only sporadically, and largely unconvincingly. I suffered a bad loss in the internal Surbiton championship when an old rival who was not an especially strong player defeated me with ease. I was lost after 20 moves following a miscalculation in a simple position. The only positive aspect of this grisly period was that I took Kingston II to promotion from division four of the Surrey League, and even there I infringed league rules by putting our side in the wrong board order and incurred a penalty which cost us an important match. Fortunately we still secured promotion by the narrowest of margins and the late Chris Clegg's memory was honoured. If my error had cost us promotion, I don't think I could ever have shown my face at the club again.

Spring brought a tiny ray of hope. I had been avoiding playing since haphazardly steering Kingston II to promotion, but eventually succumbed to my other club Surbiton's blandishments and played for the B team against Hammersmith A. I had black against a veteran graded 148 – the Doc told me later he had played him way back in 1970. My opponent played my old bête noire, the English opening, and I was soon on the back foot. I had to be very careful and that ate into my time, so I was in trouble on both the board and the clock. But I was never quite out of the game and eventually managed to land a tactical blow that gave me the edge. I made the 35-move time control with 20 seconds remaining, at which point my opponent reluctantly and in an undertone resigned, adding – with what I thought was extremely ill grace – that I'd only won because I whistled as I played.

Now, I am an inveterate hummer when I concentrate, and it's quite possible that I make involuntary sounds mid-game, but it's far too late to mention it after the game's over – the time for a protest is while the game is in progress – and when I asked my team-mates whether I did whistle at the board they reassured me that I didn't. Eat, drink, grimace, gurn, sigh, shuffle and jump up and down to go to the loo, yes, but whistle, no. My opponent was just trying to justify his defeat to himself. 'It's extraordinary the excuses people find for defeat,' one of my team-mates said. 'Either they are tired, ill or annoyed by the antics of their opponent.' Some players just can't accept they have lost fairly and squarely – even after they've been playing the game for half a century. I was, of course, not entirely innocent of such moral failings myself, and remembered Captain Kennedy's first rule on how to behave at the chessboard: 'When you have lost a game or games, never be guilty of the preposterous silliness of allowing that you are fairly mastered by the more expert skill of your antagonist.' His advice was still being faithfully followed almost 150 years later.

A week or so after this unexpected triumph I played in my first tournament for a couple of months – at Imperial College London. I'd played here before, but this time I was in with the big boys (or at least the bigger boys) in the under-175 section. Previously I had played with the under-140s, but because my grade had edged up that was no longer an option. I was being forced out of my comfort zone and wasn't much looking forward to the experience. I took a bye in the Friday evening game – guaranteeing me at least half a point in the tournament – and headed up to South Kensington early on a damp Saturday morning in late April to join the fray. My expectations were again low, not least as I had been unsettled by another sad piece of news – the death of Colin Crouch, an affable IM I had seen coaching children whenever I played at Harrow Chess Club and who seemed to me to represent everything that was good in chess. Here was a very strong player giving his time freely to help kids, showing no ego, no 'Look at me, I'm an international master' arrogance. If I had been that good, I just knew I would have had to show it, to swank about and demand attention.

I had studied – in my own, entirely non-systematic way – Crouch's book *Why We Lose at Chess* the previous summer, was considering meeting him to get some tuition and had just bought another of his concise, no-nonsense primers, *Analyse Your Chess*. As a writer, Crouch was a delightful guide. 'A Dutch IM once characterised me as a chess artist, rather than a practical player,' he says in *Why We Lose at Chess*, explaining that the book would examine games of his own in which he went wrong. He was happy to show a 20-move loss in which he played horribly to demonstrate a point (not something top players, who tend to anthologise their glorious victories, are usually willing to do). The ego-free chess player – how refreshing. But there was something else significant about Crouch: in 2004 he had a stroke which left him partially sighted. Despite this his ECF rating was still around 200 – well down on his peak but very strong – and his love of chess remained undimmed. He fought back tenaciously from his stroke, showing us not just how to play but how to live. That he had another productive decade as player, writer and chess teacher after his stroke was little short of miraculous. But his sudden death of a brain haemorrhage at the age of 58 cast a pall, especially so soon after that of Chris Clegg. British chess players did not seem to enjoy great longevity – a combination of stress, a sedentary lifestyle, bad diet and too much beer – and a generation who had grown up playing the game in the 1950s and 1960s was passing.

As I sat nursing a cappuccino before my opening game, I doubted whether I had the will to make much of a fist of the tournament. But for once my fears were unwarranted. In the first game, against a wild-haired man I'd drawn with in the British championship at Torquay a couple of years earlier, I got an advantage in the middle game and clung on to it tenaciously as we moved into a long ending. The game took more than four hours, but I finally prevailed to record what was probably my best win of the year so far. The afternoon game was another marathon – more than 60 moves played over four hours. We both made lots of mistakes in what was a tactical mêlée from the start, but my opponent made the most egregious error – dropping a piece for very little compensation – and, even though I was in severe time trouble and played poorly in the endgame, I managed to hang on for a win. To my surprise I was 2.5/3 overnight, and would be playing on top board when we resumed on Sunday. Vertigo was a certainty but for Saturday night at least – and despite all the anxieties that had been dogging me – I felt like a chess player again.

As if to prove that state of mind was not, whatever Carrera says, precisely linked to results, I tanked on Sunday, losing both my games despite feeling relaxed, focused and confident. Perhaps too confident. In the morning game I was up against a thoughtful player who exuded concentration at the board. He had the edge in the opening, despite playing black, but I fought back and had one crucial chance where I had a choice of pushing two pawns to put his king under dire threat. Naturally, I chose the wrong pawn, opting for my usual one-dimensional 'caveman' attack where I needed something subtler. I blew the chance and in the end he made me pay, though we both made numerous errors in a complicated tactical struggle. The afternoon game was even more disappointing because I made all the running with black, got an advantage but then overplayed my hand, leaving my king centralised and vulnerable as I attempted to land the knockout blow. 'You were a little rash not to castle,' my opponent said to me after he had administered a simple mate. 'Bold is the word you are looking for,' I suggested frostily.

The defeat meant I ended the event with 2.5/5 and a FIDE rating performance of 1700, which was respectable but not earth-shattering. I could, with more accuracy, have won both the Sunday games but let them slip because of familiar failings. In my emailed lament to the Doc, I revised my Saturday night euphoria. I was still *almost* a chess player. I couldn't quite seem to find the pinpoint accuracy to make the leap to the next level. Andrew Martin had told me really good players have an intuition about the key points of a position. Yes, they calculate, but they calculate on the basis of a strategic understanding of what is going on. In critical situations in my games that intuition failed me. I was still guessing – and good players never guess.

H7: WHAT'S UP, DOC?

After my close-but-no-cigar performance at the Imperial Congress and my laughable loss in the final game I hit a strange psychological barrier. I almost couldn't bear to look at a chess game; I barely played online; chess suddenly felt foreign to me. There was only one thing to do – I had to call for the Doc. When we met, I asked him whether in his 30-plus-year career as a competitive player he had suffered motivational ups and downs. He said he had and that the downs came when 'other parts of his life' weren't working very well. It was a Carrera-esque answer. He told me not to worry about my flagging motivation: 'These things just come and go. Maybe you are over-chessed. One answer to that is not to play, and come back later refreshed. Another answer is to be more selective.' Set targets; play in tournaments I really wanted to play in; avoid routine chess; take every game seriously.

I didn't really yet want Saunders' verdict on whether I had failed in my quest to become a good player – I was saving that for the post-mortem which traditionally follows a chess game – but he gave me his thoughts anyway. 'I can't remember what your original objective was,' he said. 'It's like the First World War. You start off, "What is our objective?" It's to defend little Belgium, and after a while you're in the trenches and you don't know what you're doing there.'

It was a point well made. The problem with chess is that there is no way of measuring success. Was a grade of 141 a success, or was I desperate to get to 150? If I reached 150, wouldn't I just start eyeing 160? And so on for ever. The Doc used a favourite metaphor of his: playing chess was like climbing a mountain; you get to the top of a ridge and there in front of you is another ridge. 'You keep going and going, and you realise that even to get to the top of some pathetic mountain in Wales is quite hard work.' And if you do reach the top, as Bobby Fischer did, you have a panic attack when you peer over the other side and realise the only way is down. Even Magnus Carlsen, atop that mountain, might be eyeing the Chinese teenagers – especially Wei Yi, a grandmaster at 13 and the youngest player to reach a rating of 2600 – coming up behind him. There is no security in chess, no contentment, only pain, paranoia and eventual failure. In the long run we're all dead – or mated. 'That's why I don't play chess now,' said Saunders. 'I just don't need it any more. I've come through it, and I don't want to be dragged back into it. It's a magnificent obsession, playing chess, *amour fou*, but it's a young man's game.'

There could, in that sense, be no true end to my journey. I wanted to be a chess 'expert', but who was the true arbiter of expertise? Malcolm Pein – an international master, long-time chess correspondent of the *Daily Telegraph* and the most powerful person in British chess because of his work with the London Classic and Chess in Schools and Communities – cheered me up by telling me anyone with a grade above 120 was a strong chess player. All things are relative – and I had made the top few thousand active players in the UK. The mountain still loomed ahead of me, dark, forbidding, apparently unconquerable, but a few hillocks – Chester, Bury St Edmunds, the Surrey individual championship (aka the Felce Cup) – had been negotiated. I cradled my cup and read my name on its polished surface, trying to forget that soon it would have to be given back and a new champion crowned. Whether the cup was half full or half empty depended on the way I was feeling when I posed the question.

The heart-to-heart with the Doc had been enough to galvanise me. It got me thinking about chess and playing online again. I entered the Slater-Kennington Cup – division two of the Surrey championship, a sizeable step up from the Felce. I was up against an old adversary from Surbiton in the first round, a nice man who always seemed to beat me despite his rating being lower than mine. He knew his openings and surprised me once again in a Queen's Gambit Declined, but I fought back, he went wrong in time trouble, lost his advantage and we agreed a gentleman's draw after a tense three-hour struggle. When I had last played in the Slater-Kennington, I managed half a point in six games, so to have reached that score after just one game was very satisfactory, though there were some strong opponents waiting for me in later rounds.

My second Slater-Kennington game was against a player who, though past 70 and not as strong as in his pomp, still had a grade in the 170s. I had black and feared the worst, but managed to play a reasonable game and we adjourned with a tricky endgame. The computer gave me a tiny edge, but it was almost certainly illusory, and when he emailed a week or so later to offer a draw, I took it eagerly: 50 per cent at this relatively exalted level was not to be sneezed at. I also took a quick draw in my third game in the competition, and felt as if I was back on a more or less even keel – holding my own against decent players. I had my mojo back and felt I wanted to play. The crisis seemed to have passed.

We had a memorial tournament for Chris Clegg, the man who had devoted his life to Kingston Chess Club. It was a pleasant event, held on a sunny afternoon in early summer, attended by 30 of his friends and won by grandmaster John Nunn – still loyal to chess and intensely competitive after half a century spent playing and analysing the game. Nunn had been a member at Kingston in the late 1960s and recalled playing Clegg. It was a fitting send-off, with Clegg's photograph displayed in a corner of the room in which the tournament was held, and a candle burning in a kind of makeshift shrine. It was a blitz tournament and my play was absurdly ambitious throughout, pursuing brilliancies with very little time to calculate and generally coming a cropper. I managed a draw and five losses, though I thought I had the better of the game in two of those losses until time or excessive boldness got the better of me. At least I performed better than in the Andrew Whiteley Memorial, and on this occasion didn't score nought. I was glad to have played, proud of the club for holding an event in Clegg's memory, and especially pleased that Malcolm Pein, in his chess column in the *Daily Telegraph*, featured Nunn's winning games in the final of the tournament under the headline 'In Honour of Clegg'. How rare for someone who never thrust themselves forward to get recognised at the end of so long a struggle.

H8: BOURNEMOUTH REVISITED

A couple of weeks after the Clegg Memorial I set off for Bournemouth, scene of my humiliation three years earlier when I went home prematurely – distraught, depressed, tail firmly between the legs – after scoring 0/3 on the first two days. I had always sensed I would end my quest at Bournemouth, trying to gain vengeance on all those balding, retired accountants who seemed to be in the preponderance at this tournament. Journeys are often circular, and this one was to be no exception. I had in my mind T. S. Eliot's lines from 'Little Gidding': 'We shall not cease from exploration/ And the end of all our exploring/Will be to arrive where we started/And know the place for the first time.'

By now I realised there would be no blinding flash of revelation. I would not become a chess superstar; I would not be a new person; the battle – to play better chess, to be a more focused, more complete person – would go on, would always go on. There were no magical transformations. There was just the challenge – day by day, game by game – to improve on the way you did things before. As the German grandmaster Robert Hübner said, 'Those who say they understand chess understand nothing.' You would never get to the bottom of chess, and you would never get to the bottom of life. You just had to give it your best shot.

There was, though, one problem with my desire to beat the baldies and come out of the tournament in Bournemouth in credit. I had a cold. It had been lurking for a few days, but I felt OK when I arrived in the town on a sun-drenched Friday afternoon and stupidly went for a swim on the lovely beach. The water was icy – it was mid-June and summer had hardly begun – and within a few hours I was running a temperature and feeling very sorry for myself. Inevitably I was up against one of those tough old chess technicians in the first round, and he ground me down over the course of four hours in which my condition steadily deteriorated. Far from getting revenge and redemption I now feared the tournament would be a repeat of the original nightmare. That had been an under-155 event; this was an under-165 one, so was in theory a little stronger than last time. I worried that I would be facing humiliation all over again. Bad for the soul – and even worse as the last stop on my odyssey. I knew this square was black, but hoped the blackness might have the merest chink of light in it somewhere. Surely I had made *some* progress along the way.

I felt terrible on Saturday morning and was popping paracetamol to try to counter my headache and rising temperature. I had white against another middle-aged man, who steadily built up an advantage and managed to set a passed pawn – one with the potential to get to the eighth rank and get magically transformed into a queen – running. It did not look good for me, and I was getting terrible sensations of déjà vu, but I got lucky: for once it was my opponent who was not precise enough; he blundered away the pawn and suddenly I was on top. We reached an endgame in which I had an advantage, but I was also short of time and feeling exhausted, so when he offered a draw I grabbed it, happy to have scored a half-point – the first time I had got on the scoreboard in five attempts at Bournemouth. In a way it was feeble, because there was a possible victory there and any self-respecting tournament player would have gone for it, but I took the line of least resistance and snatched what was going. I was finally off zero.

The afternoon may have been my finest hour – or four hours – of the weekend. I was up against the highest-graded player in the field, another of those aged grinders, who quickly got me in a bind and looked to have yet another passed pawn. But I fought, tried to make it difficult for him, and lo and behold he, too, went wrong as we both ran short of time. He lost the pawn, I had a better position but played an abysmal sequence of moves, and suddenly he was pressing again. I offered a draw, he turned it down determined to fight on, my position creaked, and for a moment I thought I had thrown it away, but in the end I found a way to force a draw. I was ecstatic – or maybe the ecstasy was a reflection of the delirium produced by my illness. I was on 1/3 overnight – hardly wonderful, but those two draws in the face of adversity and against tough opponents gave me more pleasure than almost anything that had gone before. Winning the Felce Cup and the tournament at Bury St Edmunds were obvious high spots in my chess 'career', but this felt just as good. I could easily have succumbed just as I had in my original outing at Bournemouth, but I didn't. I fought and I came through. I was a chess player. Not a great one, or even a particularly good one, but someone who, even when the odds were stacked against him, could play a reasonable game and hold his own against men who had played all their lives.

The next day I was feeling much improved and won a crushing victory against a much lower-graded opponent. Now, on 2/4, I really was feeling good about myself. As ever hubris produced immediate disaster and in the afternoon I was crushed by a player against whom I had managed a draw 18 months earlier in Hereford. He took apart the Scandinavian I played as black – the Doc was right, it really was time to junk this opening – and launched a powerful kingside attack that had me hopelessly beaten in 30 moves. He was wonderfully calm and gracious in victory – if I had won in such fine style I doubt whether I would have managed such equanimity. It was a pleasure to play him; almost (though not quite) a pleasure to lose to him.

I did not beat myself up: I had given a reasonable account of myself; I had, despite illness, seen the tournament through to the end; I had avoided coming last. It was not revenge or anything like it; indeed, it was still, after all this time and all this effort, no better than a middling performance. But it was a vindication, or something close to it. I had done my best – I had played close on 20 hours of chess while feeling decidedly under the weather. I was proud of my win, satisfied with my two draws, and even in my two defeats I had had one or two reasonable ideas. The catastrophe of three years earlier had been assuaged. I went back to my hotel, bought myself a large glass of Sauvignon at the bar, sat on the terrace and stared out to sea as the light dimmed. 'And all shall be well and/All manner of things shall be well.' It was over. I had neither won nor lost, but I had come through with my spirit intact. In the end that is all any of us can hope for.

POST-MORTEM

'A bad day of chess is better than any good day at work'
— Anonymous

Clearly I didn't win the game on which I embarked with such optimism more than three years ago, but nor do I think I lost it. Of course, I have to make this claim – otherwise this odyssey, as I have styled my ramshackle progress across the board, might be seen as a complete waste of time. But for now I am going to claim a draw, an honourable – if at times slightly turgid – draw. My grade did improve – from 133 to 142; I established myself on the lower rungs of division two of British chess; I won a couple of decent tournaments; I believe I understand what it is to be a high-standard competition player, even if I have yet to become one.

'It's a great huge game of chess that's being played – all over the world,' declares Alice as she stumbles into a 'curious country' neatly divided up into squares on the other side of the looking-glass. That, at times, was how I felt: as if nothing in life mattered except for the moves we were all playing. 'Life, what is it but a dream?' as Lewis Carroll, an inveterate player of games and aficionado of puzzles, writes at the end of *Through the Looking-Glass*. Board as world; game as occupation; illusion as reality. To echo Alice again: 'Oh, what fun it is! How I *wish* I was one of them!' She meant a piece, preferably a queen. I aspired to be a player, a proper one, an expert.

The problem was that, after I had been in that chess-playing bubble for a while, life would intrude. I would have to go back to

369

the day-job, the day-life. For chess pros, the board is their life and they never leave the bubble. They eat, drink and breathe chess. As Vlad Tkachiev told me, the grandmaster always has a position in his head, even when he is making love. Immersion in the chess world has not yet cured my tendency to dip into the sea (I'm thinking metaphorically here, not of that ill-judged swim at Bournemouth) rather than allow myself to be swallowed by it. The great chess player – or writer or musician – doesn't just use the board (or novel or instrument) to express himself: he inhabits it; even becomes it. The identification is total. Expert players do not need a board to play chess; they can play it in their heads; it has become part of their mental furniture and they dream chess moves.

Bobby Fischer said, 'You can only get good at chess if you love the game', and I don't think I ever quite loved it enough. I wanted to get really, really good, but wasn't prepared to work hard enough to get there. I wasn't obsessed enough to bury myself in positions for hours on end. I always wanted the instant solution, the quick fix. Playing blitz, a form of throwaway chess, always appealed more than working at the game to log something that would last. But I have to clutch at straws. I stuck with it, I got a bit better, I have a much broader understanding of chess and the people who play it, I made good friends in Russia and the US, and both chess-playing communities are now firmly on my radar. I loved the chess atmosphere in Greenwich Village, and hope one day to return and hustle there for a summer. And along the way I came to understand the enduring appeal of the game.

Part of that appeal, as I realised at the outset, was that it was a sealed world with a clear set of rules and one overriding objective that appealed to people who found life, 'real' life, challenging. It offered a straightforward narrative in a messy world. But there was also the fact that you could meet the greatest players in the world on common ground. Yes, your abilities were wildly different, but you talked roughly the same language and could exchange a few words. If I went into the boxing ring with the heavyweight champion of the world, I would be lucky to last 20 seconds and would almost certainly end up in intensive care. But I once played a blitz game against world champion Magnus Carlsen, and almost got to 30 moves – he even congratulated me on one move. I was playing the same game as Staunton and Morphy, Capablanca and Alekhine, Karpov and Kasparov; nothing like as well, of course, but we were in the same ballpark.

By Malcolm Pein's definition I was already a strong chess player, but I knew I still had a long way to go to be truly expert. A grade of 160 had seemed possible, and I still believe I can make it with more application (and possibly by retiring from everything else), but Saunders is doubtful. 'I'm sure the Chelsea FC school of management would recommend sacking the coach,' he emailed me when I told him my grade had edged up to 142. 'I guess it reflects your solid 140 credentials. A very respectable grade. Some focused work could see you pitch camp at the 150 mark, but you now appreciate how damnably steep and unforgiving the chess mountain is; 160 may be a ridge too far.' How odd that, when I set out, I had hoped to resolve great questions of truth and beauty, madness and genius, art and life, and here I was fretting about my grade. But chess does that to you. There are beautiful things in it, it aspires to be an art form, but in the end what matters most is that you beat the other guy and gain some rating points. That's how you get to sleep at night.

'Chess, despite its deep and subtle content, is just a game,' insisted Emanuel Lasker. The world is forever looking for metaphors in chess – madness as an expression of genius (Nabokov and Zweig); entrapment and oppression (the human chess game in *The Prisoner*, which echoes Alice's bafflement with the world she finds through the looking-glass); sex (*The Thomas Crown Affair*); death (Ingmar Bergman's *The Seventh Seal*) – and the game does contain them all. There are mad chess players; we are, at a banal level, all pawns in a game; chess does have a somewhat perverse sexual dimension, with its quest for control and domination; and every defeat is a sort of death. But in the end, as my idiosyncratic muse Hein Donner so pithily says, 'Chess is only chess.' The non-chess world might want to mythologise it, and the chess fraternity will play along because they are desperate for any attention, but for most players – amateur and professional – it is a technical struggle, a daily battle to survive in a dog-eat-dog world. Sex and death, art and beauty can go hang. What is my rating? That's what determines whether my ego remains intact.

Throughout my wanderings I worried for the future of the game. Capablanca was on the cover of *Time* magazine in 1925. Bobby Fischer was a global phenomenon and his match with Boris Spassky in 1972 even inspired the musical *Chess*, written by Tim Rice, with music by Benny Andersson and Björn Ulvaeus of ABBA. Garry Kasparov, with a bit of help from the supercomputer Deep Blue, also broke through to the broader public. But that connection has been lost: world championship matches are now largely ignored by the mainstream media; even the ascent of the prodigious Magnus Carlsen, the highest rated player of all time, to the world title failed to ignite mass interest, except in his native Norway; and no one is going to try to set the careers of Levon Aronian or Boris Gelfand to music. The sense of a grand narrative that underpinned the east v west struggles of the 1960s and 1970s (chess as the games-playing equivalent of space exploration) has been lost and the breaking of the bond between players and society at large constitutes a crisis for the game. Without a wider news resonance, or a public interested in the personalities and politics of chess, it ceases to be a sport and becomes a pastime. The best hope for the future lies in the emergence of a woman who could vie for the world title as Hungary's Judit Polgar once came close to doing (she reached the penultimate stage of the convoluted process to determine the world champion), or in the rise of China as a great chess power, bringing with it a new geopolitical dimension. It seems that to reach a wider public chess needs to be a metaphor for some broader struggle.

I initially thought the period between the First and Second World Wars, when Capablanca and Alekhine vied for supremacy, was the game's golden age – even more so than the Fischer-boom period, because public interest was more sustained and deeper rooted. But the more I read, the more I realised there had been many golden ages: the rise of the great Spanish players in the 16th century; François-André Danican Philidor's reign in the 18th century; the coming of fully fledged international competition in the second half of the 19th century; Fischer's dismantling of the Soviet machine in the early 1970s. Who is to say chess might not rise again and prove the doubters, me included, wrong? Golden ages are for romantics (mainly amateurs like me).

One question kept recurring throughout my odyssey: why do we play chess? Hans Ree hymns its eternal beauty; Emanuel Lasker relished the fight; Fischer enjoyed crushing his opponents psychologically; Botvinnik sought to establish a scientific method; Tal loved the tactical possibilities; Bronstein delighted in the free play of the imagination; Arnold Denker saw it as an act of rebellion; Jon Speelman seeks transcendence; the chess hustlers in Washington Square – not unlike pros all over the world – are trying to earn a few dollars. But in the end I came back to Danny Gormally's simple, honest and, I suspect, true explanation: 'Chess players are notoriously lazy and basically incapable of doing anything else, so chess is what we do.' Professional chess is an affirmation of individuality, a cry for freedom – and a way of staying in bed until midday.

I have spent three years in this strange land, got to know its contours, started to speak the language, and now, for better or worse, have become a native of sorts, hanging about on the fringes, on nodding (and peeing) acquaintance with the demigods of the game. It didn't solve my midlife crisis; I didn't stop being a dilettante; but just occasionally I play a game I'm proud of and my heart leaps a little. I will never be a Mikhail Tal, but for me, too, the board has become a testing ground, a barometer of my mental and physical well-being, a world entire unto itself. I may not yet be an expert, but nor am I any longer a rookie. I am on the mountainside, still inching upwards, trying not to look down for fear of falling. In chess, as in life.

ALGEBRAIC NOTATION EXPLAINED

Standard (or 'algebraic') chess notation is used to record games, comprising at its simplest an upper-case letter to represent the identity of the piece moved, followed by a two-character square reference indicating the destination square. Each of the eight files on the chessboard (a file being defined as the eight squares in a straight line going across the board from each player to the other – see the diagram of a board on page 7) is assigned a letter, starting on white's left: a, b, c, d, e, f, g, h (always given in lower case). Each of the eight ranks (defined as the eight squares going across the board at right angles to the files) is given a number, from 1 to 8, with the rank numbered 1 being nearest white, and the rank numbered 8 nearest black. The file and rank references are then combined so that each of the 64 squares is assigned a unique reference such as a1, d6, f7, etc., all the way to h8 (which happens to be the nearest square to where black sits at the board, to the extreme left).

The letters used to represent the pieces in English notation are K (king), Q (queen), R (rook), B (bishop), N (knight – as K is already taken). If no upper-case letter is given, just a square reference, then it means the piece moved is a pawn. Moves are numbered in pairs, with white's move given first. Thus, for example: 32. Re4 Bd6 means that, on the 32nd move of the game, white moves a rook to the e4 square and black replies by moving a bishop to the d6 square.

A capture is usually indicated by the insertion of the letter 'x' between the piece identifier and the destination square. If it is a pawn making the capture, then its original file is given as well as the destination square. Thus 45. f5 gxf5 means that, on the 45th move, white moves his pawn forward from f4 to f5, and black replies by capturing the white pawn on f5 with the one currently standing on g6. And 50. Rxf5 Rxf5 means that, on the 50th move, white captures whatever enemy piece happens to be standing on the f5 square and in reply black captures the white rook on f5 with his own rook.

Occasionally ambiguities have to be resolved. In our earlier example, 32. Re4 Bd6, if both white rooks were legally able to play to the e4 square (let's assume they currently stand on e1 and h4), then it is necessary to add an identifier of the original square after the piece identifier to make it clear which rook moves. Thus, 32. Ree4 (or 32. R1e4 – either code will serve) indicates that it is the rook on the e-file (or the first rank) that is to move to e4. If it were the other rook (on h4) moving there, the correct notation would be 32. Rhe4 (or 32. R4e4). If the rooks were already on the same file (e.g., e1 and e8), then the rank number must be used to resolve the ambiguity (e.g., 32. R1e4 or 32. R8e4). Similarly, if the rooks were both on the fourth rank (e.g., at b4 and h4), then it would be necessary to specify the file in order to resolve the ambiguity (e.g., 32. Rbe4 or 32. Rhe4, or if an enemy piece is on e4, 32. Rbxe4 or 32. Rhxe4).

Castling has a special notation identifier. Castling kingside is shown as 0-0 and castling queenside as 0-0-0.

Note that, when reference is made to a black move on its own in a chess article, it is conventional to refer to the move with an ellipsis after the move number, e.g., 'In this position a good move would be 37 ... Rxf4,' when the ellipsis makes it clear to the reader that a black move is being referred to.

Though not strictly necessary, checking moves are usually indicated in notation by a + sign after the notation. Thus 42 ... Qb2+ indicates that black, on the 42nd move, plays the queen to b2, giving check to the white king.

The result of the game is usually given at the end of the recorded moves by 1–0 (white wins), 0–1 (black wins) or ½–½ (game drawn). If the game ends in checkmate, the final move may be shown with a hash sign following, thus 52. Re8# means white plays rook to the e8 square, checkmate.

In competition play, players are supposed to indicate where they have offered a draw by writing '(=)' after the move when it was offered, but the rule is relatively new and seems not to be well-known and/or ignored by many players. This information is rarely given in scores of games printed in books and magazines.

Annotated games in books and magazines use a small number of other codes to indicate the value of the moves in the eyes of the annotator. An exclamation mark after a move means it is 'good' and two exclamation marks mean it is 'excellent'. Conversely, a question mark after a move signifies that it is 'bad' and two question marks that it is awful – chess players nearly always describe such a move as a 'blunder'. A move marked thus – 14. Re7!? – signifies that the move is 'interesting' but not necessarily good or bad. Where the exclamation and question marks are reversed, eg 22. cxb4?!, the corresponding adjective is 'dubious'.

Note: in older chess books you may see unfamiliar chess notation such as P-K4, QKt-Q2, R-R1, etc. This is called

English descriptive notation and it has nearly died out, being used only by a dwindling number of older players in English-speaking countries. It is not used in this book and is worth learning only if you wish to read pre-1980s chess books or magazines.

MY TEN KEY GAMES

Annotations by John Saunders,
Italicised Comments by the Author

!	good move
?	bad move
!?	interesting move that might be questionable
?!	questionable move that might be interesting
!!	excellent move, potentially decisive
??	outright blunder, likely to be enough on its own to lose the game
+	check
#	checkmate
1–0	win for White
0–1	win for Black
½–½	draw

Game 1: Blundering in Bournemouth

(Moss playing White)
The game that sealed my awful first tournament at Bournemouth. I played a neat knight sacrifice and really should have got something out of this game, but when I failed to do so I never recovered and ended up going home early.

1. e4 Nf6 2. Nc3 e6!? Unusual but OK. If White wants to exploit this he could try 3. e5 but the text is fine.
3. d4 d5 The opening has transposed into a known variation: French Defence, Burn variation.
4. e5 Nfd7 5. Nf3 c5 6. Bb5 Nc6 7. Bxc6 bxc6 8. 0–0 cxd4 9. Qxd4 Qb6 10. Qg4 g6 11. Rb1 Ba6 12. Re1 c5 13. Bg5! Stephen's attacking instincts are acute: he was already thinking about 13. Nxd5, with a view to opening up an attack along the e-file, but he was right to delay it.
13. ... Bg7? Black is oblivious.

14. Nxd5! exd5 15. e6 Nf6 Black could run away and hide with 15 ... 0–0, but it is clear that White will be much better after winning back the piece.
16. exf7+ Kxf7

17. Ne5+ ?? A tragic missed opportunity. A bit more thought and Stephen might have found 17. Bxf6!, which leads to an overwhelming position. For example, 17 ... Bxf6 18. Qd7+ Kf8 19. Re6 when White regains his sacrificed piece with a massive attack to boot.

379

17. ... Kg8 18. Bxf6 Qxf6 Stephen thought Black had to recapture with 18 … Bxf6 after which he saw that 19. Nd7 was good.

19. Qd7 Rd8 20. Qxa7 h5 Black is now defending well.

21. Qxc5 Kh7 22. Rbd1 Computers suggest 22. Nf3 with the sneaky threat of 23 Re6! White, material down, should be looking for tactical tricks.

22. ... Bb7 23. Qc7 Rhe8 24. Nd3 Qc6 25. Qxc6 My preference would be to keep the queens on with 25. Qg3 in pursuit of tactical tricks, but computers prefer the text. In the interests of keeping things messy, I still think keeping queens on is a better bet.

25. ... Bxc6 26. c3 Ba4 27. Rxe8 Rxe8 28. Re1 Rxe1+ 29. Nxe1 Again, computers advocate all these exchanges but from the pragmatic point of view I think it is tantamount to resignation. Maybe I'm wrong and the three pawns are worth more than I think.

29. ... Bb5 30. Nf3 To the annotator's amazement, the strong computer engine Rybka assesses this position as more or less equal. From my experience of club chess I'd expect Black to win about nine times out of ten.

30. ... Bc4 31. a4 Bf6 32. Nd4 Bxd4 33. cxd4 I poured scorn on some of these moves when Stephen and I looked at the game (without recourse to a computer), as I don't think Black should be allowed to liquidate. But computer engines give this as slightly better for White! I am astonished: computers may be able to analyse chess positions but they have no notion of 'coarse chess.'

33. ... Kg7 34. f3 Kf6 35. Kf2 Ke6 36. Ke3 Kd6 37. h4 37. Kf4 looks much more natural.

37. ... Bb3

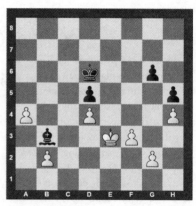

38. g4?? Stephen and I didn't look at this in any depth and the basic fundamentals of the position didn't immediately impress themselves on us but the obvious try 38. a5 has to be right. After that, I'm no longer at all sure that Black can win, e.g. 38 … Kc6 39. Kf4 Kb5 40. Kg5 Bc2 41. b4! Bd3 42. g4 hxg4 43. fxg4 Kxb4 44. a6 Bxa6 45. Kxg6 and it's clearly drawn. Well, it's clear now; but it wasn't anywhere near as clear at the beginning of the line. The point is that such positions are harder work for the defender. In real life the odds are on the defender making an error and the extra piece triumphing.

38. ... Bxa4 39. Kf4 Bd1! Unfortunately for White, this completely snookers any hope of counterplay.

40. gxh5 gxh5 41. Ke3 Ke6 42. b4 Ba4 43. Kf4 Kf6 44. Kg3 Kf5 45. Kf2 Kf4 46. Kg2 Bb5 47. Kf2 Bc4 48. Kg2 Be2 49. Kf2 Bxf3 50. b5 Bg4 51. Kg2 Bc8 0–1

Game 2: Failing to rock in Gibraltar

(Moss playing Black)
The knife-edge game which, because I lost after a tense four-hour struggle, kept me off

the showboards in Gibraltar. So near and yet so far.

1. d4 d5 2. e3 You have to hate chess with a passion to play negative moves like this. Grandmasters would never play such a move but, sadly, many club players resort to this dreary sort of chess. Just play through the moves quickly: I'll wake you up when something interesting happens ...
2 ... Nf6 3. Bd3 e6 4. Nf3 Be7 5. 0–0 0–0 6. Nbd2 b6 7. Ne5 Bb7 8. Qe2 Nbd7 9. b3 c5 10. Bb2 Nxe5 11. dxe5 Nd7 12. f4 f5 13. Rf3 a6 14. Rh3 White's jejune plan is to play Qh5 and take on h7 but it is easily averted.
14 ... Qe8 15. c4! Well, I have been unkind to White with my commentary so far but I am reluctant to admit that his plan is succeeding quite well. He hasn't got much by way of play, but he has more than Black, who has nothing and just has to sit and wait.
15 ... dxc4 16. bxc4 Rd8 17. g4 g6 18. gxf5 gxf5 18 ... exf5, keeping the g-file closed, looks better, although the White e5 pawn would become passed and there might be danger along the a1–h8 diagonal one day.
19. Kf2 19. e4 looks promising for White.
19 ... Kh8! 20. Rg1 Rg8 21. Rgg3 Computers are of the opinion that 21. e4 is close to winning for White, as the b1–h7 is likely to open up to strong effect, but it is by no means clear to mere mortals.
21 ... Qf7 22. Rh5 Rxg3 23. hxg3 Kg8! Moving away from the long diagonal as otherwise White has the sneaky threat of 24. Rxf5! exf5 25. e6+, discovering an attack on the queen.

24. e4 White finally plays the thematic push but overlooks a sharp rejoinder.

24 ... Nxe5!! Very well played tactical idea, helping Black out of his difficulties.
25. Bxe5 25. fxe5?? fxe4+ would turn the tables and win for Black.
25 ... Rxd3! 26. Rh6 The point is that, after 26. Qxd3 Black has the reply 26 ... Qxh5 but perhaps White should play it anyway.
26 ... Rd8 27. g4 Bf8 27 ... fxe4 would have set a delicious trap, albeit one which only a tactical wizard would be capable of seeing: if then 28. Nxe4 Black has 28 ... Rd4!! with the point that 29. Bxd4 Qxf4+ 30. Qf3 Qxh6 wins a second pawn.
28. Rh5 Qd7 29. Ke3?! This looks very fishy, moving the king into danger.
29 ... Bxe4 30. Nxe4 fxe4 31. Kxe4 Qd2 Black liquidates down to an endgame a pawn up, which doesn't by any means look a bad plan, but the computer thinks it would much better to keep the queens on and play 31 ... b5! when White's king is in the centre and should be vulnerable to tricks and traps.
32. Qxd2 Rxd2 33. f5 Re2+ 34. Kf4 exf5 35. gxf5 Rxa2 36. f6

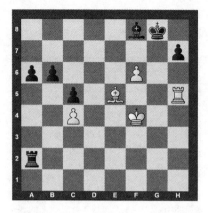

Game 3: Triumph in Torquay

(Moss playing White)
A pleasing win in the British Championship at Torquay against a player graded 170 that made me believe I could play chess. Later results undermined that belief. My opponent was Chris Kreuzer, who later became my team-mate and good friend when he started playing for Kingston. Doc Saunders, showing his musical and literary leanings, immediately christened the game 'The Kreuzer Sonata'. It remains one of the high spots of my not terribly illustrious playing career. Because all the games at the British Championship are put online, it has an existence – one hopes for all time – on the internet. After all the rubbish I played has been forgotten, perhaps this will bamboozle people into thinking that I could play chess.

36. ... Rc2?? A mistake and, as it turns out, a game-changing one. With a bit of thought about what the opponent is doing, Black might have found 36 ... h6! followed by Kf7, defending against White's kingside threats, before mopping up the queenside.

37. Kf5 h6 38. Ke6 It may not be immediately obvious why, but White's advanced passed pawn and invading king win the game for White and there is not too much to be done about it. It's often said that there is no luck in chess but I can't help thinking White was enormously lucky that this desperate little trick turned out to work quite so well.

38 ... Rxc4 39. Rh2 Rg4 40. Rd2! Black has prevented a rook invasion via the g-file but White has the option of the d-file. And, very unluckily for Black, there is nothing to be done about it.

40 ... h5 41. Rd8 Re4 42. f7+ Kh7 43. Rxf8 Kg6 1–0 A sad end to a hard-fought game by Black. Just the one mistake but it was unfortunately a fatal one.

1. d4 Nf6 2. Nf3 e6 3. c4 Bb4+ 4. Nc3 c5 5. e3 Ne4 6. Qc2 d5 7. Bd3 Qa5 8. Bd2 White can play 8. 0–0!? here, when 8 ... Nxc3? 9. bxc3 Bxc3 10. Rb1 and Black, despite his extra pawn, has a major problem extricating his bishop.

8 ... Nxd2 9. Nxd2 cxd4 10. exd4 dxc4? White now gets an alarming lead in development. Instead, 10 ... Nc6 11. Nb3 Qd8 seems playable.

11. Nxc4 Qg5 12. 0–0 Bxc3? Giving up his only developed minor piece is an act of criminal folly. 12 ... Nc6 is better but does not oblige White to defend the d-pawn, e.g. 13. Rad1! Nxd4 14. Qa4+ Nc6 15. Ne4 and White has a massive initiative for the pawn.

13. bxc3 Nc6

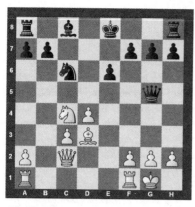

14. f4! When Stephen's attacking juices are flowing, his pieces tend to find the right squares.

14 ... Qd8 15. f5 h6 16. Rae1 0–0 17. f6!

17. ... g5? After this final error, Stephen's final simple task is to arrange his firing squad in seniority order. Instead Black would do better to take his chances with 17 ... gxf6 18. Re3 f5 19. Qd2 Qf6 20. Rh3 Kg7, when White is obviously much better but there is still a little more work to do.

18. Qe2 Nxd4 19. Qh5 1–0

Game 4: Dutch delight

(Moss playing Black)
My best game at the ten-day tournament I played in the Dutch resort of Wijk aan Zee, against the player who was probably the strongest in our group. Hinges on a nice tactic, though the computer shows I could have played it one move earlier. I am really proud of this, and especially of move 28 ... Qb4! when for once I avoided trading pieces when I had my nose in front and went for something more dramatic – and definitive.

1. d4 d5 It may seem curmudgeonly to start criticising Stephen's play at such an early stage of the game, but as his regular coach my heart sinks when I see him play 1 ... d5 against 1. d4 (and indeed against 1. e4). I'd prefer to see him play something a little more punchy against 1. d4 as he is an initiative player who is at his best when taking the fight to his opponent. However, his more restrained play in this game does suggest that he can be just as effective a 'grinder' as a 'thumper'.

2. c4 e6 3. Nf3 Nf6 4. g3 Be7 5. Bg2 0–0 6. 0–0 Nbd7 7. Qc2 b6 8. Nc3 Bb7 9. Ne5 c5 10. e3 Qc7 11. Nxd7 Qxd7 12. dxc5 Bxc5 13. cxd5 exd5 14. Rd1 Rfd8 15. b3 Rac8 16. Qd3 Qe7 17. Ne2 Ne4 18. Bb2 Re8 19. Nf4? Pretty sensible play all round until here, but this is a tactical error. 19. Nd4 was solid and stops all the tricks.

19 ... Rcd8 20. Rac1

20. ... Nxf2! As Stephen says in his preamble, he could have played this one move earlier but he does well to spot it anyway. **21. Qc3** After 21. Kxf2, Black has the devastating 21 … Ba6!! 22. Qxa6 Qxe3+ and mate next move.

21 … d4! Necessary as White was threatening a sneaky mate in one by Qxg7. **22. Rxd4 Bxd4 23. exd4 Rc8!** Another very precise choice. Other moves win but not as decisively.

24. Qd2 Rxc1+ 25. Qxc1 Bxg2 26. Kxg2 Ng4 27. d5 Qe4+ 28. Kg1 Qb4! Stephen likes this but I would have been just as happy to see him liquidate with 28 … Qe1+ 29. Qxe1 Rxe1+ 30. Kg2 Rd1 when White has negligible counterplay.

29. Qc3 Club players tend to fold and blunder when in lost positions. White could have staggered on with 29. Nd3,

when there doesn't appear to be a bone-crushing finish.

29 … Re1+! Stephen has a good instinct for a mating finish.

30. Kg2 Qe4+ 31. Kh3 Nf2+ 32. Kh4 Qe7+ 33. Kh5 g6+ 34. Nxg6 fxg6+ 35. Kh6 Ng4# 0–1

Game 5: Salvation in Chicago

(Moss playing Black)
My tournament in Chicago was something of a disappointment. I was tired, confused, found it hard to concentrate. At one stage, I stood at one out of five and was in danger of finishing rock bottom. But in round six I played this nice game against a player who was far too passive. The exchange sac which finishes the game was largely instinctive. I couldn't analyse to the end, but it just felt right. And so it proved.

1. e4 d5 2. exd5 Nf6 3. Nf3 Nxd5 4. Bc4 Bg4 5. 0–0 e6 6. d3 Be7 7. Nbd2 0–0 8. Re1 c5 9. h3 Bh5 10. Nf1 Nc6 11. Ng3 Bg6 12. a3 Qc7 13. Bxd5 White has adopted a very craven opening strategy, and giving up bishop for knight in this way is deeply unimpressive.

13 … exd5 14. c3 Bd6 15. Nf1 Bh5 Unchallenged, Black has established a stable, solid positional advantage.

16. d4 cxd4 17. cxd4 Qb6 Another very effective plan to exploit White's passivity is to play 17 … Bxf3 18. gxf3 Qd7 19. Kg2 Ne7, etc, when the Black kingside is a ruin and ripe for invasion.

18. g4 18. Ne3 is a possible reply, but after 18 … Bxf3 19. Qxf3 Nxd4 20. Qxd5 Rad8 Black is still calling the shots. **18 … Bg6 19. b4 Rae8 20. Be3 Qd8 21. Bg5 Qd7 22. Rxe8 Rxe8 23. Nh4 Re4 24. Be3 Qe7 25. Nxg6 hxg6 26. Nd2?**

White's stubborn defence had held out to here but this allows an instinctive winning exchange (rook for bishop) sacrifice. Instead, something like 26. Qd3, maintaining a multiple defence of d4 and e3, leaves Black with more work to do.

26 ... Rxe3! 27. fxe3 Qxe3+ 28. Kg2 Qg3+ 29. Kf1 Qxh3+ 30. Ke1 Nxd4 A simpler win is perhaps 30 ... Bg3+ 31. Ke2 Nxd4+ 32. Kd3 Be5+ when White has to surrender his knight with 33. Nf3. **31. Rc1** 31. Nf1 is the most stubborn move, but then 31 ... Qc3+ 32. Kf2 Qb2+ should wrap things up fairly quickly.

31. ... Bg3# 0–1

Game 6: A sucker punch

(Moss playing White)
Round two of the 2014 edition of the Felce Cup was a funny game, though not for my opponent, who went wrong in the opening, then thought he saw an opportunity to trap my queen, but was so fixated on it that he missed the imminent checkmate. The mate came on the ninth move, and a game that was scheduled to last for three hours was over in barely 20. I was ecstatic, of course, but tried to hide my pleasure. Winning with grace in chess is even more important than losing with grace.

1. d4 d5 2. Nf3 Nf6 3. c4 c6 4. e3 dxc4 More experienced players will shake their head at this move. In many positions of the Queen's Gambit it is usually a better idea to play this after White has moved his light-squared bishop, thereby forcing him to make a second move of the bishop in recapturing.

5. Bxc4 Bf5? A more serious error, allowing two of his pawns to be attacked simultaneously.

6. Qb3 Nd5 6 ... e6 is better, when 7. Qxb7 Nbd7 8. Qxc6 a5 9. 0–0 Be4 10. Qa4 Bxf3 11. gxf3 Bd6 when Black has some sketchy compensation for the two pawns lost (better development and an outside chance of being able to exploit White's broken kingside).

7. Qxb7 Nb6 8. Ne5

Suddenly Black has a revelation, but there's a snag.

8. ... Bc8 For what shall it profit a man, if he shall gain a whole queen ...

9. Bxf7# 1–0 ... and lose his own king? Here endeth the lesson.

Game 7: The end of a dream

(Moss playing White)
Joint second going into the fourth round of the British under-140 championship, I was

filled with hope. I really believed I was in with a chance of winning the title. My youthful opponent quickly disabused me of that notion, playing a confident game as Black which left me reeling.

1. d4 g6 2. c4 Bg7 3. Nc3 c5 4. d5 Bxc3+ 5. bxc3 f5 A very unorthodox treatment by Black but there is method in his madness. A lot of books and articles get written about such offbeat openings as this and they can be very effective if met by routine chess. Black's strategy throws down a gauntlet to White, who needs to realise from the off that his pawns must be pushed forward or else he will be saddled with a horribly static position indefinitely. **6. Qc2** White does better to react immediately with something like 6. e4! fxe4 and 7. f3!, gambiting a pawn in order to open the position and exploit the dark-squared weaknesses in Black's position. Another idea might be to play an early h4, launching a kingside attack.

6 ... Nf6 7. Bh6 Rg8 8. Nh3 Qa5 9. f3 d6 10. Bg5 Stephen is caught a bit flat-footed here, not able to discern anything direct enough to whet his attacking appetite. He needed to crack on with development, hence 10. e3 Nbd7 11. Be2 Ne5 and now maybe 12. Bf4

10 ... Nbd7 11. Rb1 Nb6 12. e4 The first serious mistake, allowing Black to damage the kingside pawn structure.

12 ... fxe4 13. fxe4 Bxh3 14. gxh3 0-0-0 Ordinarily two bishops for two knights might be considered an advantage but here it definitely isn't because the bishops have so little scope.

15. Be2 Rgf8 16. 0-0 The computer suggests 16. Rb5!? Qa4 17. Qb1 and evaluates this as equal. I'm not sure I entirely agree – the white king looks a bit unhappy, but at least White has his own chances.

16 ... Kb8 17. Rb3 17. Rb5 is the right move.

17 ... Qa4 18. Rfb1 Rf7 19. Bd3!

Setting a cheap trap (Black plays Nxc4, White plays Rxb7+ and then snaps off the queen). I greatly approve of cheap traps, especially when one is floundering in a fog of planlessness.

19 ... Nfd7 20. Qc1? Black had averted the trick (curses!) but not in the optimal way. Here White could play 20. e5!, exploiting the fact that Black can't take with the knight (as the trap would then be sprung with Rxb6!). After 20 ... dxe5 comes 21. d6!? and suddenly White is back in the game. Not easy for a human to spot this idea – perhaps a strong amateur would find it with a few minutes' thought.

20 ... Ne5 This cements Black's advantage and leaves White with an utterly passive and depressing position.

21. Be2 Nexc4 22. Bxc4?

Wrong on a number of levels: (1) exchanges ease the winning player's task; (2) it is better leaving the black knights to defend each other as they tend to get in each other's way; (3) it allows the black queen to dominate from c4.

22 ... Qxc4 23. Qe1 h6 I'm a bit surprised Black didn't continue with 23 ... Rdf8, with some direct threats of Rf1+, etc.

24. Bxh6 Rh8 25. Qd2? Depression leads to loss of concentration: 25. Qe3, defending the e4 pawn, is a lot more resilient.

25 ... Qxe4 26. R3b2 Kc8 27. c4 Qxc4 White attempts a last, desperate cheapo with 27 ... Nxc4 28. Rxb7, hoping to give mate with Rb8+ and R1b7, but even that doesn't work after 28 ... Qxb1+ 29. Rxb1 Nxd2, etc.

28. Qa5 Qd4+ 29. Kh1 Qxd5+ 30. Kg1 Kb8 31. Be3 Rxh3 32. Rb3 Rff3 33. Ra3 Rxe3 34. Qxa7+ Kc8 35. Rxe3 Rxe3 36. Qxb6 Re2 0–1

Games 8 and 9: Banishing the demons

(Game 8: Moss playing White)
This was the first game in the final of the 2014 Felce Cup. I had always thought I could win this competition – for Surrey players rated less than 140 – and now it was in my grasp. I had played my opponent, David Cachet, on several occasions, and thought I had a decent chance, especially as he was prone to time trouble. In this game, he got an edge in the opening; I fought back and got a plus; then trapped his knight and had a winning advantage which I did my best to dissipate. If he had played f5 on move 37, he could have got a draw. Happily for me, he didn't and I was one up with one to

play. All I needed now was a draw in game two, when I would be playing Black, to lift the trophy.

1. e4 d6 2. d4 g6 3. f4 Bg7 4. Nf3 c5 5. Bb5+ I'm not keen on this as I prefer Stephen to keep his pieces on the board and use them to checkmate his opponents. The exchange makes Black's defensive task a little easier, or should do.

5 ... Bd7 6. Bxd7+ Nxd7 7. c3 Qb6 8. e5 dxe5 9. fxe5 Nh6 10. Na3 cxd4 11. cxd4 Rd8 12. Qa4 0–0 13. Nc4 Qa6 14. Qxa6 bxa6 15. Bd2 Nb6 16. Ne3 Nd5 It's been a somewhat erratic opening so far, with White getting a slightly better position than he deserves. Here Black passes up his second or third opportunity to play a thematic 16 ... f6 move, to chisel away at White's pawn centre.

17. 0–0 Nxe3 18. Bxe3 Nf5 19. Bf2 h5 20. Rfd1 Bh6 21. h3 Rd5 22. Rd3 Rfd8? Black overlooks a tactical possibility for his opponent. 22 ... e6 23. g4 hxg4 24. hxg4 Ne7 is at least playable.

23. g4!

Stephen spots the flaw in the black plan.

23 ... hxg4 24. hxg4 Nxd4 After the only safe move of the knight, 24 ... Ng7 White has 25. g5!, trapping the bishop.

25. Rxd4 Rxd4 26. Bxd4? White blunders in return. Fortunately for him, it is a blunder of a smaller denomination, leaving him enough in the bank to win anyway. 26. Nxd4 would have been all over bar the shouting.

26 ... Rxd4 27. Nxd4 Be3+ 28. Kg2 Bxd4 29. Rd1 Bxe5 30. Rd7 Bxb2 31. Rxa7 e5 32. Kf3 Kg7 32 ... f5 is quite hard to break down. White should win with best play, but how many of us can deliver such a commodity?

33. Rxa6 Kh6 34. Rb6 Bd4 35. Rb4 Kg5 36. Rxd4?! Whoa! White should at least give 36. a4 a try first before plunging into a king and pawn endgame.

36 ... exd4 37. a4

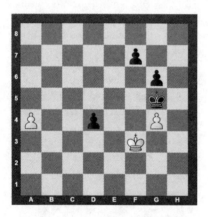

37. ... d3?? Well, I suppose the counter-argument to my last comment is that it might be better to give Black a 'fifty-percenter'. An old chess friend of mine gave that name to a move where a player has a 50% chance of getting it right, and 50% of blundering. Anyway, Black finds the blunder. Instead he could have drawn with 37 ... f5! though he would have had to be a reasonably strong player to evaluate all the ramifications: 38. gxf5 (if 38. a5 fxg4+ 39. Kf2 d3 40. a6 g3+ and it's a draw) 38 ... Kxf5 and Black's king is 'in the box', i.e. the square formed by the pawn and its path to the queening square

(a4–a8 forming one axis, and a4–f4 the other). Even the humblest club player ought to be familiar with this sort of thing. 39. a5 g5 40. a6 g4+ 41. Kg3 d3 42. a7 d2 43. a8Q d1Q 44. Qf8+ Ke4 45. Qe7+ Kd3 46. Qd8+ Ke2 47. Qxd1+ Kxd1 48. Kxg4

38. a5! Now the a-pawn scoots through to queen and the Black pawns aren't in time to organise the coronation of one of their own number.

38 ... d2 39. Ke2 Kf6 40. a6 Ke6 41. a7 1–0

1. Nf3 d5 2. d4 Nf6 3. e3 e6 4. Bd3 Be7 5. 0–0 0–0 6. c3 Nbd7 7. Nbd2 b6 A desperately dull opening, for which I would normally give Stephen my slightly more middle-class version of the Alex Ferguson hairdryer treatment, but since he only needed a draw, it was forgivable just this once.

8. e4 dxe4 9. Nxe4 Bb7 10. Ng3 c5 11. Be3 cxd4 12. cxd4? Unnecessarily isolating his pawn and leaving the e3 bishop in the lurch. 12. Bxd4 is much better.

12 ... Nd5 13. Qe2 Nb4!

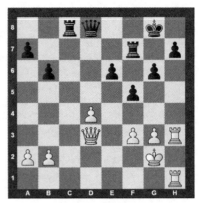

When not bearing down on his opponent's king, Stephen's second best natural instinct is when he harries and nags at his opponent's pieces in such positions. White should respond by shifting the bishop to c4 or b5, but instead he plays a routine developing rook move. And, as in the previous game, it's a blunder, although just a positional one this time.

14. Rfd1? Nxd3! 15. Qxd3 15. Rxd3? loses to the mundane skewer 15… Ba6

15 … Bxf3 16. gxf3 Nf6 Black has the simple plan of Nd5, followed by Bg5, strongpointing the f4 square for future operations against the white king. White has no viable counterplay.

17. h4 A desperate thrust but Black is not impressed.

17 … Nd5 18. Bd2 If 18. h5 then 18 … f5, threatening f5–f4 and various other unpleasantnesses.

18 … Bxh4 19. Kg2 Bg5 20. Rh1 g6 21. Ne4 Nf4+ 22. Bxf4 Bxf4 23. Rh3 f5 24. Ng3 Bxg3 The computer prefers other plans but this liquidation seems very natural and reasonable.

25. fxg3 Rc8 26. Rah1 Rf7

White's attack is all too easily parried and only encourages Black to set up an invasion battery of his own.

27. Rh6 Rfc7 28. g4 Qg5 29. R1h4 Qf4 30. Kf2 Rc2+ 0–1

Game 10: My Cup runneth over

(Moss playing Black)
A month or so after winning the Felce, I played in the Bury St Edmunds Congress. I was leading the intermediate section (for players graded under 145) after the fourth round and needed a draw to guarantee a share of victory in the tournament. A win would secure the first prize of £200 outright. My opponent was half a point behind me, and was hell-bent on victory. Afterwards, he admitted he had been too gung-ho and went for the jugular too soon. He also missed a draw by perpetual check when his attack was running into the sand. It was a thrilling game and my win made sure of victory in the competition. Rather than elation, I felt relief at having survived the onslaught, and sat down afterwards to analyse in gentlemanly

fashion with my friendly and gregarious opponent a game in which we had both sought to attack. Relief, then, but some pride too. After being becalmed for so long, my chess finally seemed to be on the up.

1. e4 d5 2. exd5 Nf6 3. d3 If cricket legend Geoff Boycott were a chess commentator, he would know what to say about such a move. Probably something colourful, involving his grandmother's dexterity with a stick of rhubarb. Not coming from Yorkshire, I'm going to settle for the adjective 'insipid'. I'm certainly not seeing anything 'gung ho' at this stage of White's game, but these are early days, I suppose.
3 ... Nxd5 4. g3 e5 5. Bg2 c6 I see no reason not to continue active development with 5 ... Nc6
6. Nf3 Bd6 7. 0–0 0–0 8. Nbd2 Bg4 9. Nc4 Bc7 10. Re1 Nd7 Here the consolidating 10 ... f6 was screaming to be played.
11. Qd2 White should simply put the question to the bishop with 11. h3, when Black either has to cede the defence of the e5–pawn or else play 11 ... Bxf3 12. Qxf3 and then perhaps 12 ... f5, with a fairly level position.
11 ... Bxf3 Again 11 ... f6 was called for.
12. Bxf3 f5 13. Qd1 f4 14. Bg4 fxg3 15. hxg3

15. ... N7b6? An error, putting the knight offside. I'm surprised Stephen wasn't drawn to 15 ... Qf6, defending the e5 pawn and also creating pressure along the f-file.
16. Be6+ 16. Nxe5!? looks more direct. If then 16 ... Qf6 17. Nf3 h5 18. Be6+ Kh8 19. Kg2, and there doesn't seem to be a way for Black to exploit the impression of weakness in the White kingside.
16 ... Kh8 17. Qg4 Now 17. Nxe5 Qf6 18. Ng4 looks shakier, though computers don't come up with a refutation.
17 ... Nxc4 Once again refraining from 17 ... Qf6!?, which looks pretty good for Black.
18. dxc4 Nf6 19. Qh3 Bb6 Finally the game has started to open up and Black has his eye on the f2 square.
20. Bg5?! Black had planned his tactical shot against Rxe5 but now finds it works just as well against Bg5. Instead, 20. Bf5 Qd4 21. Rf1 Qxc4 22. Bg5 would have led to a very sharp position which would have been unfathomable to all but the finest and/or silicon-enhanced brains. But it is going to be sharp enough anyway.
20 ... Bxf2+!

Spectacular but there is plenty of chess left in this yet.
21. Kg2 21. Kxf2? Ne4+ 22. Kg2 Rf2+ 23. Kg1 Nxg5 24. Qg4 Qd2 would be

terminal but, intentionally or not, it turns out that White has quite a lot of play for the loss of the exchange and pawn.

21 ... Bxe1 22. Rxe1 Qe7 If you feed this position into a computer, you may find it suggesting some quite outlandish moves hereabouts, but the analysis is beyond human comprehension. This is a desperately hard position for a human player to evaluate accurately, so the players go with their instincts. They do a pretty good job for the next few moves.

23. Rh1 h6 24. Qf5 Rae8 25. Bxh6! gxh6 26. Rxh6+ Nh7

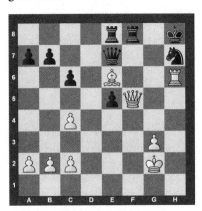

27. Qxe5+?? Finally White loses his bearings. Instead he should sacrifice a second rook: 27. Rxh7+! Qxh7 28. Qxe5+ Qg7 29. Qh5+ Qh7 30. Qe5+ secures a draw by perpetual check.

27 ... Rf6 27 ... Qg7 also wins for Black. **28. Rxh7+ Kxh7 29. Qh5+ Rh6 30. Bf5+ Kg7 31. Qg4+ Kh8 32. Qd4+ Qe5 0–1**

ACKNOWLEDGEMENTS

As will be clear from the text, John Saunders has been a central figure in my chess 'journey', as mentor, technical adviser, annotator of my games, and friend. He also kindly supplied the note on algebraic notation. My unwillingness or inability to follow John's advice infuriated him, but our friendship was never seriously tested and I owe him a great deal, including a curry at the very good Bangladeshi restaurant close to where he lives.

I have numerous other debts, too, and just as I forget what I'm supposed to be playing when I'm at the chessboard, so I am sure to omit key people. Apologies to those I have left out. But these are names I have remembered: grandmaster Stuart Conquest, another mentor and friend, and an inspiration both in his love for the game and in the creativity of his play; grandmaster Jonathan Rowson, with whom I had an early conversation about the possibility of writing a book on chess and whose reflections on the game have been wonderfully thought-provoking; grandmaster Vladislav Tkachiev for spending so much time with me in Moscow and being such a vivid, inspiring and insightful companion; chess writer Steve Giddins for pointing me towards Tkachiev; the legendary grandmaster Yuri Averbakh, then aged 92, for allowing me to interview him while in Moscow; grandmasters Genna Sosonko and Hans Ree for allowing me to interview them in Amsterdam; Eddy Sibbing for guiding me round the Max Euwe Centre and telling me about grassroots chess in Holland; Leonard Barden, chess correspondent of *The Guardian*, for his support over my almost three decades at the paper and for taking my interest in chess seriously; Malcolm Pein, international master and chess correspondent of the *Daily Telegraph*, for illuminating conversations and help in locating players willing to subject themselves to my questioning; grandmasters Keith Arkell, Sabino Brunello, Stephen Gordon, Danny Gormally, David Howell, Gawain Jones, John Nunn, Yasser Seirawan, Nigel Short, Jon Speelman, Peter Svidler and Jan Timman, international master and former British champion William Hartston, international master and five-time British women's champion Jovanka Houska, woman grandmaster and two-time US women's champion Jennifer Shahade, and all the other great players who have given freely of their time when I have buttonholed them at tournaments and demanded to know why they devote their lives to this infuriating pursuit; Alina Frolenko for help with accommodation in Moscow; Alexander Kostyev, founding director of the chess faculty of the Russian State Social University, for allowing me to visit; international master and super-trainer Igor Yanvarjov and youthful grandmasters Vladimir Belous and Andrey Stukopin for being willing to be interviewed during that visit; chess trainer Aleksander Nikitin for talking to me about his work with Garry Kasparov and explaining how they plotted the downfall of reigning world champion Anatoly Karpov; chess journalist and administrator Mark Gluhovsky for giving me an overview of the chess scene in Russia; Konstantin Gumirov, Dmitrii Loev, FIDE master Arman Erzhanov, Marshan Karaketov and woman grandmasters Eugenia Chasovnikova and Elmira Mirzoeva for their help and advice during my stay in Moscow; Mike Klein for helping me plan my US chess expedition; the staff at the Marshall Chess Club in New York for letting me play there during my stay; FIDE master Asa Hoffmann for showing me the treasures at the Marshall and playing some blitz against me; grandmaster Andrew Soltis for meeting me in New York and illuminating the American chess scene; international master Jay Bonin for telling me about the life of the American chess pro; Frank Brady, Bobby Fischer's biographer, for describing this great, complex, endlessly fascinating champion; nonpareil tournament organiser Bill Goichberg for sharing his reminiscences of Fischer and explaining competition chess in the US; David in Washington Square and all his fellow 'hustlers' for showing me what street chess – and the double-edged freedom that comes with it – is really about; Elizabeth Spiegel, for letting me spend the day watching her teach chess at the Eugenio Maria de Hostos Intermediate School (aka IS318) in Brooklyn; John Galvin at IS318 for his help in making my visit possible; Mike Wilmering for making sure the St Louis leg of the US trip worked out; Rex Sinquefield for showing me his collection of Bobby Fischer memorabilia; grandmaster Ben Finegold for telling me with characteristic ebullience and good humour about his life in chess and playing a fun (yet serious!) game against me; grandmaster Maurice Ashley for telling me about his million-dollar tournament in Las Vegas; Andrea Griffini and all my friendly rivals at Wijk for making the tournament there so pleasant – sorry I messed it up at the end; Kaarlo Schepel for describing his unusual life in chess; journalist Peter Doggers for help throughout and especially during my stay in the Netherlands; Brendan O'Gorman, a fixture on the British chess scene and mainstay of the 'Barmy Army', for sharing his love of the game; tournament organiser Adam Raoof for sage advice on what might loosely be called the entrepreneurial side of chess; Phil Ehr, former chief executive of the English Chess Federation, for explaining chess politics to me; Stephen Carpenter and Oliver Condy for fruitful conversations about music and chess; Steven Poole for instructive conversations when I was considering this undertaking; Ronan Bennett and the rest of *The Guardian* chess club (now sadly defunct) for reactivating my interest in the game a decade ago; international master Andrew Martin and up-and-coming players Michael Healey and Tom Villiers for extra coaching; John Foley, Ken Inwood, Nicholas Grey, Christopher Kreuzer, Alan Scrimgour, Julian Way and all my fellow players at Kingston Chess Club for help and advice; Chris Briscoe, Paul Durrant, David Morant, Gonzalo Shoobridge and the large (and happily fast-growing) membership of Surbiton Chess Club for demonstrating that there is still life left in British club chess; Charles Cumming and my fellow players at the delightfully informal Capablanca Chess Club (a template for the future perhaps); chess journalist (and keen amateur player) Matt Read for help on many fronts; Adrian Waldock for several instructive games and much good advice; David Cachet for a series of enjoyable games and for losing to me in the final of the Felce Cup; Luke Boumphrey for analysis of his games at Aberystwyth; Paul Haddock for interesting conversations whenever we met at tournaments; Will Taylor for discussing his 'Road to Grandmaster' blog and for playing for Kingston II in a key Surrey League promotion clash – greater love hath no chess player; antiques dealer Luke Honey for guiding me through the rich history of chess sets; Paula Cocozza and Jill Tilden for translating parts of Pietro Carrera's *Il Gioco degli Scacchi*, a rare copy of which is held by the British Library; Steve Peters for giving me psychological advice on how to play; the staff at the Chess and Bridge Shop in Baker Street, London, for their help and advice in locating books and DVDs, and for the discount they gave me on the proper chess set I eventually treated myself to; Jim Falzarano, Sean Ingle, Tony Paley, Mark Rice-Oxley and Maxton Walker for chess chat at *The Guardian*; Jeremy Alexander for reading the proofs with characteristic rigour and for removing several thousand unnecessary commas and other excrescences; Ian

Katz for sending me to Iceland in pursuit of Bobby Fischer in 2005; Mike Herd for pointing me in the direction of Walter Tevis's novel *The Queen's Gambit*; and Philip Oltermann for drawing my attention to Thomas Glavinic's novel *Carl Haffner's Love of the Draw* and for sending me his essay on Stefan Zweig and hypermodernism. I should also put on record my thanks to all my colleagues at *The Guardian* for putting up with my idiosyncrasies – and occasional chess-related absences – over many years. I have at various times interviewed Magnus Carlsen, Bobby Fischer, David Howell, Garry Kasparov and Judit Polgar for *The Guardian* – meetings which both encouraged me to think about writing this book and which then informed some of the writing.

My captain at Kingston II, Chris Clegg, died as my odyssey was drawing to a close, a great loss for the club. Soon afterwards the international master Colin Crouch also died at far too young an age, and these two deaths perhaps encouraged my view that I was writing an elegy for a chess age that was disappearing. They were part of the fabric of British chess, and I would like to acknowledge their selfless contributions and commitment to the game.

This book started to form in my mind at least a decade ago. It has been godfathered by my long-suffering agent David Miller at Rogers, Coleridge & White, to whom no amount of thanks are sufficient. It took concrete form at a dinner with Matthew Engel, whose suggestion that I write a book about horse racing somehow turned into a contract to write a book on chess. My editor Charlotte Atyeo has been patient, endlessly encouraging and necessarily meticulous. Thanks to her and to Ian Preece, who together have turned rough-hewn text into a book that I hope will interest both the chess aficionado and the general reader. Julie Kemp dealt admirably with the complex issues surrounding permissions. I am grateful to Jonathan Rowson, Robert Desjarlais and Fred Waitzkin for permission to use extracts from their respective works. Thanks also to James Watson for his elegant jacket design, Rosemary Dear for her work on the index, and to all the staff at Bloomsbury – not least Holly Jarrald, Henry Lord and Stephanie Morgan – for their enthusiastic championing of the book and for calmly dealing with the author's ever shifting view of what constituted good grammar. Richard Collins gave the proofs a much-needed final reading, saving the book from an excess of 'extraordinaries' and locating Kensal Green cemetery in the correct part of London.

Finally I must thank my wife Helen for her fortitude over many years and my son Tim for making my computer work and rescuing the text a few times. In a sense the fact it has made it into print is down to him, and he must therefore be held responsible for any errors or omissions. I merely played the moves, usually wildly misconceived ones.

INDEX